WARD METHOD PUBLICATIONS

MUSIC INSTRUCTION FOR CATHOLIC SCHOO



BY

**Justine Ward**

BOOK ONE – TEACHERS MANUAL

# *That All May Sing*

Revised by an International Committee of Teachers of the

WARD METHOD

New American Edition Prepared by

Theodore Marier

Published for the
CENTER FOR WARD METHOD STUDIES
The Catholic University of America
by

THE CATHOLIC UNIVERSITY OF AMERICA PRESS

Washington, D.C.

*Cover design and illustrations by PAUL FOWLER*

*Selected sketches from earlier edition by FRANCES DELEHANTY*

*Additional drawings by SISTER MARY CONNORS, F.S.E.*

*Computerization of musical scores by LAWRENCE A. HARRIS*



Second Printing 1992

## PREFACE TO THE WARD METHOD

The object of this series of textbooks is to provide a basic integrated musical education for the children in the primary and intermediate grades of Catholic schools. This progressive musical training, designed for the child's spiritual and aesthetic enrichment, begins in Grade I and continues through Grade VIII.

At every level of the WARD METHOD program, the course content is adapted to the growth and unfolding capacity of the students. Accordingly, from the outset - and continuing through the eight-book series - the children learn to:

- recognize musical tones;
- understand tonal relationships;
- associate musical sounds with printed symbols;
- transform their speaking voices into agreeable musical instruments;
- appreciate the world of ordered movement which we call rhythm;
- develop basic, and in the upper grades, sophisticated musical skills preparatory to the disciplined renditions of great music;
- share intimately in many noble works of musical art through study, appreciation and performance;
- discover the rich heritage of religious music preserved by the Church for liturgical observances through the centuries.

The principles of pedagogy applied to music in the WARD METHOD are the same as those applied to other branches of the school's curriculum. The elements of music, for example, as the elements of any language, are first studied separately, then in combination. In addition, opportunities abound for leading the students to make their own "discoveries"; for training the eyes, ears, memory, and the body muscles; for games, contests, and experiential group listening. In other words, the time-honored principles and techniques of good teaching are found here structured into the frame of a daily music period in which the entire class is meaningfully involved.

The purpose of all this, then, is: THAT ALL MAY SING!

But, what shall they sing? Indeed, if music is to help in character formation, if it is to contribute to the integration of the child's intellect with his emotional nature and lift his soul into a spiritual world of truth and beauty, then special attention must be given to the quality of the music selected for study and performance. In order to maintain a high quality of music in this series of books and, at the same time, to include music suited to the technical and emotional grasp of the children at each level of their development, the music repertoire for the WARD METHOD was selected from the best folk traditions of many countries, the works of classical and modern composers, and from the rich store of the Church's liturgical melodies.

Musical principles, finally, have been simplified in order that the regular classroom teachers can learn to teach this great art of music to their children.

Thus, ALL MAY SING, not merely a talented few, for music belongs to all of God's children.

# FOREWORD TO BOOK ONE - "THAT ALL MAY SING"

From the Writings of Justine B. Ward

## PSYCHOLOGICAL BASES OF WARD METHOD OF MUSIC INSTRUCTION

When presented to little children in a manner that is suitable to their age and when graded with the same care that is given to all other subjects in the elementary grades, music brings joy and fresh vitality into the lives of children. Even those children who appear to be tone deaf can learn to sing correctly and joyfully.

### Three Stages of Development

Imitation - A child of six years is an imitative being. In music classes the teacher will strive to give the child such models to imitate as will facilitate his development from the stage of pure imitation to that of understanding and reflection. The initial work projects of the Ward Method have this object in view.

Understanding - At this stage the child gains a firm grasp of a few basic musical truths. These values are not assimilated through the teacher's spoken words nor through memorized formulae but by action, the child's own action. Through his eyes, ears and muscles, the child receives the stimuli that deepen his intellectual understanding of musical truths or values.

Growth - In this stage of growth, the child moves from the known to the related unknown. If the child's growth is to be continuous and progressive, he ought not to sing anything that he does not understand. Teachers must, moreover, resist the temptation to employ the device of rote-teaching as this technique tends to stunt the child's normal musical development.

### How Music Becomes Functional with Children

A new musical truth or skill can become functional for a child only on the condition that it be:

Properly prepared;
Correlated with what has already been assimilated;
Based on ideas that move from the known to the related unknown;
Embodied in action of the senses.

When sound psychology is applied to the study of music in this manner, music awakens and contributes to the growth impulses of the child's mind.

Throughout this method there has been a conscious attempt to make effective application of these principles.

## Learning by Action and Gesture

Little children can learn quickly and well when they become involved actively in a learning experience. The teacher, at such times, stands apart as a catalytic agent, stimulating, encouraging and guiding. In this way the child's "watchful senses" - to use Milton's phrase - become active senses. Sight, touch, hearing, muscular movement with observation and memory, all become sensitized and ready to function at their peak of potential.

If the child is to become involved in this lively and varied way, the teacher must prepare each lesson well. There must be no fumbling for pitch, no hesitation in passing from one type of action to another.

## PRINCIPLES OF PEDAGOGY FOLLOWED IN WARD METHOD BOOK ONE

Music is a complex art. Even the simplest song embodies several elements that must be controlled if its message is to be communicated. Experienced teachers know full well that any attempt to teach all or several of these elements simultaneously is likely to fail. The procedure followed, therefore, in these books, is one in which a study is first made of the musical elements separately and then, as the skills for their proper rendition are developed, these elements are re-assembled. An outline of the procedure follows.

### Music Elements Taught Separately

Timbre - Tone Quality: Discovering and developing the singing voice is surely one of the first areas of music that a child needs to explore. Having first discovered his singing voice, the child must then learn to use it properly.

Voice Placement: By means of the single syllable "Nu," a light quality of voice characterized by a free head resonance is called into play. This one syllable, practised at different tonal levels and in a variety of melodic formations, is used throughout BOOK ONE for this purpose. Later, other vowels are similarly drilled for placement in the cavities of the head where the child's voice finds it most attractive and controllable quality. Sixteen different Vocal Exercises on the syllable "Nu" are used in BOOK ONE.

In the beginning of the training period, the teacher gives a model of the tone quality that a child is expected to imitate. From then on selected children give the models.

Tonal Range: During the first year, only the fixed pitches between *F* (above middle *C*) up to Soprano *E* are recommended.

Factors related to breathing, posture and common faults that need to be corrected will be found treated in the course of the lessons.

Rhythm - Measure: Rhythm is the "ordered movement" of musical tones, the rise and fall, tension and relaxation. In Measure (also referred to as time or meter), we identify the relationship of short tones to long tones and indicate the regularity of short-long patterns by means of measure bars. In BOOK ONE, rhythmic control is developed by means of physical gestures and dictations.

Rhythm Gestures: Since rhythm implies movement, children learn it best by motion: movements of the whole body that bring large muscles into play. A rhythm thus becomes a muscular experience and in time, from this experience, the child develops muscular memory. As the child's movements become more precise and orderly, the art of beautiful movement will be reflected in the artistry of his musical renditions. Throughout BOOK ONE special expression is given to this principle.

Metrical Gestures: Special hand and arm gestures are used for counting pulses within a rhythmic movement, for measuring prolonged notes by pressure, and for indicating rests or measured silences.

Rhythmic Dictations: In these a child is tested for his ability to grasp a phrase as a whole and not piecemeal. In the presence of a rhythmic musical stimulus, the child is required to react physically and accurately, controlling his muscles and taking careful note of what he hears and feels.

Notation: Several systems of notation are used in the Ward Method. These are presented in progressive sequence and are adapted to the unfolding capacity of the students. For example:

Melodic Gestures
Finger Notation
Number Notation
Staff Notation

Dynamics - Expression: The quantitative elements of the loudness or softness of musical tones are not stressed in BOOK ONE. As a general rule, it is recommended that gentleness and moderately soft singing should prevail through all exercises and renditions. In later books, the controlled disciplines of tone and rhythm having been implanted, phrase dynamics and levels of tone will be taught.

Words - Song Texts: Although not specifically a musical element that must be considered separately, words or song texts are intended to be sung and obviously need to be studied for understanding, articulation and control. Since song texts are combined with musical tones, they will be treated under: Music Elements Combined.

**Intonation - Pitch:** Skills in handling pitches, that is, high and low tones, scale-line tonal groupings, skips, etc., are developed in a variety of ways.

**Intonation Exercises:** By means of charts, diagrams and drills arranged in the order of progressive difficulty, the horizontal, vertical and oblique reading skills are developed. BOOK ONE includes 50 Intonation Exercises and 12 Diagrams interspersed over 23 chapters.

**Ear Tests:** Sometimes referred to as melodic dictations, these tests are given daily to assist the child in assimilating the pitch sequences of the exercises. In the course of the tests the child must identify correctly the pitches announced by the teacher. Each chapter contains numerous tests which are given in the appealing form of guessing games. (*See:* APPENDIX I.)

**Eye Tests:** Look-and-remember games. (See: APPENDIX I.) In these games the child develops the habit of storing a brief phrase in the memory. When rendering the phrase, he depends on his memory image to inform him of that which he perceived through his visual sense. Visual memory tests are given daily in the form of pitch and rhythm dictations. (*See:* APPENDIX I.)

**Arm and Finger Gestures:** Measuring the height of a tone with the arm or "making the fingers sing" are devices used daily for strengthening the child's perception of musical tones.

<u>SPECIAL NOTE</u>

Throughout the Ward Method of Music Instruction, children are taught to sing according to the system called the <u>Moveable DO</u> or <u>Relative Pitch</u>. In this system, the tones of the scale and their Number Notation equivalents are given as:

| SOL | LA | TI | DO | RE | MI | FA | SOL | LA | TI | DO | RE | MI |
|---|---|---|---|---|---|---|---|---|---|---|---|---|
| $\underset{\cdot}{5}$ | $\underset{\cdot}{6}$ | $\underset{\cdot}{7}$ | 1 | 2 | 3 | 4 | 5 | 6 | 7 | $\dot{1}$ | $\dot{2}$ | $\dot{3}$ |

This entire series of pitches, or fragments thereof, may occur any place in the total gamut which the human voice is capable of sounding. The arrangement of whole steps and half steps is in no way affected by the location of the starting pitch.

The teacher will be careful to notice, however, that the letters *C, D, E, F, G, A,* as given in this book, are <u>Fixed Pitches</u> and are to be played on a pitch-pipe or some other musical instrument in order to establish the exact starting point of the tonal groups to be sung.

## Music Elements Combined

Having considered the music elements of timbre, pitch, rhythm, and notation separately, there remains the task of making combinations of these elements and gradually extending the combinations to the construction and performance of complete songs.

Songs Without Words: More than 50 songs without words that combine pitch, rhythm and notation in a variety of ways are included in BOOK ONE. In addition to these there are:

Vocalizations: Combinations of timbre with rhythm and pitch.

Intonation Exercises. Combinations of pitch and rhythm in the form of melodic applications of the scale tones under study. These are sung on names of the scale tones.

Rhythm Patterns: These combine with pitches to form rudimentary melodic designs. They are sung on names of the scale tones.

Notation Drills: Combinations in various oral and written forms of rhythm patterns and tonal groupings.

Improvisations: Combinations of pitch and rhythm in the form of question and answer games and in the simple song structures where repetition, variation and balance are discovered. These also help to reveal the meaning of partial and final cadences.

Songs With Words: In verbal melodies all the musical elements studied are combined and in so doing make the greatest demands on the child's powers of concentration. If the child is able to control the musical elements of tone quality, pitch, rhythm, words, then the rendition of a complete song will bring him the full musical rich experience that lies there waiting to be summoned forth. The child's vocabulary of songs will thus increase as his skills in rendering them increases. Although few in number, the verbal melodies included in BOOK ONE have been carefully chosen to correlate with the child's known vocabularies of tone and rhythm.

Words are combined with pitch and rhythm in a variety of ways.

Pitch Calls: Combining familiar verbal phrases with tones.

Refrains: Simple melodic settings of words like *Amen* and *Alleluia* are used either alone or in dialogue songs between teacher and child.

Improvisations: Combining words spontaneously with melodic fragments.

## LESSON PLANNING FOR BOOK ONE

Ideally, the teaching of music in a classroom situation should take place daily along with the other subjects of the curriculum. Based on this premise, the content of BOOK ONE has been planned for a full year of daily classroom music periods in the First Grade of a parish or church affiliated elementary school. This daily music period should be of 20 minutes' duration and should be conducted by the classroom teacher. Given these circumstances the content of each chapter can be presented in five to eight music lessons. As aids to the teacher in preparing and giving a lesson, the following are offered:

1. FIVE MODEL LESSONS for teaching content of Chapter One. (*See:* Pages 5 - 24 inclusive.)

2. CONTENT AND PEDAGOGY of Chapter Two. (*See:* Pages 27 - 35 inclusive.)

3. LESSON PLANS for Chapters Two, Three, Four, Five, Nine, Fifteen, and Eighteen, preceding each chapter.

4. CHAPTER SUMMARIES for all Twenty-Three Chapters. (*See:* APPENDIX II.)

5. TEN SUGGESTIONS FOR TEACHERS (*See:* APPENDIX I)
   "How to.... Plan a lesson
   Teach a vocal exercise
   Help non-singers to find their singing voices
   Teach an intonation exercise
   Play "listening" games
   Play "look-and-remember" games
   Study rhythm patterns
   Give rhythm dictation
   Teach a song without words
   Teach a song with words

### SPECIAL NOTE

It is understood that variations in lesson planning are possible and, in fact, are often imposed by unalterable circumstances. For example:

One who is teaching this method for the first time will need more time than a teacher who is experienced in Ward methodology.

A large class can effectively slow down the teaching pace and so more lessons per chapter will be required than are indicated here.

A music specialist giving the course, who comes two or three times per week, will have to make special plans to cover the year's content.

Children of more advanced years, say of 10, 15 years - even adult beginners - will require a faster pace and special lesson plans.

| Under no circumstances is it advisable to omit or to alter in any way the sequence of the training program as given in this book. |
|---|

## RECOMMENDED EQUIPMENT FOR TEACHING BOOK ONE - "THAT ALL MAY SING"

To satisfy the functional needs of teaching the content of all the chapters of BOOK ONE, the following equipment is strongly recommended:

Pitch-pipe (chromatic F to F) or instrument capable of sounding accurate fixed pitches such as a piano or organ.

Blackboard space and colored chalk.

Overhead projector and box of acetates.

Tape cassette or record player on which to play a recording of the accompaniments to rhythm gestures.

24-inch pointer painted red at one end and green at the other to be used for "think" and "sing" indications shown in the intonation exercises.

*The Composer*

# TABLE OF CONTENTS

# Chapter One

*A summary of the chapter content is given first, that is, drills and exercises under the headings of* VOCAL TRAINING, INTONATION, CREATIVE ACTIVITY, NOTATION, RHYTHM, DICTATION, *and* SONGS. *The pedagogy that follows is presented in the form of five model lessons, each of approximately 20 minutes' duration. In these lessons the chapter content is presented in detail.*

## CHAPTER CONTENT SUMMARY

## Vocal Training

*Begin to classify voices*

Vocal Exercise 1

*1 = $A^b$ – Bb – C*

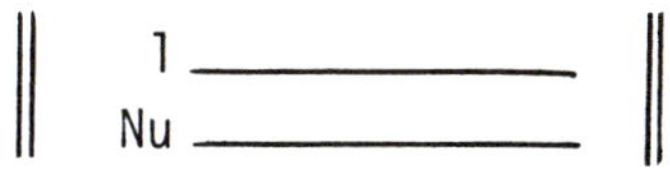


*Timbre alone*

Vocal Exercise 2

*1 = $A^b$ – F – G*

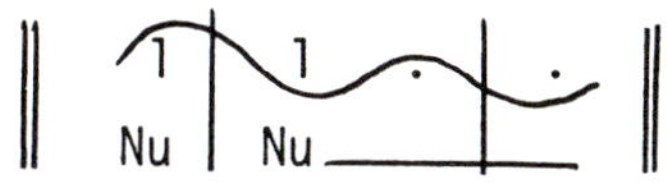


*Timbre and rhythm*

## Intonation

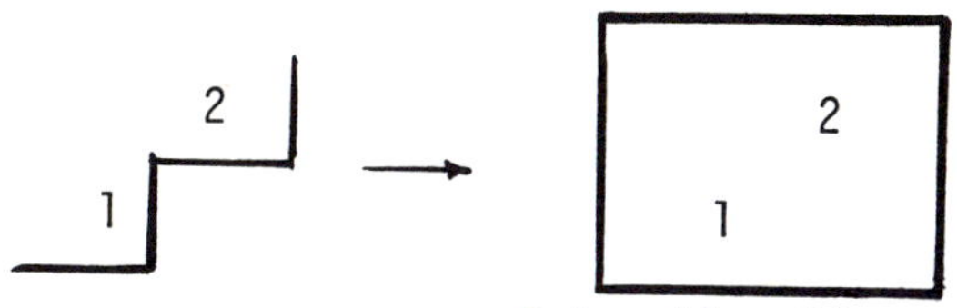


Intonation Diagram 1

Intonation Exercise 1 *Teach on* Diagram 1

*(1 = Ab)*

| 1 | 2 | | | | | 2 | | 1 | | |
|---|---|---|---|---|---|---|---|---|---|---|
| 1 2 1 | | 1 2 2 | | | | 1 2 | | 1 2 1 | | |

Intonation Exercise 2 *Teach on* Diagram 1

*(1 = Ab)*

| a) | b) |
|---|---|
| 1 1 1 2 1 | 1 2 1 1 1 |
| 1 2 2 2 1 | 1 2 1 1 2 |
| 1 2 2 1 1 | 2 1 2 1 1 |
| c) → | |

# Rhythm

## Rhythm Patterns - Series 1

*Meaning of the signs:*

*One stroke, that is,* **I** *= note of one pulse duration.*

*Each dot adds one pulse duration to the note.*
*For example:* **I .** *= two pulses*

**I . .** *= three pulses*

*Metrical Language:*

la = **I** *Note of one pulse duration.*

long = **I .** *Note of two pulses duration. This word is also used for notes of more than two pulses duration.*

*RHYTHM PATTERNS*

*a)* 

*b)* 

*c)* 

Measure bars have their usual funtion of defining the metrical units of the rhythm, whether these be two beats, or three or more beats.
Curved lines indicate the UP and DOWN of rhythm gestures.

## Rhythmic Gesture I

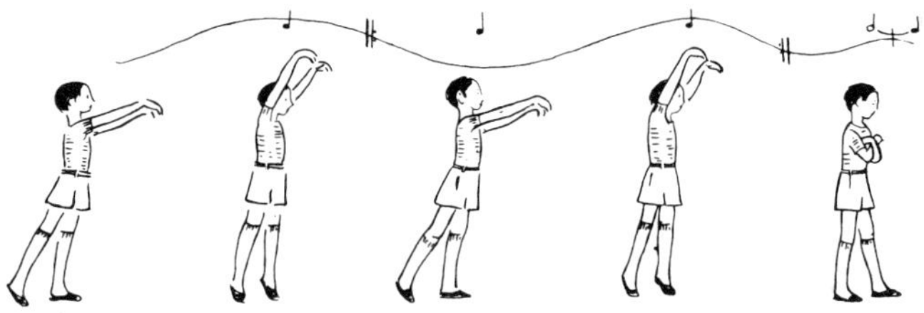

## Rhythmic Gesture II

## Metrical Gesture I

Right hand touches palm of left hand for each pulse of the rhythm (shown as a single stroke in the rhythm patterns.) Right hand presses palm of left hand gently for each dot.
For each single stroke say: la.
For each long note say: long.

# Creative Activity

Step 1 - Improvisation. *Thinking in terms of musical tones. Musical conversation, pitch calls and tone-matching games. Question (or statement) and response on same tones.*

**The Ball Game** *($\dot{1}$ = $B^b$)* The children do not need to know the names of the notes they sing.

| | | | | |
|---|---|---|---|---|
| | $\dot{1}$ ———— $\dot{1}$ 6 | | $\dot{1}$ $\dot{1}$ 6 |
| *Teacher:* | Here comes the red ball. I throw it. | *Children:* | I catch it. |
| | 5 ———— 5 $\dot{1}$ | | 5 5 $\dot{1}$ |
| *Teacher:* | Here comes the green ball. I throw it. | *Children:* | I catch it. |
| | $\dot{1}$ ———— $\dot{1}$ 6 4 | | $\dot{1}$ 6 4 |
| *Teacher:* | Here comes the blue ball. I throw it. | *Children:* | I catch it. |

**Musical Conversation** *(1 = $B^b$)* *Color game - Finding objects - Activities - Identity*

| | | | |
|---|---|---|---|
| | $\dot{1}$ ———— 6 | | $\dot{1}$ ———— 6 |
| *Teacher:* | What is your name?<br>What color is the sky?<br>Where is the clock? | *Children:* | My name is John.<br>The sky is blue.<br>The clock is on the wall. |
| | 5 ———— $\dot{1}$ | | 5 ———— $\dot{1}$ |
| *Teacher:* | What color is the grass?<br>Where do you live?<br>How old are you? | *Children:* | The grass is green.<br>I live in New York.<br>I am six years old. |
| | $\dot{1}$ ———— 6 4 | | $\dot{1}$ ———— 6 4 |
| *Teacher:* | Do you like to sing?<br>What color is the snow?<br>How do you feel to- day? | *Children:* | Yes, I like to sing.<br>The snow is white.<br>I feel fine to- day. |

# Notation

**Number Notation** 1 = DO *Pronounced as in "dough"*
2 = RE *Pronounced as in "ray"*

**Finger Notation** *Teacher uses left hand. Child uses right hand as if looking in a mirror.*

1 = DO  2 = RE 

**Measuring (Melodic) Gesture** *Teacher uses left hand. Child uses right hand.*

DO

RE

# *Dictations*

**Eye Tests** (1 = A♭)

*"Look-and-Remember" Games*

*Dictations are given with pointer at* Diagram 1 *on the board; with finger and/or arm gestures; by visual memory, i.e., teacher writes numbers on the board and erases them from left to right; children observe, then turn away and sing from memory.*

| | | | |
|---|---|---|---|
| 1 2 | 1 2 2 | 1 1 2 | 1 2 2 1 |
| 2 1 | 2 1 1 | 1 2 2 | 1 1 2 2 |

**Ear Tests** (1 = A♭)

*"Listening" Games*

*Teacher sings a group of tones on the syllable* Nu *(as in "noon"). Children must identify the tones sung by pointing to the correct numbers on the chart, or by showing the appropriate* Measuring Gesture. *Same tests as those given above may be used.*

**Rhythmic Dictations**

(1 = A♭)

*Teacher sings on* Nu *while making* Rhythmic Gesture I *or* II.

# *Songs*

*Melodic application of* Rhythm Patterns - Series 1.

**Song 1** (1 = A)

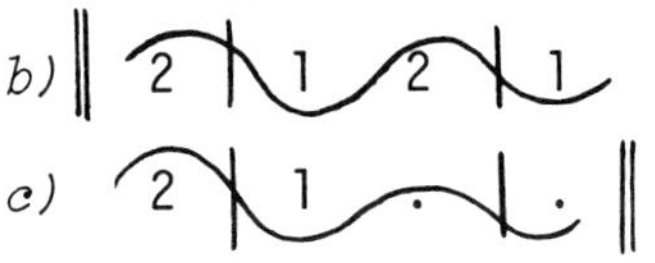


**Song 2** (1 = A)

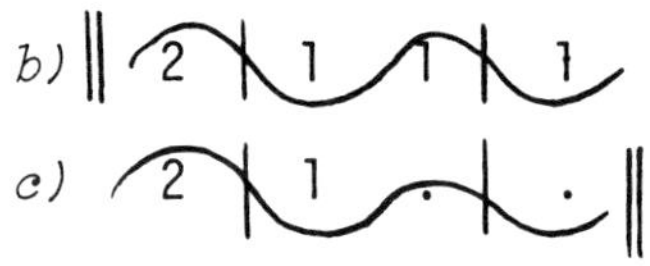


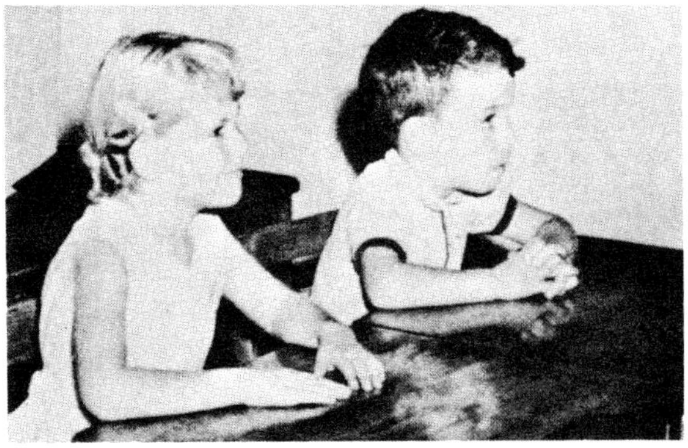

*"Look and remember"*

# PEDAGOGY FOR CHAPTER ONE

## FIRST DAY

*The teacher's first task is to group the children as follows:*

1. *Those who can hear and imitate different pitches. For the time being these children will be called* Bluebirds. *Listen especially for clear resonant tone.*

2. *Those who cannot do so, who merely drone and mumble. For the time being these will be called* Sparrows.

*This grouping is very important - although difficult - and the teacher must attend to it at the very beginning of the school year with a new class. The Sparrows should be seated together and separated from the Bluebirds. In the beginning, they will do more listening than singing. The reason for insisting on this separation of the groups is this: unless droners are temporarily silenced no child in the room can ever hear an accurately matched pitch. Droners eventually find their singing voices if they listen attentively to the children who do sing on pitch. Now and then the teacher will test the Sparrows as a group by offering them a lower pitch than that given the singers. Bluebirds do not sing while Sparrows are being tested.*

### Vocal Exercise 1

*Teacher blows A or* $A^b$ *on pitch pipe. Teacher then sings a prolonged* Nu *(pronounced as "oo" in the word noon ) on the same pitch.*

*Children are invited to imitate.*

*Teacher listens attentively, showing no surprise at the chaos of sounds. The children who match the given pitch accurately are separated immediately from the others. They will henceforth be called Bluebirds.*

*Teacher repeats* Nu *and then explains that we all have two voices:*

1. *A speaking voice for talking - "as I am talking to you now;" and*

2. *A musical voice for singing. Teacher gives an illustration.*

*CHILDREN STAND*

*"Some children take longer than others to find their singing voice. It may be hidden like a secret. But it is there. How can we find it? By listening."*

*Teacher sings* Nu *on the pitch C. Children imitate.*

*Teacher sings* Nu *on A or B. After two or three trials, children imitating, teacher turns to the next segment of the lesson.*

First Day

Intonation Exercise 1 *Presentation of* DO *and* RE.

*CHILDREN SIT*

*While singing the syllable* NU *twice on the pitch* $A^b$, *the teacher makes the* Melodic Gesture *for the tone* DO, *pronounced as in "dough". The teacher uses left hand for the gesture.*

*Children imitate using right hand for the gesture.*

*Teacher: "How many* DO*'s did you sing?*

*After the children answer, the teacher again sings two tones on* NU, *but this time the pitch of the second tone is different from that of the first tone. For example, the teacher sings* NU *on the pitch of* DO, *then, with a large upward gesture of the hand and forearm, sings the second pitch one step higher, that is,* NU *on the pitch of* RE, *pronounced as in "ray".*

*Teacher: How many tones did I sing? (Two)*

*Teacher: Were they both alike? (No)*

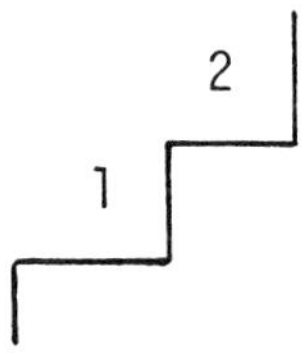


*Teacher draws two steps of a stairway and places the numbers* 1 *and* 2 *as illustrated at right.*

*Teacher sings two tones again on syllable* Nu *while making* Melodic (Measuring) Gesture.

*Teacher invites Bluebirds to sing the same two* Nu*'s while making* Melodic Gesture. *Sparrows make the gesture but do not sing.*

*Teacher announces that each tone has a name. These two tones are called* DO *(as in "dough") and* RE *(as in "ray").*

*Teacher erases stairs and places the two numbers in a frame. This produces* Intonation Diagram 1.

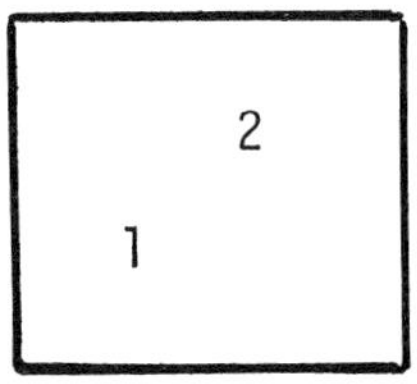


Diagram 1

*Using pointer, teacher will show and sing the first line of* Intonation Exercise 1*:* (DO = 1, RE = 2).

1 2 2 1

*Making* Melodic Gesture, *Bluebirds imitate. Sparrows listen.*

First Day

## Rhythm Gesture 1

*CHILDREN STAND* *assuming positions that leave their arms free to move without touching others.*

*All take "Starting Pose" and hold it momentarily. (Bluebirds and Sparrows.)*

*All take "Up Pose" and hold it.*

*All take "Down Pose" and hold it.*

*Up and Down postures are now alternated slowly. End with arms folded as shown in drawing.*

*The gesture must be made quite slowly until the total body movement has been grasped: arms moving freely from the shoulders; wrists loose and flexible; fingers drooping - on the UP pulse of the movement as well as the DOWN pulse; weight of body on left foot, while right foot, set at an angle, provides equilibrium.*

*The gesture does not become rhythmic until it can be repeated several times without stopping rather quickly.*

*After six or seven up-and-down movements have been linked together, the teacher turns again to Intonation.*

## Intonation Exercise 1

*CHILDREN SIT*

*Teacher shows* Diagram 1 (DO *and* RE) *then sings Line 2 of the exercise pointing to numbers while singing:*

1 2 1  1 2 2  1 2  1 2 1

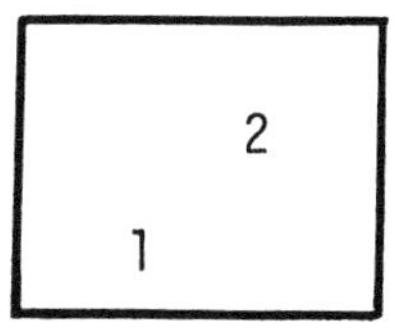


*Bluebirds imitate while making* Melodic Gesture. *Sparrows make the same gesture but do not sing.*

First Day

## Finger Notation

*For variety, the tones* DO *and* RE *can be shown on fingers.*

*Teacher shows* DO *and* RE *while singing the two tones. Teacher uses fingers of left hand while children, facing teacher, use fingers of right hand.*

1. *Teacher shows* DO RE. *Bluebirds sing same tones.*

2. *Teacher sings* DO RE. *Bluebirds show tones on their fingers.*
   *Sparrows too can show them but they will not sing.*

## Melodic Dictation

*Teacher: "We are going to play a guessing game. You look at the diagram and guess the names of the tones I sing."*

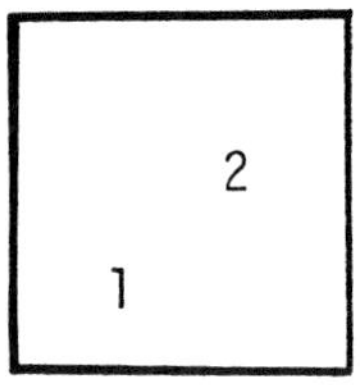


*Teacher sings pitches* DO and RE *using the syllable* NU.

*All make* Melodic Gesture *but only Bluebirds sing note-names.*

*Teacher: "Could anyone step down the stair and sing* RE DO?" *Teacher points to tones and sings them.*

*Children imitate. Teacher sings two tones again. Children imitate.*

## Vocal Exercise 1

*CHILDREN STAND*

*1 = A*$^{b}$

*Teacher gives pitch and invites Bluebirds to sing it. Teacher repeats pitch and invites Sparrows to try to sing it.*

## Vocal Exercise 2

*1 = A*$^{b}$

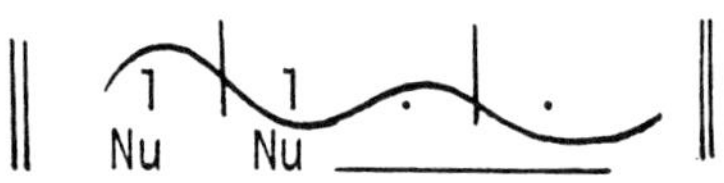


*Teacher sings exercise first. Children imitate.*

First Day

## Visual Memory

*Teacher announces a new game with* DO *and* RE.

*"Watch the notes I point to on the Diagram and remember them."*

*Teacher sings "This is* DO*," (on A♭), then points to* 1 2 2 .

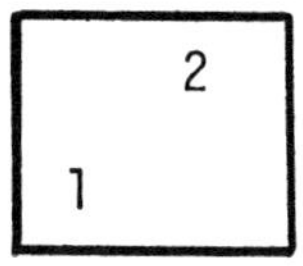


*Children look, remember and sing:* 1 2 2
DO RE RE

*Repeat, using fingers instead of board diagram.*

1. *Teacher sings while showing tones on fingers.*
2. *Children observe, remember and sing while using their own fingers.*

*Sparrows may join the finger game but in silence.*

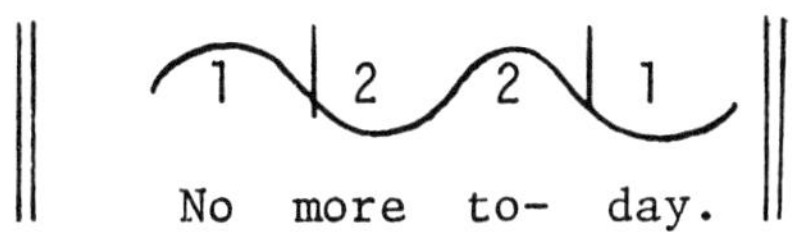


End of First Day

## SECOND DAY

*Prepare on board:*

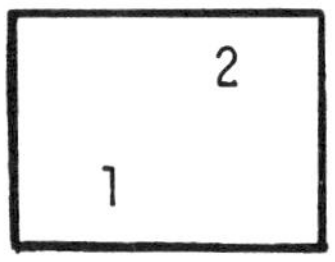

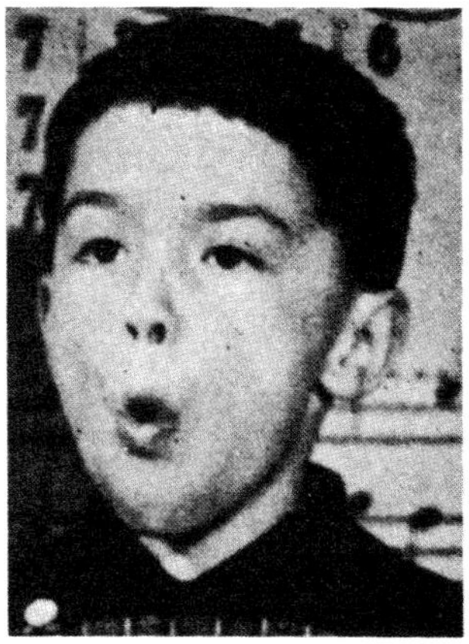

*Follow same plan as on first day.*

### Vocal Exercise 1 *CHILDREN STAND*

*Teacher sings* Nu *on C exaggerating the initial N.*

*Bluebirds imitate.*

*Teacher sings* Nu *on* $E^b$ *and invites Sparrows to imitate it. As the Sparrows respond, teacher will listen carefully to discover children who try very hard to match the pitch and who sometimes do match it. They are to be separated from the droners and placed in a separate category, for example,* Robins, *as soon as possible.*

*Remember that vocal exercises are to be sung slowly with mouth slightly open in the shape of an egg up and down for the vocalising syllable* Nu.

### Intonation Exercise 1 - Line 2 *CHILDREN SIT*

Teacher: *"Who remembers the names of the tones we sang yesterday? Who can show them on fingers?"*

*"Listen to what I sing. Then you show it on your fingers."*
*Sings* 1 2 1 1 2 2 *several times with* Melodic Gesture *for* DO RE.

*Each time children respond with fingers.*

*(1 =* $A^b$*)* *Using* Diagram 1, *the teacher invites the Bluebirds to follow the pointer, singing the correct tones as directed.*

*The Robins and Sparrows will also try to sing the line but at a lower pitch level, for example on F or E. All use* Melodic Gesture.

Second Day

## Rhythm Gesture 1 *CHILDREN STAND*

*Teacher will insist on precision and unity of action. The class can be divided so that one half can watch while the other half practises the gesture. Note position of arms, wrists and feet.*

= *One rhythm. Like breathing: inhale (Up); exhale (Down).*

## Dictation - Ear Tests *CHILDREN SIT*

*After reviewing the tones of* Diagram 1, *teacher says:*

*"Listen carefully, I will begin with* DO *and you will guess the other tones."*

*Teacher sings on* Nu *while making* Melodic (Measuring) Gesture*:* 1 2 2

*Children sing* 1 2 2 *on* Nu *while making gesture.*

*Children repeat singing names of tones:* DO RE RE.

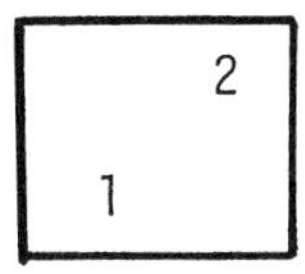


*Finally they all show* 1 2 2 *on fingers.*

*Repeat process for* 1 1 2 *and for* 2 1 1.

## Dictation - Eye Tests (Visual Memory)

*Teacher: "Children, look and remember!"*

*Teacher sings* DO *and points in silence to numbers on* Diagram 1:

1 2 2 1

*Children name notes. Bluebirds sing note names. Robins and Sparrows make gesture.*

*Teacher sings* DO *and indicates pitches on fingers of left hand silently:*

1 1 2 2

*Children name notes. Bluebirds sing notes. Robins and Sparrows show notes on fingers.*

## Vocal Exercise 1 *CHILDREN STAND*

*1 = A Show how lips come forward as when whistling and mouth opens by dropping chin. Divide class so that each group sings and each in turn watches and listens.*

Second Day

## Pitch Calls and Tone Matching

<u>*The Ball Game*</u>. *Teacher pretends to toss a ball to someone in the class while singing. Child catches the ball if he matches the pitch in his response. If response is made on an incorrect pitch, child did not catch the ball.*

$\dot{1}$ ________________ $\dot{1}$ 6 — $\dot{1}$ $\dot{1}$ 6
*Teacher:* Here comes the red ball, I throw it. *Child:* I catch it.

5 ________________ 5 $\dot{1}$ — 5 5 $\dot{1}$
*Teacher:* Here comes the green ball. I throw it. *Child:* I catch it.

$\dot{1}$ ________________ 6 4 — $\dot{1}$ 6 4
*Teacher:* Here comes the blue ball. I throw it. *Child:* I catch it.

## Rhythmic Dictation *CHILDREN SIT*

*Teacher sings a single rhythm while making gesture:*

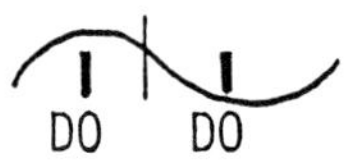


*Children imitate.*

*Teacher: "Can you find this pattern on the board?" One child is invited to come forward and point to it.*

*Teacher: "We shall try to draw this figure while we sing." One child draws on board without chalk, Others draw in the air.*

*Teacher sings* DO DO *while making two strokes clearly on the board.*

*Child at board repeats, passing a finger precisely where teacher has made the two strokes.*

*Others sing and make gesture in air. Repeat several times until accuracy is achieved.*

## Song 1 *(1 = A)* *CHILDREN STAND*

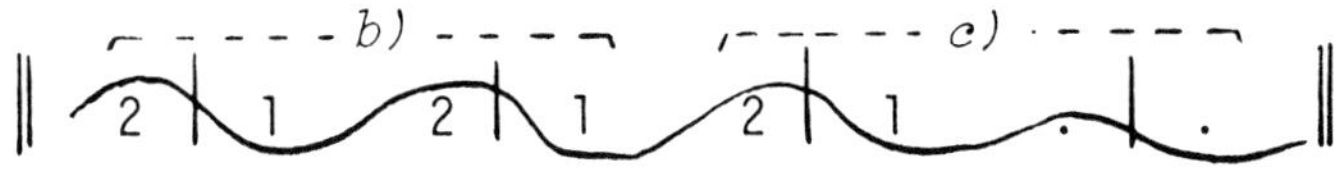


*Teacher shows Pattern 1 on board and sings it once while making* Measuring Gesture.

*Teacher repeats while making* Rhythm Gesture I.

*Children imitate: Bluebirds first; then Robins. Sparrows make gesture without singing.*

*Sing single rhythmic unit three times in succession. Take final posture of repose at end.*

End of Second Day

## THIRD DAY

*Prepare on board:*

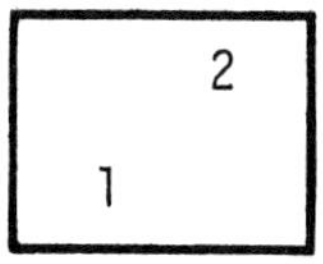

*Follow plan of first and second days.*

*By this time the grouping of Bluebirds, Robins and Sparrows should be quite well advanced so that good tones can be heard. Bluebirds usually sing first so that a pure tone can be heard by all. Then Robins will follow. Some among them may be promoted as soon as they can sing on pitch. Even Sparrows should be given a moment's test - as a group, not singly.*

### Vocal Exercise 1 *CHILDREN STAND*

*Teacher sings:* *1 = B* || 1 ________ Nu ________ ||

*Children listen. Bluebirds sing several times trying to obtain a feeling of resonance in head cavities.*

*Robins imitate Bluebirds trying to match their tone quality.*

*Sparrows sing on F after teacher has sung model.*

*During these vocalises the teacher should move through the groups listening for droners and for those children who are improving in accuracy.*

### Pitch Calls and Tone Matching

*Continue with Ball Game giving special attention to Sparrows on lower pitches such as F or* $E^b$.

### Intonation *CHILDREN SIT*

*Show* Diagram 1 *already drawn on board. Using pointer, teacher sings* DO RE.

*Children imitate, making* Melodic Gesture *as they sing.*

*Teacher:* *"Now, let us step down stairs." Sings* RE DO *using* Melodic Gesture *with left arm. Children imitate, using right arm for gesture. Practise* RE DO *on fingers.*

Third Day

## Intonation Exercise 2 *CHILDREN SIT*

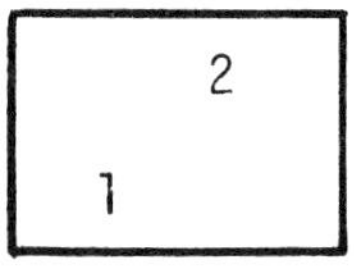


Diagram 1

*Teacher points to notes of* Intonation Exercise 2 *on* Diagram 1 *with pointer. Bluebirds try to follow. Use only three lines of segment a).*

*a)* →

| 1 | 1 | 1 | 2 | 1 |
|---|---|---|---|---|
| 1 | 2 | 2 | 2 | 1 |
| 1 | 2 | 2 | 1 | 1 |

## Tonal Dictation (Ear Tests)

*Following the Intonation Exercise, teacher gives melodic dictation. Keeping* Diagram 1 *in full view of class, teacher sings* DO *(1 = A♭), pauses, then sings on syllable* Nu:

2 2 2 1
Nu Nu Nu Nu

*A child is invited to come to the board and identify correctly the pitches sung by pointing to numbers of the diagram.*

*A second dictation is given by the teacher:* 2 1 2 1 *A second child is invited to come to the board to identify and sing the pitches given.*

## Visual Memory (Eye Tests)

*Teacher shows four notes* *silently* *in one of the following ways:*

*Pointing to notes of* Diagram 1
*On fingers* - Finger Notation
*With* Measuring (Melodic) Gesture

*Children try to remember and repeat by* *singing* *and at the same time giving the correct note-names of the pitches dictated:*

1 2 2 1
2 1 2 1
2 1 1 1

*Teacher can vary the presentation by:*

*Writing four notes on board ;*
*Letting children study briefly the phrase given;*
*Erasing numbers slowly from left to right.*

*Children then try to sing correctly the dictated notes identifying them by their correct note-names.*

Third Day

## Ear Tests

"Teacher: "*Listen and tell me the names of the notes I sing.*"

1 2 2 1
Nu Nu Nu Nu

*Children repeat tones also on* Nu, *then sing them on note-names while making* Melodic Gesture.

*Teacher then uses fingers to dictate while singing on* Nu: 1 2 2

*Children use fingers, then* Melodic Gesture. *Finally, they sing note-names.*

*Repeat procedure for additional tests:* 2 2 1

2 1 1

1 2 1

## Rhythm Gesture I *CHILDREN STAND*

*Starting Pose*

*Up....*

*Posture of Repose*

*Children stand at posture of repose: arms crossed, weight of body on right (rear) leg. (See below.)*

Teacher: *"Prepare for eight rhythms, that is, UP-DOWN eight times."*

*"Now take starting pose." Children stretch arms horizontally. Weight on left (forward) leg. Hold this position until teacher gives the command:*

*"Up-Down now start," moving hands up and down in time with the command.*

*Children begin rhythm gesture.*

*There should be no hesitation nor pause between teacher's command and children's response. While moving they count:*

*Up - One*

*Up - Two. . . etc. until at*

*Up - Eight they take posture of repose again.*

*Repeat for precision.*

Third Day

Notation - *Rhythm Strokes - Rhythm Curve - Measure Bars*

*Presenting written form of* Rhythm Patterns - Series 1.

*1.* Pattern *a)*

*Teacher draws two vertical strokes on board using white chalk while singing* DO DO. 1 1

*A child is invited to board to trace strokes with index finger. Same child then draws* 1 1 *on board with same index finger. (No chalk yet.) If gesture is precise, child is permitted to draw two strokes on board with chalk in strict time.*

> *At same time, all other children make two strokes in the air. Bluebirds sing* DO DO *on one pitch (1 = A), while drawing strokes in air.*
> *Robins and Sparrows make stroke but only whisper* DO DO.

*Teacher sings* DO DO *while drawing rhythm wave with a different color of chalk.*
*Children imitate tones and the curving gesture.*

*Teacher draws bar lines between the two notes with a third color of chalk.*

*2.* Pattern *b)*

*Same procedure as above. Then pointing to* Pattern *b) prepared on board:*

*"How many* DO*'s ?"*
*"How many UP? How many DOWN?"*

*CHILDREN STAND*

*On another part of the board teacher writes* Pattern *b) in strict time: notes, rhythm wave and bar lines.*

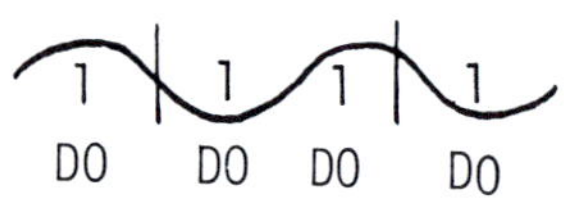


*Bluebirds invited to sing four* DO*'s while making* Rhythm Gesture 1. *All others make gesture but do not sing. (1 = A)*

*Bluebirds invited to sing four* RE*'s. All others make gesture.*

*"We have sung* DO *and* RE *four times each. Who can sing this?"*

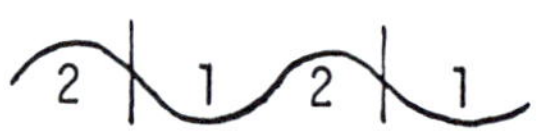


*Child who sings phrase correctly comes to front of class and repeats exercise while making gesture. Robins repeat. Sparrows make gesture.*

## Third Day

### 3. Pattern *c)*

*"If dots are added to a rhythm, that means the tone is held for a long time. For example, let us sing one rhythm:*

*Now I shall add two dots to the last note and listen to what happens:"*

*Teacher sings rhythm on* DO DO *holding the second tone for two more counts. assuming posture of repose on the last dot.*

*"Did you notice what happened?"*

*Bluebirds sing* DO DO *and hold second tone to posture of repose. Others repeat gesture.*

### Rhythmic Dictation

*With three patterns of the series being studied in full view of the class, teacher sings one of them while making gesture.*

*"Which of the three did I sing?" All repeat with gesture.*

*Teacher sings another pattern. "Which one did I sing that time?" All repeat with gesture.*

*Teacher sings third rhythm.*

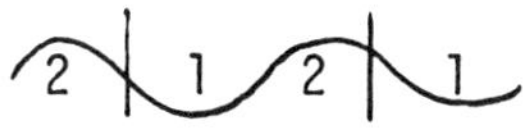


*All repeat while making rhythmic gesture.*

*"Repeat after me:"*

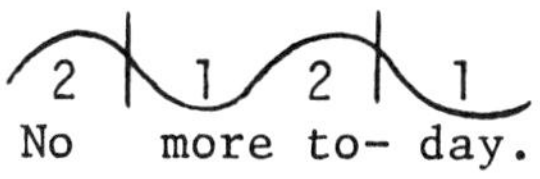


### End of Third Day

## FOURTH DAY

*Prepare on board:*

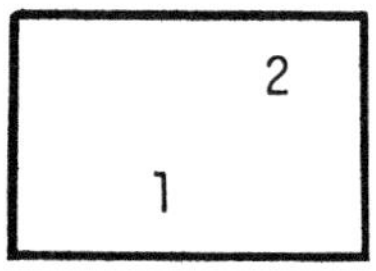


Diagram 1

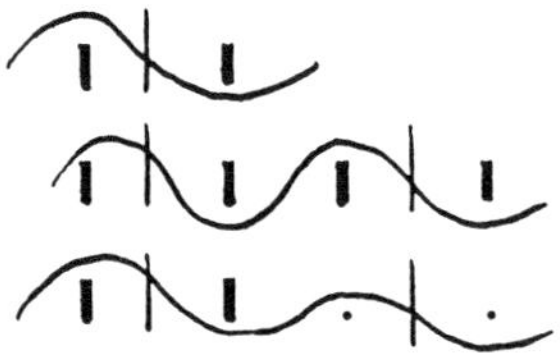

*Children take their special seats for music class according to groups:*

*Bluebirds*
*Robins*
*Sparrows*

Vocal Exercise 1 *CHILDREN STAND*

*1 = D* ‖ 1 ________ ‖
Nu ________

*Teacher sings long* Nu *on D, exaggerating Nnnnn sound. Bluebirds imitate exaggerating Nnnnn sound. Robins also imitate. Sparrows listen.*

*A child is singled out whose voice is clear and well focused to sing alone. All others listen. Bluebirds imitate. Robins likewise.*

*A lower pitch - F or G is given for Sparrows. Teacher listens for those who are really trying to match pitch.*

Tone Matching and Conversation *CHILDREN SIT*

*Teacher selects phrases not used thus far and calls on children who have not as yet volunteered. All children must be given an opportunity to participate.*

Intonation Exercise 2 On Diagram 1

*b)* ⟶
| 1 2 1 1 1 |
| 1 2 1 1 2 |
| 2 1 2 1 1 |

*Teacher uses pointer and invites children - in groups - to follow the pointer. Others listen. Exercise can also be given with* Melodic Gesture *and* Finger Notation.

## Fourth Day

**Rhythm Gesture II** *See text - Page 2.* *CHILDREN STAND*

*Same as* Rhythm Gesture I *but arms are extended out to the sides like bird wings. The UP - DOWN movement is the same. Repeat eight times with teacher counting:*

*Up-one, up-two, up-three . . . . to up-eight.*
*Children then assume posture of repose.*

*Two children who are especially precise and graceful come to front of class to demonstrate and lead the others.*

**Dictation** *CHILDREN SIT*

**Ear Tests** *With diagram in full view of class, teacher sings on* Nu *while children listen:*

*a)* 1 1 2 2 *b)* 1 2 2 2 *c)* 2 2 1 1 *d)* 1 2 1 1

*After each dictation is sung, children are asked to identify pitches sung by pointing to notes on diagram and singing tones while pointing. If correct, all children - group by group - repeat.*

**Eye Tests** *Teacher points silently - but rhythmically - to numbers on diagram. At the same time, children try to find notes dictated by making arm gesture or on fingers:*

1 1 1 2 2 2 2 1 1 1
1 1 2 1 1 2 1 1 2

*Teacher may also give dictation silently with* Melodic Gesture *or on* Finger Notation. *Children must identify (singing) by name all pitches dictated by teacher all the while repeating the teacher's gesture.*

**Vocal Exercise 2** *CHILDREN STAND*

*This exercise should be sung with a light but springy up-pulse and a smooth connection through* Nnnn *to the long tone on the down-pulse.*

*Teacher sings exercise while making* Rhythm Gesture I.
*Bluebirds repeat. Then Robins repeat. Sparrows listen but make gesture.*

$1 = B^{\flat}$

*Teacher gives pitch of G or F and tests Sparrows as a group listening for those who are showing signs of improvement.*

Fourth Day

<u>Metrical Gesture *and* Metrical Language</u> *(See page 2 of text)*

*"For each rhythm stroke the finger of the right hand touches the palm of the left hand. Each time you do this you say:* la.

*Let us practise."*

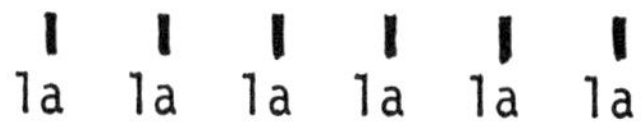


*Pointing to* Rhythm Patterns - Series 1, *teacher says:*

*"Let us now sing one rhythm:"*

*(1 = A) Repeat several times pausing between each repetition.*

*"Let us now sing the second pattern:"*

*Repeat several times.*

*"You notice that the third pattern has a long note. How can you tell? By the dots that are added. When you see dots beside a note, you say* long *for that note and press into the palm of your hand for each dot. For example:"*

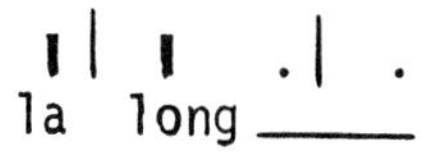


*Repeat several times.*

## Song 1 *(1 = A)*

*"We are now going to combine the second and third patterns to make up a song. Let us sing the rhythms first while making the gesture we just learned."*

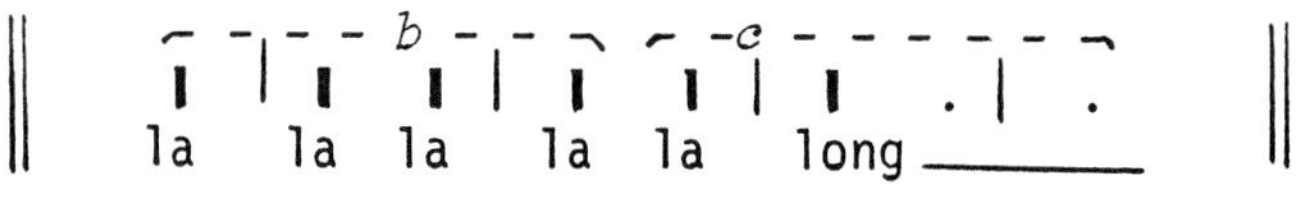


*"Instead of singing the rhythm words, we shall now sing the note names."*

<u>*CHILDREN STAND*</u>

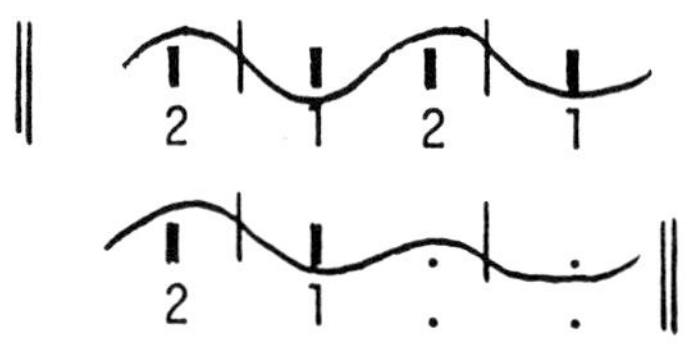


*Teacher sings with* Rhythm Gesture I *on syllable* Nu

*Children imitate.*

*Teacher sings with note names while making gesture. Children imitate - one group at a time.*

*Teacher:*

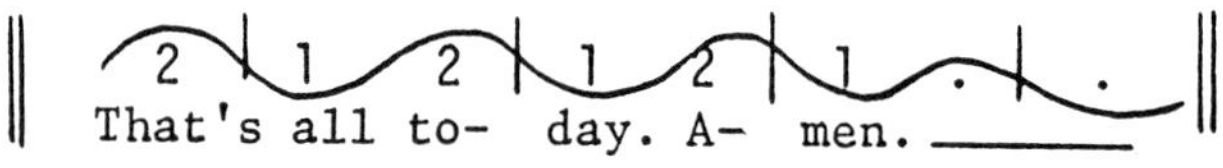


*Children repeat.*

<u>End of Fourth Day</u>

## FIFTH DAY

*Prepare on board:*

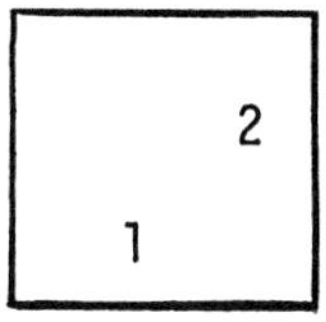


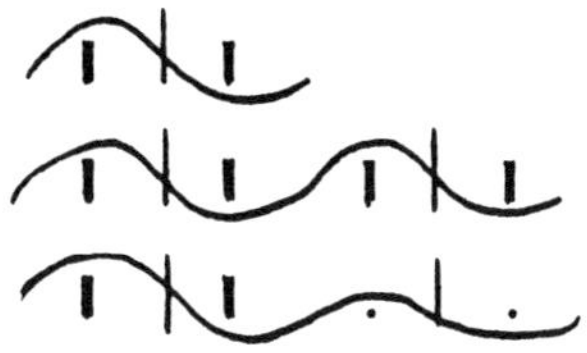

### Tone Matching and Conversation *CHILDREN STAND*

($\dot{1} = B^b$) *Teacher:* $\dot{1}$ ______ 6
Good morning, Bluebirds.
Good morning, Robins.
Good morning, Sparrows.

*Children:* $\dot{1}$ ______ 6
Good morning, Teacher.

*Teacher:* 5 ______ $\dot{1}$
How are you to- day?

*Children:* 5 ______ $\dot{1}$
We are fine, thank you.

### Vocal Exercise 1

*"Let us sing a nice long tone like this:"*

*1 = C* ‖ 1 ______ ‖
Nu ______

*Teacher sings exaggerating* Nnnn.

*Bluebirds repeat.*

*1 = G for Robins.*

*1 = C for Bluebirds.*

*1 = A for Robins.*

*1 = F for Sparrows. (Do not spend too much time here.)*

### Intonation Exercise 2 *with* Diagram 1 *CHILDREN SIT*

*1 = A* *Bluebirds follow pointer for segment a).*
*Robins follow pointer for segment b).*
*Bluebirds and Robins follow pointer for segment c).*

*Segments of exercise may also be shown on overhead projector.*

Fifth Day

Rhythm Patterns Series 1  CHILDREN STAND

1. *Practise using* Metrical Gesture *and* Metrical Language.

   *Review* I = la    I . . = long

   *1 = A*

   I | I
   la la

   I | I   I | I
   la la la la

   I | I  . | .
   la long______   *(Remember: right hand presses into palm of left hand for each dot.)*

2. *Repeat each line several times while singing* DO *and making* Rhythm Gesture 1. *Work for precision so that large body muscles will learn to coordinate with and reinforce the eye and ear perceptions.*

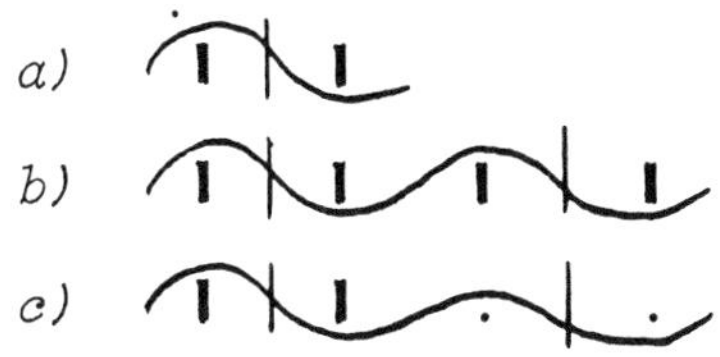


3. *Repeat several times on note names while making rhythm gesture.*

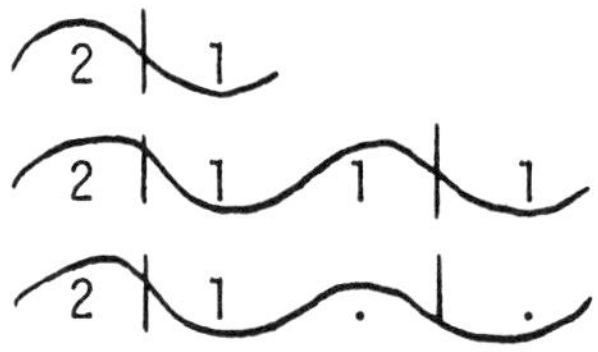


**Song 2** *Melodic application of patterns b) and c).*

*(1 = A)*   *Teacher sings first line while making* Rhythm Gesture 1.
*Bluebirds and Robins repeat.*
*Sparrows make gesture but do not sing.*

*Teacher sings second line to posture of repose. Bluebirds and Robins repeat. Sparrows make gesture but do not sing.*

*Bluebirds invited to sing two lines without stopping. Robins repeat.*

Ear Tests - Diagram 1 CHILDREN SIT

*After announcing the pitch of* DO *(1 = A), teacher sings one of the following:*

| 1 1 2 2 2 | 2 2 1 1 1 | 1 2 1 2 1 |
|---|---|---|
| Nu Nu Nu Nu Nu | | |

*Children respond by offering to "discover" notes on diagram or their fingers.*

Fifth Day

## Eye Tests *"Look and remember"*

*Teacher dictates silently one of the following note groups while pointing to numbers on the diagram or by using finger notation.*

| | | |
|---|---|---|
| 1 2 2 | 2 2 1 | 1 2 1 |
| 1 1 2 | 2 1 1 | 1 2 1 |

*Sparrows show notes on fingers while Bluebirds and Robins sing.*

## Vocal Exercise 2

*1 = C*

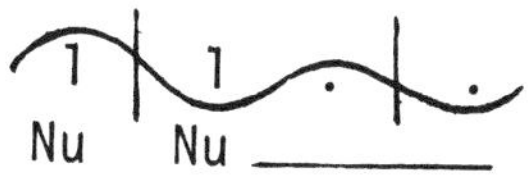


*Work for good lift on the up-pulse and for precision of posture of repose on long note. Try individuals in this exercise. Test Robins and Sparrows for possible promotions.*

*Teacher gives first model followed by Bluebirds. Then Robins.*

## Tone Matching - The Ball Game

*Teacher selects child to whom the "ball" will be thrown. Child is said to catch the ball only if he succeeds in matching the pitch. Several others try to catch it.*

| | |
|---|---|
| $\dot{1}$ ______ 6<br>Here comes the red ball. I throw it. | $\dot{1}$ $\dot{1}$ 6<br>I catch it. |
| 5 ______ $\dot{1}$<br>Here comes the green ball. I throw it. | 5 5 $\dot{1}$<br>I catch it. |
| $\dot{1}$ ______ $\dot{1}$ 6 4<br>Here comes the blue ball. I throw it. | $\dot{1}$ 6 4<br>I catch it. |

*A child could also be invited to throw the ball to a friend using one of the above formulae.*

## Rhythm Gesture 1 *CHILDREN STAND*

*Check starting pose, lift* *__from the wrist__* *for the up-pulse and posture of repose.*

*Bluebirds and Sparrows make gesture while Robins. say:*
*"Up one, up two, up three, up four."*

*Robins and Sparrows make gesture while Bluebirds continue:*
*"Up five, up six, up seven up eight."*

Fifth Day

Metrical Guessing Game *CHILDREN SIT*

*Teacher writes three patterns on board and then with the pointer taps one of them. Children tap same patterns and identify the correct one.*

*Children repeat using* Metrical Language *and* Metrical Gesture.

*a)* 2 | 1

*b)* 2 | 1 1 | 1

*c)* 2 | 1 . | .

*CHILDREN STAND*

*Children sing note names while making* Metrical Gesture *(1 = A)*

*Individuals invited to sing Patterns b) and c) while making* Rhythmic Gesture 1. *Others follow in groups.*

|| 2 1 1 1 2 1 . . ||

*Teacher:* That's all to- day. A- men.

*Children repeat to posture of repose.*

End of Fifth Day

PRINCIPLES OF PEDAGOGY APPLIED IN PRESENTING CONTENT OF CHAPTER ONE

By the end of this series of lessons - offered as a model for presenting the content of Chapter One - the children should have:

1. Progressed from known to related unknown;
2. Assimilated a variety of musical ideas through the senses of touch, hearing, seeing, and through the use of large body muscles.

Furthermore, several important musical elements have been introduced and explored, such as: moments of intense activity followed by moments of intense concentration involving children in tones and pulse mechanisms; variations in posture for ear and eye tests and rhythm drills; attentive listening to models of accurate pitch and good tone. All of these have been presented in planned sequence for five full 20-minute periods.

SUMMARY OF GOALS ACHIEVED THUS FAR

Several important baselines have been set which will prove indispensable for teaching the remainder of the book.

1. Class has been grouped, at least tentatively, into three sections:

   Bluebirds who can readily match pitches;
   Robins who try and often succeed in matching pitches;
   Sparrows who have not as yet become aware of pitch.

2. Voices have been guided toward the resonating cavities of the head.

3. Rhythm, in its most elemental form (Up-Down), has been taught through: muscular coordination and control; visual and aural memory; physical response in gestures.

4. Tonal relationships have been established. DO and RE have been taught in a variety of ways. Two tones are not many, but the manner of presentation and learning help to establish a foundation for future development.

5. While some imitation has been used in these lessons, it should be noted that even in this elementary stage of training, children must be encouraged to measure time and pitch distances on their own. In this way they will become musical "thinkers" and not just parrots.

SUGGESTIONS FOR TEACHERS

In presenting a lesson, teachers must keep verbal commentaries down to a minimum. Talking instead of singing can use up too much time and is most often indulged in by the teacher to no particular avail as far as the children or music are concerned.

Teacher ought to avoid singing <u>with</u> the children as much as possible. Listening to the children as they sing can exert a strong effect on their concentration.

FINALLY

Teachers who have aroused the children's interest in music after these lessons can be considered successful.

# Chapter Two

| | 1 | 2 | 3 | 4 | 5 |
|---|---|---|---|---|---|
| Stand<br>**Vocal Training** | Tone matching and greeting | Voc. Ex. No. 1 | 1 ___ Nu ___ | | |
| | Group I 1̇ ___ 6<br>*Ball Game* | Concentrate on Group II<br>1 ___ 3<br>*What Is Your Name?* | Concentrate on Group III<br>1̇ ___ 6<br>*Ball Game* | Groups I and II<br>Matching tones in conversation. Finding things (1-5) | Groups I and II<br>Color Game 1̇ ___ 6 ___ 4<br>Test Group III |
| Sit<br>**Intonation** | **Present:**<br>*Intonation Diagram 2*<br>[diagram: 1, 2, 3]<br>*Int. Ex. 3a*<br>Pointer with Groups I and II<br>Measuring Gestures – Gr. III | **Review:**<br>Intonation Diagram 2 →<br>Int. Ex. 3a with pointer<br>3b Measuring Gesture<br>Groups I and II | Groups I and II:<br>Int. Ex. 3b: on Diagram 2 →<br>Group III: Measuring Gesture<br>Show MI on fingers<br>3 2 1<br>3 2 1 1 1<br>3 3 3 2 1 | Group I<br>Int. Ex. 3c – Diagram 2 →<br>1 1 1 2 3<br>3 3 3 2 1<br>Group III Measuring Gesture | **Rev.** Int. Ex. 3a, 3b, 3c<br>Groups I and II Measuring Gesture<br>Group III – Finger Notation |
| Stand<br>**Rhythm**<br>Gestures | **Rev.** Rhythm Gesture I<br>Establish posture<br>Make gesture to rhythm of breathing 1 1 | Rhythm Gesture II →<br>New posture<br>Same rhythm of breathing<br>Repeat 4 times | Sing Rhythm Pattern b) after teacher on DO RE MI<br>Note deep breathing<br>Wrists loose on up-pulse<br>Steady rhythm<br>Include Group III → | Group I sings Rhythm Pattern b) on DO RE MI Group II answers<br>Practise stop with graceful precision → | Rhythm Pattern c)<br>Teacher sings<br>Students follow<br>Check individuals |
| Sit<br>**Dictations** | PREPARE BY SINGING NOTES AGAIN FROM DIAGRAM 2 | | | | |
| | **Ear Tests**<br>1 2 3<br>1 2 3 3<br>**Eye Tests** (Pointer)<br>1 2 3 3 3<br>1 1 1 2 3 | 1 2 3 3 2 3<br>1 2 3 2 3<br>(Arm Gesture)<br>1 2 3 3 2<br>1 2 3 3 2 1 | 1 1 2 3 2 3.<br>3 2 3 2 1<br>(Fingers)<br>1 1 2 3 2 1<br>1 2 3 3 | 1 2 3 2 3<br>2 1 2 3<br>(Arm Gesture)<br>1 1 1 2 3<br>2 1 2 3 | 1 2 2 1 1 2 3<br>1 1 1 2 3<br>(Fingers)<br>1 1 2 3<br>2 3 2 1 |
| Stand<br>**Vocal Training** | Vocal Exercise 2: 1 1 . . | | Voc. Ex. 3 1 1 1 1 . . | | Voc. Ex. 2: 1 1 . . |
| | Test each group<br>I – Bb II – Ab III | Group I Ab Bb<br>Group II G Ab | Group I – A Bb Group II – Ab<br>Group III – G Work with individuals | | Group III Listen for promotions |
| Sit<br>**Rhythm**<br>Rhythm Patterns | [rhythm gestures] | Metrical Language<br>la la la la<br>la long | Rhythm Patterns *Series I*<br>Metrical Language<br>Combine b) and c) | Combine b) and a) | Combine a) and c) |
| Dictations | 1 1 2 3 | 1 1 2 3 3 3 . | 3 2 . | 3 3 2 1 | 2 3 2 1 . |
| Stand<br>**Songs** | Teacher: 1 2 2 1<br>Al - le - lu - ia<br>Students: 2 1 . .<br>A - men. ___ | Song 3 1 1 2 3<br>3 3 . .<br>3 2 2 1<br>1 1 . .<br>Group I – Sing melody<br>Groups II and III make gesture | Song 4 2 1 2 3<br>3 2 . .<br>2 1 2 3<br>2 1 . . | Song 5<br>1 1 1 1 2 3<br>3 3 3 3 2 1 | Song 6<br>1 1 2 3 .<br>2 1 1 1 . . |
| | | | End class with: 1 2 2 1 2 1 .<br>Al - le - lu - ia. A - men. ___ | Teacher-children dialogue: *Hail, Holy Queen*<br>Groups I and II sing with gesture<br>Group III makes gesture only | |

# Chapter Two

*A suggested plan for teaching content of Chapter Two in five lessons is offered on page opposite. The pedagogy for this chapter is given in the pages that follow.*

## CHAPTER CONTENT SUMMARY

### Vocal Training

*Study of vocal timbre with and without rhythm. Continue to group voices.*

*Review* Vocal Exercise 1 — $1 = A^b - B^b - C$

*Review* Vocal Exercise 2 — $1 = A^b - B^b - C$

Vocal Exercise 3 — $(1 = A^b)$

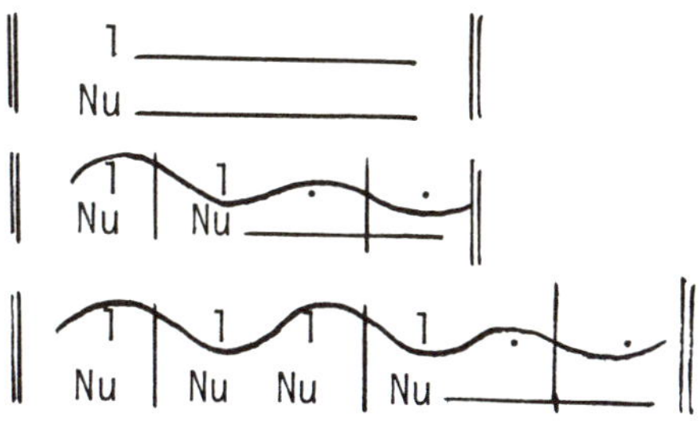


### Intonation

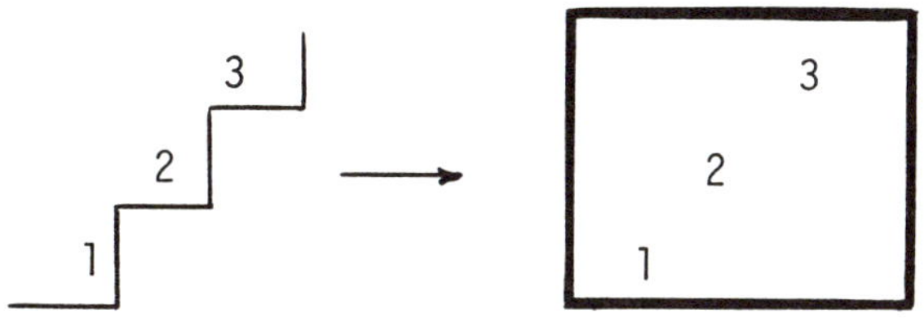


Intonation Diagram 2

Intonation Exercise 3 *Teach on* Intonation Diagram 2

*(1 = $A^b$)*

a) 1 2 3 | b) 3 2 1 |

| 1 2 3 3 3 | 3 2 1 1 1 |

| 1 1 1 2 3 | 3 3 3 2 1 |

c)

### Creative Activity

Step 1 - Improvisation *(Continued)*

*Review musical conversation as given in Chapter One. Add new verbal phrases and melodic patterns. Teacher's greeting.*

| $\dot{1}$ — 6 | 1 — 3 | 4 — 6 — $\dot{1}$ |
|---|---|---|
| Good morning, Bluebirds. | What is your name? | Where is the clock? |

# Notation

<u>Number Notation</u> 1 = DO

2 = RE

3 = MI *Pronounced as in "me"*

<u>Finger Notation</u>

DO  RE  MI 

<u>Measuring (Melodic) Gesture</u>

# Rhythm

*Review* Rhythm Patterns - Series 1 *and melodic application*

*a)*
*b)*
*c)*

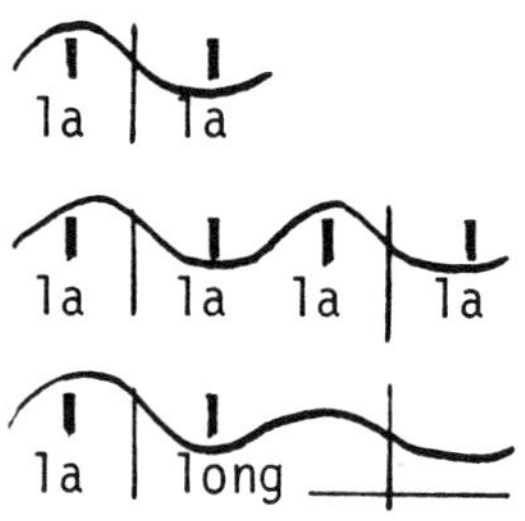


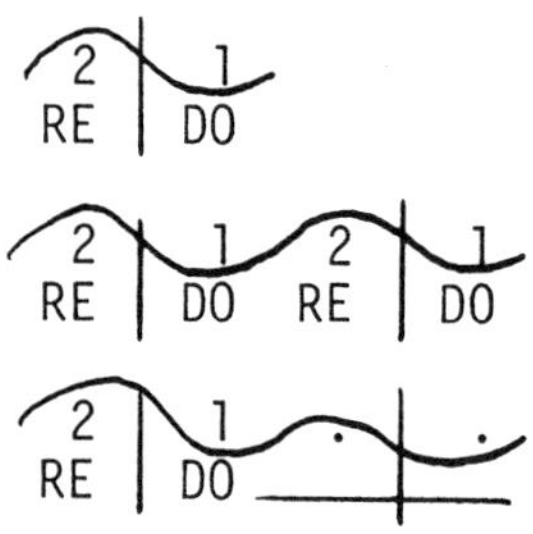

Rhythm Gesture II

*Review* Metrical Gesture I *as in Chapter One*

*Sing with* Metrical Language *and* Metrical Gesture I; *with* Rhythmic Gesture II.

N.B. *See Page 33 for* Melodic Application *of* Rhythm Patterns *in the form of a dialogue between Teacher and Children.*

# Dictations

*"Listening" Games*

<u>Ear Tests</u>

1 2 3 3 2 1     1 2 3 3 2 3     1 2 3 3 3

1 2 3 3 2     1 2 3 2 3

*"Look-and-Remember" Games*

<u>Eye Tests</u>

1 2 3 3 2 1 *(See Lesson Plans for additional tests.)*

1 2 3 2 1

1 2 3 3 2 3 2

3 2 3 2 1     1 1 1 2 3

<u>Rhythmic Dictations</u>

1 | 1 2 | 3     3 | 3 . | .

# Songs

*Application of* Rhythm Patterns - Series 1 *to melody*

**Song 3** *(1 = $A^b$)*

b) ‖ 1 | 1 2 | 3
c) 3 | 3 . | .
b) 3 | 3 2 | 1
c) 1 | 1 . | . ‖

**Song 4** *(1 = $A^b$)*

b) ‖ 2 | 1 2 | 3
c) 3 | 2 . | .
b) 2 | 1 2 | 3
c) 2 | 1 . | . ‖

**Song 5** *(1 = $A^b$)*

‖ 1 | 1 1 | 1 2 | 3 (b: 1 1 1 1; a: 2 3)
3 | 3 3 | 3 2 | 1 ‖

**Song 6** *(1 = $A^b$)*

‖ 1 | 1 2 | 3 . | . (a: 1 1; c: 2 3 . .)
2 | 1 1 | 1 . | . ‖

WORDS AND MELODY

*(1 = $A^b$)*

‖ 1 | 2 . | . ‖
A- men___

‖ 2 | 1 . | . ‖
A - men___

‖ 1 | 2 2 | 1 . | . ‖
Al- le- lu- ia___

*See also* "Hail, Holy Queen" *and* "Hail, Mary" *on Page 35.*

# PEDAGOGY FOR CHAPTER TWO

*In presenting the content of Chapter Two, the teacher's task is easier: voices are tentatively grouped; Bluebirds always sing first; then Robins. Sparrows, for the most part, only listen to singing tones but participate in other activities such as rhythm gestures, finger notation exercises, measuring gestures, guessing games and others. If it is the classroom teacher who gives the music lesson, the Sparrows might be given special help outside the daily music lesson.*

## Vocal Training *CHILDREN STAND*

*Mouth large inside, small outside, lips in whistling position. Teacher must now be concentrating on good quality of vocal emission characterized by a clear resonant tone. (See Chapter Three, Page 37.)*

Vocal Exercise 1. *Long tone on a single pitch. Select keys best suited to Bluebirds and Robins. Periodic testing of Sparrows is given on lower pitches.*

Vocal Exercise 2. *Pitch and rhythm combined. Present this immediately after* Voc. Ex. 1. *Occasionally invite a child to give the model tone. Do not always invite the same child. Vary the solo singer. Special attention to the up-pulse.*

*Teacher should not permit a chaos of mixed pitch sounds from the class whether during vocal or intonation drills. Each group should be responsible for the true pitch requested by the teacher. If the tone is good and the pitch accurate, the teacher must say so. If the tone is not good and the pitch inaccurate, the teacher must also say so.*

*Presenting the Vocal Exercise.*

*Teacher sounds B♭ on pitch-pipe and sings* Nu *on same pitch. Children listen attentively.*

*Bluebirds and Robins (in separate groups) repeat several times, trying to produce a clear, gentle and controlled sound. A lower pitch, for example F, is chosen for Sparrows. Teacher continues to listen for possible promotions, that is, re-grouping of voices.*

Vocal Exercise 3. *Pitch and rhythm combined.*

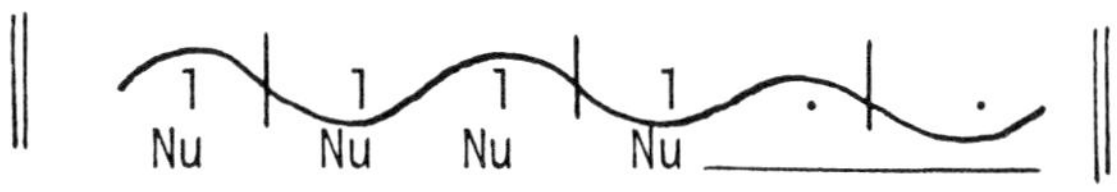


*Here again, the up-pulse must be light. As progress is noted, the teacher will raise the pitch for Bluebirds and Robins. Sparrows will listen quietly and take part in the rhythm gesture.*

INTONATION *CHILDREN SIT*

*Presenting* MI.

*The teacher points to* Diagram 1 *prepared on the board and sings* DO *on* Nu *while making the* Measuring Gesture. *Children repeat and remember the names of the tones.*

*"Listen carefully, you are going to hear something new."*

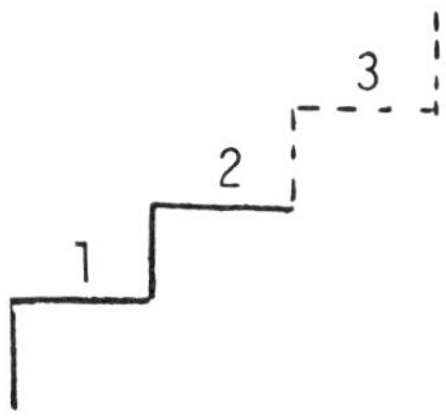



*Teacher then sings* DO *and* RE *again on* Nu *and, while making a broad* Measuring Gesture *(with the left arm), sings* MI *also on* Nu.

*Children repeat the three tones on* Nu *while making the* Measuring Gesture *using their right arms.*

*"Did you hear something new? How many singing steps do we have now?" (Three).*

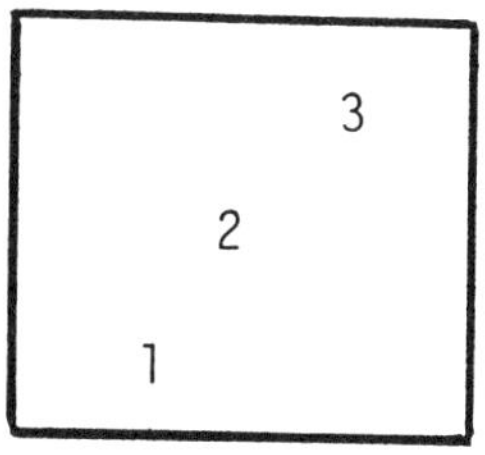



*Teacher draws three steps and writes the figure* 3 *on the third step to produce* Diagram 2.

*After singing* DO RE MI *once again slowly on* Nu, *the teacher gives the third tone its name:* MI *(pronounced as in "me".)*

*Children sing the three tones with their names while making the* Measuring Gesture.

Intonation Exercise 3

*Teacher invites children to follow the pointer and sing notes given in* Intonation Exercise 3, *arrow a). During another lesson on another day, teacher presents arrow b). Arrow c) might be given on a third day.*

*Teacher will make sure that children measure steps accurately. They should not begin to sing until their arms are in correct position. Bluebirds and Robins alternate. Sparrows make gestures but do not sing.*

*"We can also find the note* MI *on our fingers." Teacher demonstrates and children imitate.*

*Intonation exercise is now reviewed using* Finger Notation.

3 MI

*While presenting the content of this chapter, the descending progression* 3 2 1 *must also be practised. "We went up the steps, we can also come down." Progression is shown : on* Diagram 2; *with* Measuring Gesture; *and* Finger Notation.

*Descending progressions are often the sources of off-pitch singing. Care must therefore be taken to correct "flatting" as soon as it is noted. Testing at the end of each line (oftener if necessary), will serve to focus attention on this fault when it occurs.*

RHYTHM *CHILDREN STAND*

Presenting Rhythm Gesture II. *(See drawing on Page 28.)*

*The same precision of movement with equal suppleness is required for* Rhythm Gesture II *as for* Rhythm Gesture I.

*Children take posture with arms stretched to sides like wings; weight slightly forward on front foot; wrists loose; fingers drooping.*

*Practise gesture at first silently to the rhythm of the children's breathing. The action of inhaling coupled with that of exhaling comprise one rhythm. Repeat several times slowly.*

*"We shall now make eight small rhythms without stopping." Children stand in opening position and teacher gives starting command:*

*"Up down now start" Up one Up two etc...*

*At the end of series of small rhythms children assume posture of repose.*

Rhythm Patterns - Series 1. *Board preparation:*

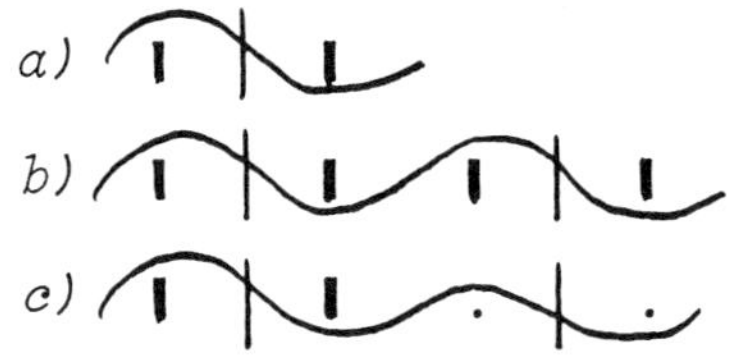


*Review rhythm patterns with* Metrical Gesture *and* Language.

*Bluebirds and Robins alternate singing rhythm patterns while making* Rhythm Gesture II.

Rhythmic Dictation

*A child is called to the board. Teacher sings Pattern b) on syllable* Nu *while making* Rhythm Gesture II.

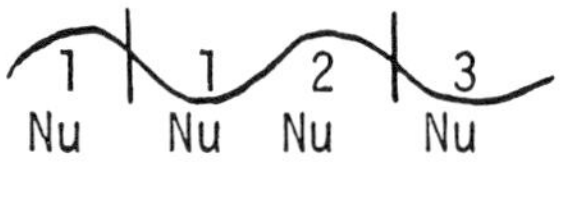


*While all the class sings it again, the child at the board draws the four strokes of* Rhythm Pattern *b), first with index finger, then with chalk, rhythmically.*

*Teacher adds bar-lines, numbers and rhythmic curve using different colored chalk for each. Bluebirds and Robins sing line over again while making* Rhythm Gesture II. *Sparrows make gesture only.*

Melodic Application to Rhythm Patterns

Pattern *b)* *1 = A*

*Teacher sings* Rhythm Pattern *b) on different pitches. Children repeat in groups immediately after each example. Each line is sung at a brisk tempo.*

*1. Teacher:*

1 | 1 1 | 1
DO DO DO DO

*Children repeat.*

2 | 2 2 | 2
RE RE RE RE

3 | 3 3 | 3
MI MI MI MI

1 | 1 2 | 3
DO DO RE MI

*2. Teacher:*

3 | 3 3 | 3
MI MI MI MI

2 | 2 2 | 2
RE RE RE RE

1 | 1 1 | 1
DO DO DO DO

3 | 3 2 | 1
MI MI RE DO

*3. Teacher:*

2 | 1 2 | 1
RE DO RE DO

2 | 1 1 | 1
RE DO DO DO

1 | 2 2 | 1
DO RE RE DO

Pattern *c)* *4. Teacher:*

1 | 1 . | .
DO DO ______

1 | 2 . | .
DO RE ______

2 | 1 . | .
RE DO ______

Ear Tests *Use* Diagram 2. *Children Sit*

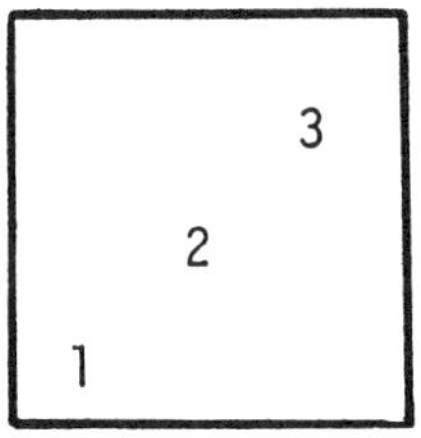


Diagram 2

*Teacher invites children to sing* 1 2 3 *(*DO RE MI*) as they make* Measuring Gesture *and follow pointer on diagram.*

*Following this, children watch diagram while teacher sings on* Nu *several times the following:*

1 2 3   1 2 3 3

*Children repeat each phrase also on* Nu. *Their attention is drawn to the repeated sounds. One child offers to identify correct pitches using note names. If the note names are correctly identified, his group repeats the notes while making the* Measuring Gesture. *Sparrows participate by pointing to notes on diagram or showing notes on fingers.*

*Teacher repeats process for other groups of notes.* *(See Page 29)*

Eye Tests *"Look and remember"*

*1. Teacher: "Pay attention to notes I point to on the diagram (or show on my fingers)."*

1 2 3 3 3

*A child offers to sing the phrase from memory on note names. If rendition is correct, the other children of his group are invited to repeat phrase from memory on note-names.*

*2. Teacher: "Pay attention to notes I am going to write on the board."*

1 1 1 2 3

*Teacher erases phrase - from left to right. A child is invited to sing phrase on note-names from memory picture.*

*These ear and eye tests should be given each day. Sample phrases are given on Page 29. Use also lines from songs being studied.*

Creative Activity *Step 1.*

*Continue musical conversation with words in which answer is melodically identical to question.*

| 1 ________ 3 | 1 ________ 3 |
|---|---|
| What is your name? | My name is John. |

Songs *SIT for preparation exercises. STAND for singing entire song.*

Song 3, *without words, links the tones* 1 2 3 (DO RE MI) *with binary rhythm beginning on the up-pulse.*

*After a short preparation from* Diagram 2 *to locate the pitches, children sing the song with* Metrical Gesture *and* Metrical Language. *Finally, Bluebirds and Robins each sing the song separately with* Rhythm Gesture I or II. *Sparrows make gesture but do not sing.*

*Repeat process for other songs selected for study and and singing. Note that the rhythm patterns are indicated for each line of a song.*

*In these early chapters it is not necessary to teach all the songs given. One or two will suffice.*

‖ 1 | 1 2 | 3
la la la la

3 | 3 . | .
la long ____

3 | 3 2 | 1
la la la la

1 | 1 . | . ‖
la long ____

Songs with Words *Close each lesson with:*

‖ 1 | 2 2 | 1 2 | 1 . | . ‖
Al- le- lu- ia. A- men.____

(Alleluia *means: Praise God.* Amen *means: So be it, or I agree.)*

*If time permits, teacher sings a versicle and children respond as follows:*

*1.* *Teacher:* ‖ 1 | 1 2 | 3 . | .
Hail, ho- ly Queen, ____

3 | 3 2 | 1 . | .
O pray for us.

*Children:* 1 | 2 2 | 1 2 | 1 . | . ‖
Al- le- lu- ia. A- men.____

*2.* *Teacher:* ‖ 1 | 1 2 | 3 3 | 3 . | .
Hail, Ma- ry, full of grace, ____

3 | 3 2 | 1 . | 2 . | .
the Lord is with ____ you. ____

*Children:* 1 | 2 2 | 1 1 | 2 . | . ‖
Al- le- lu- ia. A- men. ____

# Chapter Three

| | 1 | 2 | 3 | 4 | 5 |
|---|---|---|---|---|---|
| **Stand**<br>Vocal Training | Greeting – Tone matching<br>*Good Morning, Children*<br>1̇ ______ 6<br>Voc. Ex. 1 Group I – Bb<br>*Ball Game* Step 1 → | Feel vibration of Nnnn<br>Voc. Ex. I Group II Ab<br>*What is your name?*<br>Group III → | Voc. Ex. 1 Group III – G<br>*Step 2* – Reverse direction<br>Groups I and II:<br>*Weather* questions → | Voc. Ex. 1 Group I – C<br>Test individuals for regrouping. Step 2 – Children ask question, Teacher answers → | Group I – C Group II Bb<br>Group III – G<br>Step 2 – Musical Conversation: *Time* |
| **Sit**<br>Intonation | Int. Diagram 2 (1 2 3)<br>*Int. Ex. 4*<br>*Think Tones* (1st 2 lines)<br>1 2 3 3 2 1<br>1 2 3 • 2 1 → | Lines 3, 4, 5<br>Show on fingers<br>**Present:** *Int. Diagram 3* →<br>Int. Ex. 5<br>Line 1<br>Measuring Gesture (1 2 3 4 5) → | Lines 6 and 7 with pointer →<br>Line 2 on fingers → | →<br>Line 3 with pointer and Measuring Gesture → | Lines 1, 2, 3 with pointer and Finger Notation |
| | | | GROUP III SHOWS NOTES ON FINGERS AND BY MEASURING GESTURE BUT DOES NOT SING | | |
| **Stand**<br>Rhythm | **Review:** Rhythm Gestures I and II for precision.<br>Slowly without music, then with music either from cassette or sung by teacher.<br>Up-pulse binary rhythm tunes given in Chapter Summaries. | | →<br>Use Melodic Application of Rhythm Patterns Series 2 → | →<br>→ | |
| **Sit**<br>Dictations | | PREPARE FOR DICTATIONS BY SINGING NOTES AGAIN FROM DIAGRAMS 2 AND 3 | | | |
| Eye Tests | Pointer and Measuring Gesture:<br>1 2 3 3 3 3<br>1 2 1 1 2 3 | Pointer: 1 2 3 4 5<br>5 4 3 2 1<br>Meas. Gest.: 1 2 3 4 5<br>1 1 1 2 3 | Pointer: 1 2 3 2 1<br>1 2 3 4 5<br>Fingers: 1 2 3 2 1<br>1 2 3 4 5 | Pointer: 1 1 2 3 4 5<br>1 2 3 4 5<br>Meas. Gest.: 5 5 4 3 2 1<br>1 2 1 1 2 3 | Pointer: 1 2 3 3 4 5<br>5 4 3 3 2 1<br>Finger: 1 1 1 1 2 3<br>3 3 3 2 1 1 |
| Ear Tests | On *Nu:* 1 1 1 2 3<br>3 3 3 2 1 | 1 2 2 2 2<br>1 2 3 3 3 3 | 1 2 3 3 2 3<br>1 2 3 3 3 2 | 1 1 1 2 3<br>5 5 5 5 | 2 1 2 3 2 3<br>2 1 2 3 4 5 |
| **Stand**<br>Vocal Training | Study of Timbre and Rhythm<br>Group III makes gesture only<br>Test individuals occasionally for possible promotion | Voc. Ex. 4: | ‖ 2 1 2 1 • • ‖<br>Nu Nu Nu Nu ___<br>Group I on Ab (DO)<br>Group II on F (DO) | Group I on Bb (DO) | Group II on Ab (DO) |
| Rhythm | Rhythm Patterns Series 2<br>Lines 1 and 2 as dialogue:<br>Group I ‖ 1 1 1 1<br>Group II 2 \| 2 • \| •<br>Group II 2 \| 2 2 \| 2<br>Group I 1 \| 1 • \| • ‖<br>Group III – gestures only | R. P. Series 2 – New pattern<br>c) 2 1 2 3 2 3<br>Metrical language<br>Rhythm Gesture II | d) 2 3 2 1 • •<br>Rules for placing bar lines | c) 1 1 2 3 4 5<br>d) 5 5 5 5 • •<br>Sing on note names | → |
| | | **Sit**<br>**Dictations:** Rhythm Patterns Series 2 always in full view of class during dictations<br>1 1 2 3 3 3 | | 1 1 2 3 • • | 5 5 4 3 2 1 |
| **Sit for preparation**<br>Songs<br>**Stand for singing** | **Review:** Songs 5 and 6<br>Teacher-pupil dialogue:<br>*Hail, Mary* (Chapter Two) | Song 7<br>‖ 2 1 2 3 2 3<br>2 \| 1 2 \| 3 2 \| 1 ‖<br>**Review:** *Hail, Holy Queen* | Song 9<br>‖ 1 1 2 1<br>1 1 2 3 • •<br>3 \| 3 3 \| 3<br>2 \| 3 2 \| 1 • \| • ‖<br>**A Conversation Song:**<br>*The Flowers Awake* | Song 10<br>‖ 1 1 2 1 • •<br>1 \| 1 2 \| 3 4 \| 5<br>5 \| 5 5 \| 5 • \| •<br>5 \| 5 4 \| 3 2 \| 1 ‖ | →<br>**Review:** *Hail, Mary* |

# Chapter Three

*Beginning with this chapter, suggestions for teaching the content are given in each category of study. A lesson plan on the page opposite suggests a possible division of the matter into five lessons.*

## Vocal Training

*Begin the lesson with* Vocal Exercise 1. *Allow plenty of time for the articulation of the* N *so that the* Nu *may have all possible resonance.*

*For example:* *Place fingers on the forehead so as to feel the vibration of* NNNN. *Then link the consonant to the vowel so that the tone is propelled into the head. Be sure children pronounce* Nu *as* NOON, *not* NEEOON.

Vocal Exercise 1

*1 = A♭ – B♭ – C*

*Midway through the lesson,* Vocal Exercise 4 *is added. This exercise combines melody and rhythm in a pattern that is known. Insist that the tone be soft and gentle. Teacher should aim for quality, not loudness.*

Vocal Exercise 4

*1 = A♭ – B♭ – C – F*

*Timbre and Rhythm*

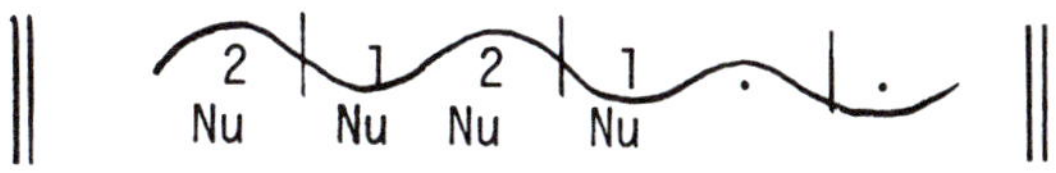


*By this time the class has been divided into three groups.*

*Bluebirds (Group I) sing first; then Robins (Group II). High pitches are selected as indicated.*

*Sparrows (Group III) listen. Occasionaly they are tested briefly on lower pitches, for example, E or F.*

| Remember that the teacher sets the model for the children but does not sing with them. |
|---|

# Intonation

Intonation Exercise 4 *Introduces the "think" tones. Teach on* Diagram 2.

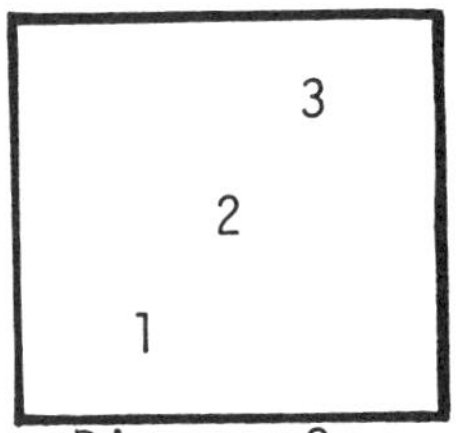


Diagram 2

*(1 = $A^b$)*

```
1 2 3   3 2 1
1 2 3   (3) 2 1

1 2 3   3 2
1 2 3   3 2 3 2
1 2 3   3 2 3

1 2 3   (3) 2 3
1 2 3 . (3) 2 3 2 1
```

*As the teacher points to the smaller number over the dot in the column being studied, children stop to "think" the note. Arriving at the "think" note, teacher points with other end of pointer and places finger over the lips to indicate silence. Teacher then proceeds to the other notes of the exercise.*

Intonation Exercise 5 *Teach on* Diagram 3.

*This exercise adds two more tones to the scale line:* 4 = FA
5 = SOL

*Teacher sings* 1 2 3 4 5 *on the syllable* Nu *using the* **Measuring Gesture** *(see page opposite) for all five tones to show their ascending stepwise progression. Then teacher constructs* Diagram III *as a staircase with five steps. After the first lesson, numbers are placed in box without steps.*

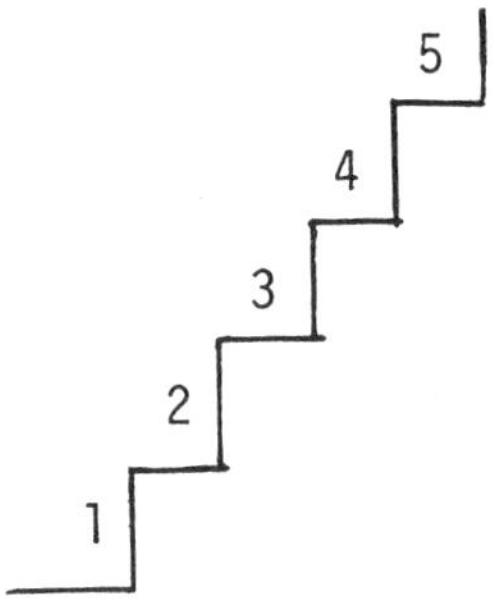


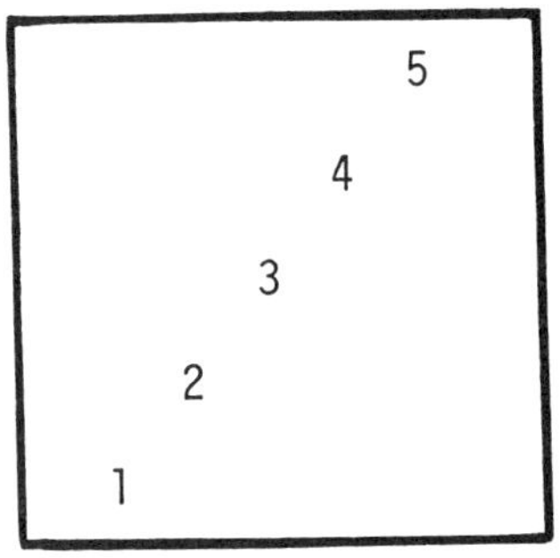


Diagram 3

*(1 = F)*

```
a)                b)
1 2 3 4 5         5 4 3 2 1
1 2 3 4 5 5 5     5 4 3 2 1 1 1
1 1 1 2 3 4 5     5 5 5 4 3 2 1
c)
```

*Pointing to the numbers, the teacher (in a speaking voice), names them:* DO RE MI FA SOL. *Children repeat naming them forward and backward so that there is no hesitation in saying the note names. Teacher sings pentachord ascending while pointing to the numbers on the diagram. Children repeat. Teacher sings pentachord descending. Children repeat. Teacher begins intonation exercise with Bluebirds first; then Robins. Sparrows listen.*

*It will be useful here to show that* FA *and* SOL *can also be shown on the fingers.* Finger Notation *and* Measuring Gesture *are necessary for giving the dictations.*

# Notation

Number Notation

4 = FA *as in fa-ther*

5 = SOL *as in solution*

Finger Notation

FA 

SOL 

Measuring (Melodic) Gesture

FA 

SOL 

# *Rhythm*

RULES FOR PLACING BAR LINES: 1) Place first bar before last note.
2) Count back by two's and place a bar after each second note.
3) If one note is left alone at front, his partner will be found at other end (whether it is a note or a dot) and each little house (measure) will have two notes in it.

## Rhythm Patterns - Series 2

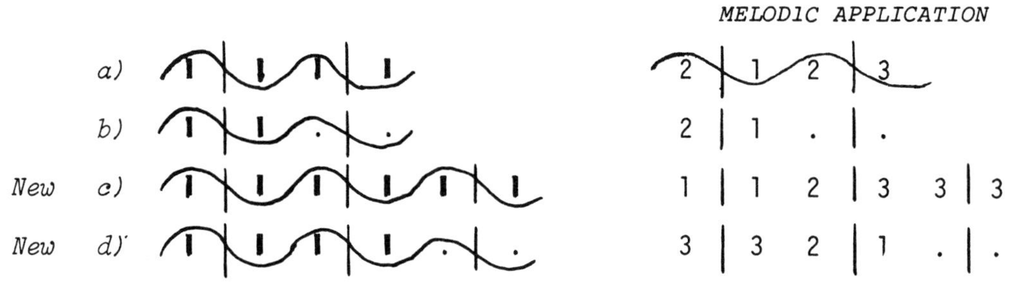


*Two patterns have already been studied, namely, a) and b).*

*Children in groups sing them first with the* Metrical Gesture, *then with the* Rhythm Gesture I *or* II. *Groups may alternate. For example:*

*Bluebirds (Group I) sing a)* 1 1 1 1 *Robins (Group II) answer b)* 2 2 . .

*Then Robins sing a)* 2 2 2 2 *Bluebirds answer b)* 1 1 . .

| Sparrows (Group III) make gesture but do not sing. |
|---|

*The two new patterns c) and d) are first sung with the* Metrical Gesture *and* Metrical Language *to make the short and long notes perfectly clear.*

*c)* la | la la | la la | la

*d)* la | la la | long . | .

*When these patterns can be sung with ease at a moderate tempo by Groups I and II, the teacher will present melodic application of rhythms, line by line.*

## Rhythmic Dictation

*Teacher places patterns c) and d) on the board. One child, preferably from Group III, is called to the board. Teacher sings pattern c) on a melodic application. For example:*

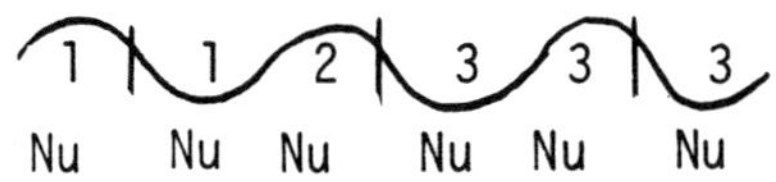


*Class repeats the pattern and the child tries to identify it from the patterns on the board. Class sings it again as the child draws the strokes, first with his finger, then with the chalk. Teacher adds bar lines and draws the rhythmic curve. All repeat with* Rhythm Gesture I *or* II. *Another day, teacher repeats gesture for pattern d):*

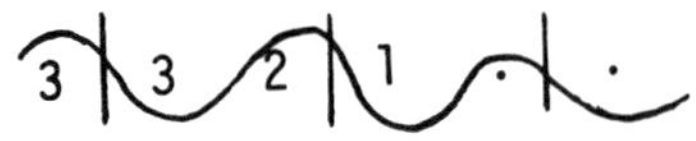

Rhythm Gestures I and II *Review for precision.*

*From a rhythmic standpoint there is no difference between* Rhythm Gestures I *and* II. *There is only a change of posture. When practising* Rhythm Gesture II *proceed as when practising* Rhythm Gesture I.

Opening position: prepare for starting, notice distribution of weight, listen for pulse, right foot forward -

Rise on the toes for the UP of the rhythm: arms remain straight without bending the elbows, wrists pulling arms above the head but not to hunch shoulders -

The silent descent for the DOWN of the rhythm: heels do not touch floor -

Repeat UP and DOWN movements several times -

Closing position at last DOWN of the rhythm: arms folded gently on chest -

*Practise making gestures* I *and* II *without music but in strict time. Then one group sings a known melody while the other group makes the correct gesture. Reverse the roles. Children who make best gestures are invited to come to the front of the class to lead the others.*

*A cassette recording especially prepared for these gestures should be played here while children adapt their rhythm gestures to the music. Teacher may also sing melodies in binary rhythm beginning on an up-pulse as given in later chapters.*

## Creative Activity

Improvisation. *Musical conversations continued.*

*Review* Step 1. *See Lesson One* - The Ball Game *and* Musical Conversation. *Tone matching.*

Step 2. *Children ask the question. Teacher demonstrates the possibility of a change of melody for the answer.*

*Example:*

| | | | |
|---|---|---|---|
| | 1 ——— 5 | | 5 ——— 1 |
| *Child:* | What is the weather like today? | *Teacher:* | Today is fine. |
| | 1 ——— 3 5 | | 5 ——— 3 1 |
| *Child:* | What time is it now? | *Teacher:* | It is ten o- clock. |

*Reverse the roles. Teacher asks the question and the children make a response with tones that are different from those used by the teacher.*

## Dictations

*Keep* Intonation Diagram 3 *in full view of class for all tests.*

*Review dictations given in Chapter Two. When children are somewhat secure in the use of* DO RE MI, *teacher commences drills to assimilate* FA *and* SOL.

Eye Tests

| | | | | | |
|---|---|---|---|---|---|
| | 1 2 3 3 3 3 | 1 2 3 4 5 | 1 2 3 2 1 | 1 1 2 3 4 5 | 1 2 3 3 4 5 |
| | 1 2 1 1 2 3 | 5 4 3 2 1 | 1 2 3 4 5 | 5 5 4 3 2 1 | 5 4 3 3 2 1 |
| | | 1 2 3 4 5 | 1 2 3 2 1 | 1 2 3 4 5 | 1 1 1 1 2 3 |
| | | 1 1 1 2 3 | 1 2 3 4 5 | 1 2 1 1 2 3 | 3 3 3 2 1 1 |

Eye Tests

| | | | | |
|---|---|---|---|---|
| 1 2 2 2 2 | 1 2 3 3 2 3 | 1 1 1 2 3 | 2 1 2 3 2 3 | |
| 1 2 3 3 3 3 | 1 2 3 3 3 2 | 5 5 5 5 | 2 1 2 3 4 5 | |
| 1 1 1 2 3 | | | | |
| 3 3 3 2 1 | | | | |

> Step-wise scale fragments used for dictations in this chapter ought not to exceed six tones.

*Instructions for giving the* EAR *and* Eye *tests will be found in the pedagogy of Chapter Two.*

Rhythmic Dictation *will be found in the section on RHYTHM of this chapter.*

# *Songs* Melodic Application of Rhythm Patterns - Series 2

**Song 7** *(1 = $A^b$)*

*c)* ‖ 2 | 1 2 | 3 2 | 3

*c)* 2 | 1 2 | 3 2 | 1 ‖

**Song 8** *(1 = $A^b$)*

*d)* ‖ 1 | 1 2 | 3 . | .

*d)* 2 | 3 2 | 1 . | . ‖

**Song 9** *(1 = $A^b$)*

*a)* ‖ 1 | 1 2 | 1

*d)* 1 | 1 2 | 3 . | .

*a)* 3 | 3 3 | 3

*d)* 3 | 3 2 | 1 . | . ‖

**Song 10** *(1 = G)*

*d)* ‖ 1 | 1 2 | 1 . | .

*c)* 1 | 1 2 | 3 4 | 5

*d)* 5 | 5 5 | 5 . | .

*c)* 5 | 5 4 | 3 2 | 1 ‖

## The Flowers Awake *(1 = F)* *A "Conversation Song"*

*Teacher:* ‖ 1 | 1 1 | 1 1 | 1 1 | 1 1 | 2
A cro- cus lifts her love- ly head to say:

*Children:* 1 | 2 2 | 1 . | .
Al- le- lu- ia! ___

*Teacher:* 2 | 3 3 | 3 3 | 3 3 | 2 1 | 2
A gold- en daf- fo- dil be- gins to pray:

*Children:* 1 | 2 2 | 1 . | .
Al- le- lu- ia! ___

*Teacher:* 2 | 3 4 | 5 4 | 3 4 | 5
Out of the earth With song- ful mirth,

5 | 5 4 | 3 3 | 2 1 | 2
The flow- ers spring. I hear them sing:

*Children:* 1 | 2 2 | 1 2 | 1 . | . ‖
Al- le- lu- ia! A- men. ___

# Chapter Four

| | 1 | 2 | 3 | 4 | 5 |
|---|---|---|---|---|---|
| Stand<br>**Vocal Training** | Greeting: *Good morning, Children*<br>1 ______ 3 _5<br>Voc. 1 and 2: Group I – Bb<br>Group II – Ab →<br>*Ball Game* Step I Groups I<br>II | Children's response on same tones: *Good morning, . . .*<br>1 = F<br>→<br>*What is your name?* Step 2<br>Groups I and II | 1 ______ 3 _5<br>→<br>Step 2 – *Finding Things*<br>Groups I and II<br>Test individuals for promotion | →<br>Step 2 – Question and answer as child asks and teacher answers | →<br>→<br>Step 1 with Group III<br>Question and answer game on same pitches |
| Sit<br>**Intonation** | Intonation Diagram 3<br>[1 2 3 4 5]<br>Int. Ex. 6a) b)<br>Group I →<br>Pointer<br>Meas. Gesture | →<br>→<br>Pointer<br>Finger Notation | →<br>Int. Ex. 7a) b) Group I<br>Int. Ex. 6a) b) Group II<br>Pointer<br>Measuring Gestures | →<br>Int. Ex. 8a) b) c) Group I<br>Int. Ex. 7a) b) Group II<br>Pointer and Finger Notation | →<br>**Rev.** Int. Ex. 6a) b)<br>Groups I and II<br>Group III makes gestures |
| | **KEEP DIAGRAM 3 BEFORE CHILDREN DURING DICTATION** | | | | |
| **Dictations**<br>Ear Tests<br>Eye Tests | 1 2 3 4 5 5 5<br>1 2 3 3 4 5<br><br>1 2 3 3 4 5 Pointer<br>5 4 3 3 2 1 On board and and erase | 1 2 3 3 2 1<br>1 2 1<br><br>1 2 3 4 4 3 2 1 Pointer<br>1 2 3 4 4 4 4 Fingers | 1 2 3 4 5<br>1 2 3 4<br><br>1 2 3 4 4 3 2 1 Pointer<br>1 2 3 4 3 2 1 On board and erase | 1 2 3 4 4 4<br>1 2 3 4 5 5 6<br><br>1 2 3 3 3 2 Pointer<br>5 4 3 3 2 1 Fingers | 1 2 2 3 4 5<br>5 4 4 3 2 1<br><br>1 2 3 4 3 2 1 Pointer<br>1 2 3 4 4 3 2 1<br>Meas. Gesture |
| Stand<br>**Rhythm** | **Review:** Gesture I (arms in front) and Gesture II (arms to side)<br>1. Without music and on inhalation and exhalation of breath. Note well positions of preparation, rise, fall, repose.<br>2. With music accompaniment such as folk songs known to children, music from cassette recording, or melody sung by teacher. Up-pulse binary rhythm. All groups participate. | | | | |
| Sit<br>**Creative Activity** | *Step 3:* Conversation without words →<br>Teacher: 1 2 3<br>Pupil: 2 1 | →<br>Teacher: 1 2 3<br>Pupil: 3 2 1 | →<br>Pupil: 1 2 3<br>Teacher: 3 2 1 | → | **Review:**<br>Step 2 – with words<br>Groups II and III |
| Stand<br>**Vocal Training** | Voc. Ex. 5: ‖ 2 1 2 3 2 1 . . ‖<br>Nu Nu Nu Nu Nu Nu ______<br>Group I – **1 = G** Groups II and III make gesture | | Group II **1 = G**<br>Group I **1 = Ab** →<br>**GROUP III CHILDREN MAKE GESTURE BUT DO NOT SING** | | Group I **1 = Bb** II **1 = Ab**<br>Group III Voc. Ex. 1<br>**1 = G** |
| Sit<br>**Rhythm** | Rhythm Patterns Series 2: Sing patterns a), b), c), d), A, with Metrical Language and Metrical Gesture on 1 pitch.<br>Repeat singing Melodic Applications.<br>Practise combining patterns.<br>**KEEP RHYTHM PATTERNS IN FULL VIEW OF CLASS DURING DICTATIONS – REVIEW RULES FOR PLACING BAR LINES** | | | | |
| Dictations: | 1 1 2 3 4 5 . . | 5 5 4 3 2 1 . . | 5 5 5 5 5 5 . . | 3 3 4 5 . . | 5 5 4 3 . . |
| Stand<br>**Songs** | **Review songs previously studied**<br>Song 11 – Lines 1 and 2<br>Identify Rhythm Patterns | Song 11 – Complete<br>Song 12<br>*Alleluia* | **Review:** Songs 11 and 12<br>*Alleluia* | Song 13<br>*Hail, Mary* | **Review:** Song 13<br>*The Flowers Awake* |

# Chapter Four

## Vocal Training

Timbre, Rhythm, Pitch, Legato - by imitation

*Begin each lesson with* Vocal Exercises 1 *and* 2. *Concentrate children's attention on quality of tone. Strive to make them critical of the timbre of their voices: Is tone light, free, smooth, clear? Initiate the vowel of the vocalise with a good firm* NNNN: *finger tips on forehead to feel the vibration. As* $\overline{oo}$ *vowel emerges, finger tips leave forehead in an upward motion like flower petals unfolding.*

Vocal Exercise 1 *(1 = $A^b$, $B^b$, F)*

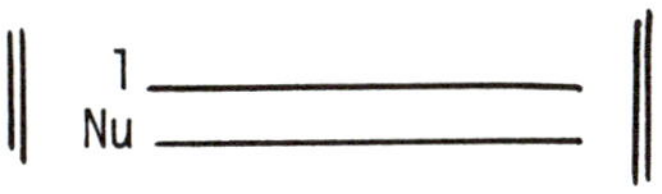


Vocal Exercise 2 *(1 = $A^b$, $B^b$, F)*

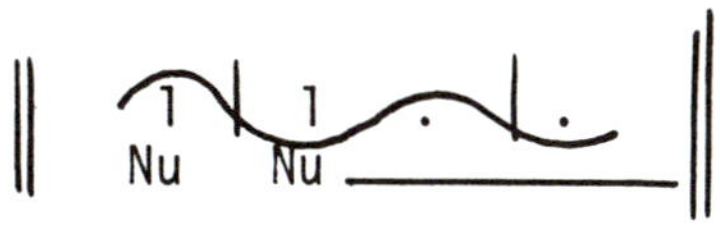


*Bluebirds and Robins first on the higher pitches. Occasionally test Sparrows on lower pitches for possible promotion.*

Vocal Exercise 5 *(1 = $A^b$, $E^b$, $B^b$, G)*

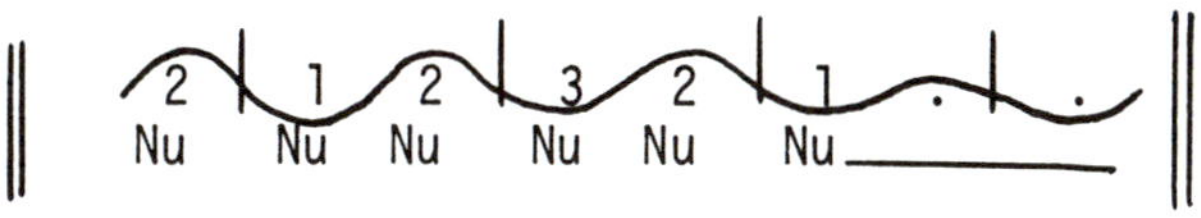


*During the second vocal period of the lesson, combine melody and rhythm with tone quality. This is done by imitation, first without rhythmic gesture, then with gesture. Link tones carefully for good legato.*

> A child's interest can be readily awakened in beauty of vocal timbre. This interest - and consequent joy - is an excellent tool for vocal formation. It is more effective than criticism.

# Intonation

All exercises given on Diagram 3

*Intonation exercises of this chapter and of Chapters Five, Six and Seven, all treat pentachord* 1 2 3 4 5 *in a variety of ways. These drills develop a working tonal vocabulary in the children, one that they can use freely and joyfully without imitation or prompting.*

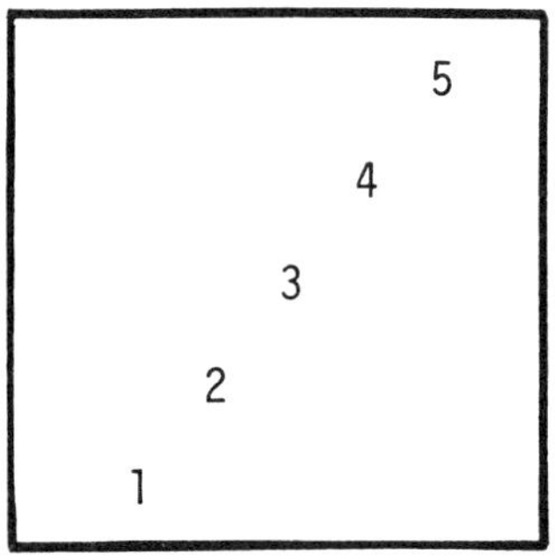


Diagram 3

**Intonation Exercise 6** *(1 = G) Stop at any point*

| a) → | b) → |
|---|---|
| 1 2 3 4 5 | 5 4 3 2 1 |
| 1 2 3 4 | 5 4 3 2 |
| 1 2 3 | 5 4 3 |
| 1 2 | 5 4 |
| 1 2 3 4 5 | 5 4 3 2 1 |

**Intonation Exercise 7** *(1 = G) Stop and repeat*

| a) → | | b) → | |
|---|---|---|---|
| 1 2 3 4 5 | 5 5 5 | 5 4 3 2 1 | 1 1 1 |
| 1 2 3 4 | 4 4 4 | 5 4 3 2 | 2 2 2 |
| 1 2 3 | 3 3 3 | 5 4 3 | 3 3 3 |
| 1 2 | 2 2 2 | 5 4 | 4 4 4 |
| 1 2 3 4 5 | 5 4 3 2 1 | 5 4 3 2 1 | 1 1 1 |

**Intonation Exercise 8** *(1 = G) Stop, repeat, continue in same direction*

| a) → | | b) → | |
|---|---|---|---|
| 1 2 3 4 5 | | 5 4 3 2 1 | |
| 1 2 3 4 | 4 5 | 5 4 3 2 | 2 1 |
| 1 2 3 | 3 4 5 | 5 4 3 | 3 2 1 |
| 1 2 | 2 3 4 5 | 5 4 | 4 3 2 1 |

*c)* →

> It is not necessary to practise each Intonation Exercise until it can be sung perfectly by all the children. Each exercise prepares for the next one which, in turn, perfects the one before it. The progression of the exercises will take care of the repetition necessary to insure free use of the pentachord by all the children.

# Rhythm

Rhythm Patterns- Series 2
Melodic Application

*Practise with:*
Metrical Gesture 1
Metrical Language
Rhythm Gesture 2

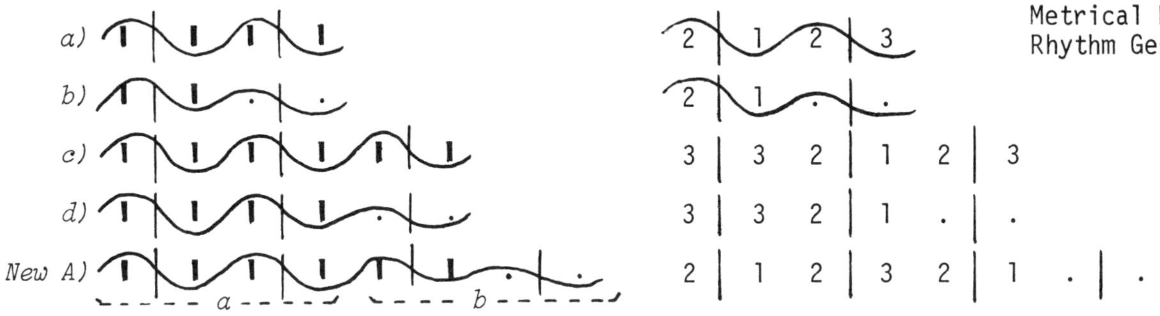

To count the pulses of long notes while making Metrical Gesture 1, press finger tips of right hand gently on palm of left hand for each dot. Be careful to avoid giving vocal emphasis to each act of pressure.
To signal the end of a rhythm, fingers of left hand clasp finger tips of right hand.

*COMBINING PATTERNS*

*Patterns a) and b) placed side by side to form longer pattern A).*

*Children sing pattern a), then pattern b) as if they were two isolated rhythmic words. They are sung first on different pitches as shown in Chapter Three. Then with melodic application as follows:*

1. *Bluebirds (Group I) sing* a) 

   *Robins (Group II) sing* b) 

   *Alternation must connect without interrupting rhythm*

2. *Robins sing* a) 

   *Bluebirds sing* b) 

   *Sparrows make gesture but do not sing*

3. *Bluebirds and Robins together sing patterns a) and b) linking them together without a break thus forming the new pattern A).*

*Teacher writes new pattern on board:*

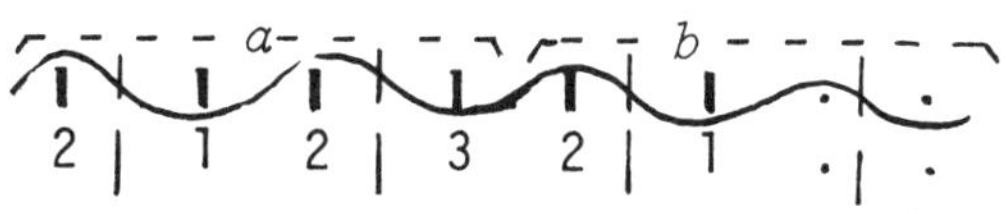


Children must become used to combining rhythm patterns as this is the basis for musical phrase construction.

# Notation

Number Notation, Finger Notation *and* Measuring Gesture, *same as in Chapter Three.*

# Creative Activity

Musical Conversation - Step 3

*Teacher suggests the possibility of musical conversation* without *words, for example, as birds converse with one another.*

*Teacher:* 1 2 (Nu Nu *or* DO RE)

*Children:* 2 1

*Teacher:* 1 2 3

*Children:* 3 2 1

*Repeat with a child asking the question and the teacher responding.*

*Review* Step 2: *Answers different melodically from questions.*

# Dictations

Diagram 3 *remains in full view of the class during the dictation tests*

Ear Tests *Teacher sings a fragment on* Nu. *Children try to find tones while silently making* Measuring Gesture.

1 2 3 4 5 5 5   1 2 3 3 2 1   1 2 3 4 4 4   1 2 2 3 4 5
1 2 3 3 4 5   1 2 1   1 2 3 4 5 5   5 4 4 3 2 1

5 4 3 2 2 3 4 5   1 2 3 4 5   1 2 3 4 4 4   1 2 3 4 5
5 4 3 2 3 4 5   1 2 3 4   1 2 2 2 2   1 2 3 4

Eye Tests *Teacher writes a fragment on board and after a moment erases it from left to right. "Who remembers what teacher wrote?" For variety, tests are also given with pointer on the diagram or on fingers.*

1 2 3 3 4 5   1 2 3 4 4 3 2 1   1 2 3 4 4 3 2 1   1 2 3 3 3 2
5 4 3 3 2 1   1 2 3 4 4 4 4   1 2 3 4 3 2 1   5 4 3 3 3 2

Rhythmic Dictation *Patterns studied in this chapter should be in full view of class during the tests.*

*a)* 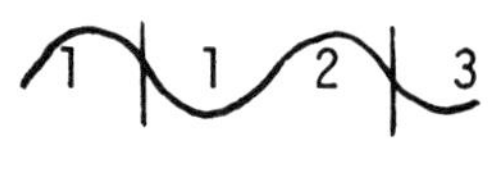


*c)* 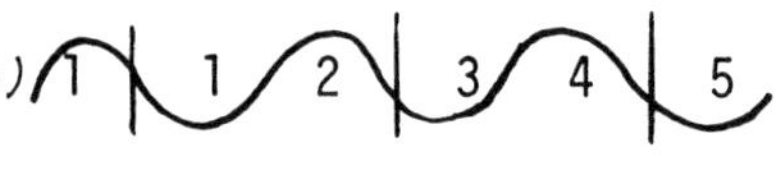

## Songs

Melodic application of pentachord 1 2 3 4 5 with known rhythm patterns and combinations

### Song 11 (1 = G)

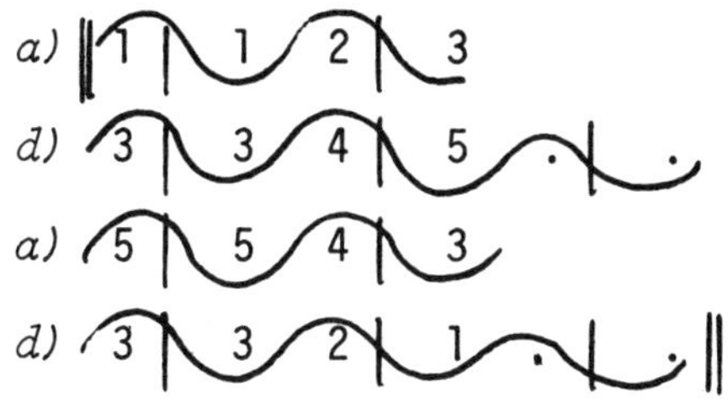


### Song 12 (1 = G)

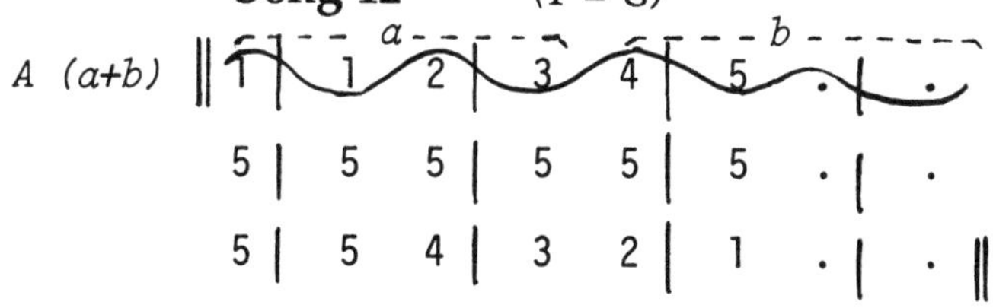


### Song 13 (1 = G)

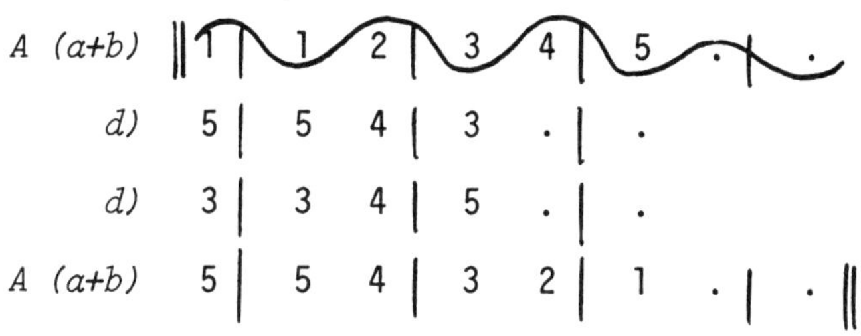


*Review songs of Chapters Two and Three*

<u>FOR MAINTAINING INTEREST DURING CLASS MUSIC LESSON</u>

1. Minimum amount of talking.
2. Do not remain on a point too long. Better to return later to a difficulty when encountered.
3. Prepare blackboard well. Have recordings and transparencies ready for instant use.
4. Vary standing and sitting postures.
5. Move swiftly from one segment of the lesson to another.

# Chapter Five

| | 1 | 2 | 3 | 4 | 5 |
|---|---|---|---|---|---|
| Stand<br>**Vocal Training** | GREETING:<br>i̇ ______ 6<br>Good morning, Bluebirds<br>Robins<br>Sparrows<br>**1 = Bb**<br>Step 1 – Answer on same tone<br><br>Voc. Ex. 1 **1 = Bb G D**<br>Test individuals of Group I | →<br><br>Test individuals of Group II | 4 ______ 6 __ i̇<br>Good morning, Bluebirds<br>Robins<br>Sparrows<br>Step 1 – Answer on same tones<br><br>Group I **1 = Bb, G, D**<br>Group II **1 = G, A, Bb** | 4 ______ 6 __ i̇<br>Good morning, Bluebirds<br>Robins<br>Sparrows<br>Step 2 – Answer on *different* tones<br>Groups I and II **1 = Bb G**<br>Strong Nnn long clear tones | →<br><br>Color Game<br>*Here comes the red ball* |
| Sit<br>**Intonation** | Intonation Diagram 3 →<br><br>*Int. Ex. 9* Pointer<br>Repeat horizontally | →<br><br>*Int. Ex. 10* Pointer<br>Repeat horizontally | →<br><br>*Int. Ex. 11* Lines 1 and 2<br>*Think* tones – Red pointer<br>Bluebirds first | →<br><br>*Int. Ex. 11* Lines 1 to 4<br>*Think* tones cont'd<br>Bluebirds and Robins only | →<br><br>Int. Ex. 11 Complete<br><br>Horizontal reading |
| | | KEEP DIAGRAM 3 IN FULL VIEW OF CLASS DURING DICTATIONS | | | |
| **Dictations** | *Nu* – 1123 33 3345 55<br><br>Red Pointer – 3321 11<br>Fingers – 5543 33 | 123 321 1234 4321<br><br>Meas. Gest. – 123 345/ 543<br>Board – 1221 123 /45 | 1234 321<br><br>Fingers – 12345 4321<br>Pointer – 123 21 / 333 221 | 1234 4321<br><br>Fingers – 12345 55<br>Board – 1234 321/ 123 | 3321 11<br><br>Meas. Gest. – 1234 4321<br>Board – 123 345 |
| Stand **Gestures**<br>**Rhythm** | **Rev.** Rhythm Gesture II<br>Special attention to Sparrows | Teacher sings a song to accompany gesture or uses cassette recording | | | |
| Sit **Patterns Study** | | Rhythm Patterns Series 2<br>Identify combinations<br><br>a+b 2 1 2 3 2 1 . . | **Present:** Series 3<br>Metrical Gesture and Language<br>Identify single *words*<br>Sing all patterns on DO | Identify combinations<br><br>a+b 1 2 2 3 2 1 . 1<br>b+c 2 3 . 3 2 1 . . | |
| **Notation** | | **Present:** Staff Notation 1<br>(staff: 1, 2) | **Rev.** Staff Notation 1<br>(staff: 1, 2)<br><br>Child fills in notes<br>**Rev.** Int. Ex. 1 and 2 | **Transcribe** from staff to numbers<br>(staff notes) | **Transcribe** numbers to staff notes<br>1 2 2 1<br>1 1 2 2 |
| **Creative Activity** | Dialogue without words<br>Step 3<br>Children: 1 1 2 3 . .<br>Teacher shows several different answers | → | Robins: 1 1 2 3 . .<br><br>Bluebirds sing answers | → | Teacher: 1 1 2 3 . .<br><br>Soloists make answers |
| Stand<br>**Vocal Training** | *Vocal Exercise 5* ‖ 2 1 2 3 2 1 . . ‖<br>‖ Nu \| Nu Nu \| Nu Nu \| Nu ___ ‖ | | Group II **1 = G** Group I **1 = Bb**<br>Work with individuals | Group III Voc. Ex. 1 **1 = A** test for promotion | |
| | | RHYTHM PATTERNS SERIES IN FULL VIEW OF CLASS DURING DICTATIONS | | | |
| Sit<br>**Rhythm**<br>Dictations | R.P. Series 2<br>2 1 2 3 2 1 . . | 1 1 2 3 2 1<br>1 1 2 3 . . | R. P. Series 3<br>2 1 1 1<br>2 1 . 1 | → | 2 1 2 3<br>2 1 . . |
| Stand<br>**Songs** | Song 14<br><br>*Hail, Mary* | Song 14<br>Bluebirds and Robins<br>Sparrows make gestures | Song 15<br><br>**Rev.** Song 14 as dialogue between Bluebirds and Robins | Song 15<br><br>Song 14 – Teacher suggests words *Before I Go To Sleep* (See Ch. Six) | → |

# Chapter Five

## Vocal Training

Timbre, Rhythm, Pitch, Legato - continued

*Review* Vocal Exercise 1 *1 = B, G, F*

*Review* Vocal Exercise 5 *1 = B, G, F*

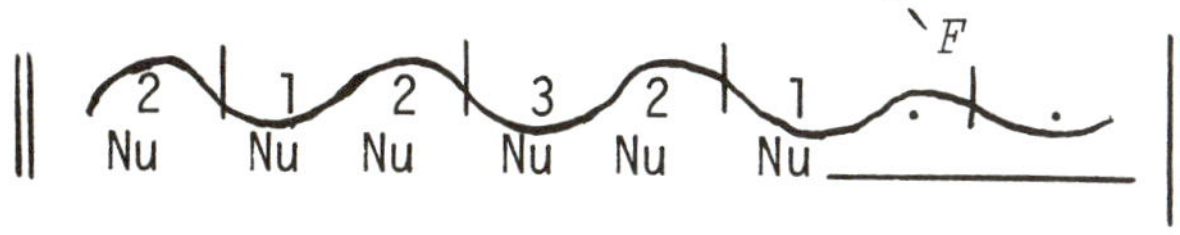


*In this series of lessons, concentrate on vocal work with groups and individuals. Select pitches according to the ability of the groups. For example:*

*Bluebirds on a high pitch - B or C*
*Robins on a lower pitch - G or A*
*Sparrows on lowest pitch - E or F*

## Intonation

*All exercises on* Diagram 3 *(1 = G or* $A^b$ *)*

### Intonation Exercise 9

*Stop and continue in same direction*

```
1 2 3 4 5 5 5   5 4 3 2 1 1 1
1 2 3   3 4 5   5 4 3   3 2 1
1 2 3 3 3 4 5   5 4 3 3 3 2 1
```

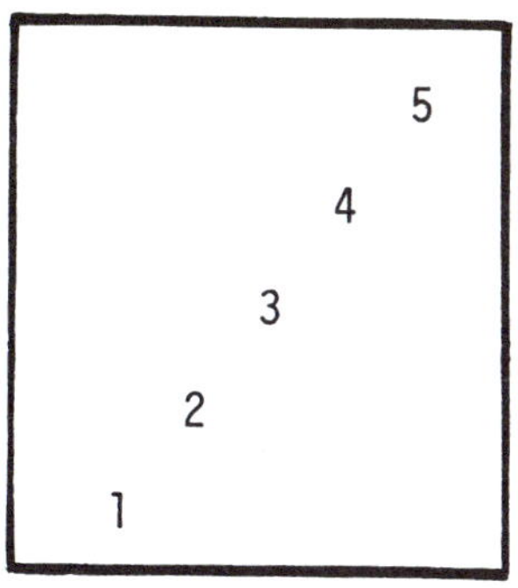


Diagram 3

### Intonation Exercise 10

*Stop, repeat, change direction*

```
1 2 3 4 5   5 4 3 2 1
1 2 3 4       4 3 2 1
1 2 3           3 2 1
1 2               2 1
1 2 3 4 5   5 4 3 2 1
```

### Intonation Exercise 11

*Stop, think repeated note on dot, change direction*

```
1 2 3 4 5   5 4 3 2 1
1 2 3 4 5   . 4 3 2 1
1 2 3 4       4 3 2 1
1 2 3 4       . 3 2 1
1 2 3           3 2 1
1 2 3           . 2 1
1 2               2 1
1 2               . 1
```

[A 24-inch wooden pointer, painted green at one end and red at the other, may be used for Intonation Exercise 11: green for singing tones; red for thinking tones.]

# Rhythm

<u>Rhythm Patterns - Series 3</u> Melodic Application

a)
New b)
c)

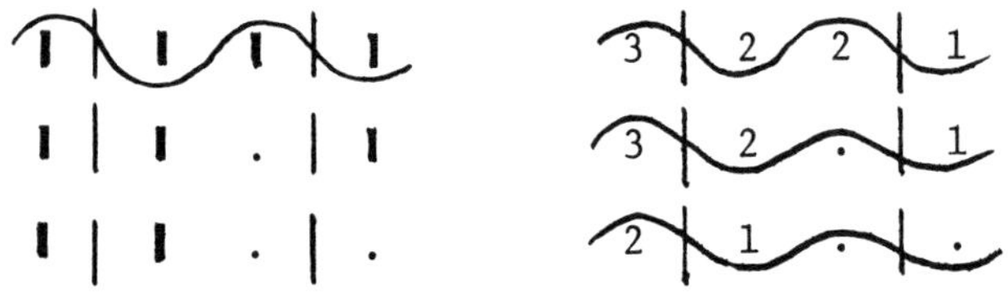


*Teach with* Metrical Language *and* Metrical Gesture I. *Then with* Rhythm Gesture II.

*Review* R.P. -Series 2

*The new rhythmic pattern uses length in another place than at the end, namely, in the middle of the line. Point this out to the class. Teach them to notice similarities and differences. Slow children will neither readily see nor hear them. For example:*

*Do you hear four short* DO's?
*Do you hear three* DO's, *the second one is long?*
*Do you hear two* DO's, *the second one is very long?*

> Colored chalk helps to clarify the visual image of the rhythm: <u>yellow</u> for numbers or rhythm strokes
> <u>red</u> for measure bars
> <u>blue</u> for rhythm wave

# Dictations

Ear *and* Eye Tests *of Chapter Four are reviewed for greater accuracy. Fragments from* Int. Ex. 9, 10 *and* 11 *may be used.*

<u>Rhythmic Dictation</u> *With melodic application of* Rhythm Patterns - Series 2

*<u>Melodies as dictated by teacher</u>* *<u>Rhythms as written by children</u>*

a)
b)
c)
d)
A)

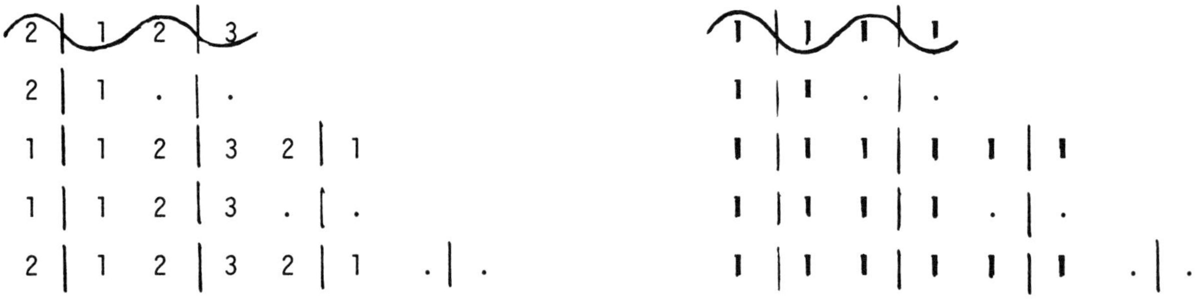

# *Notation* 

*New:* Staff Notation 1

*Children have learned the sound of the ascending and descending tones of the pentachord* 1 2 3 4 5 *by means of:* Number Notation

Finger Notation

Measuring Gesture

*All of this has been a preparation for recognizing the position of the tones of the pentachord on the musical staff.*

*Teacher draws a horizontal line on the board and writes the figure* 1 *through it. Above the line and touching it, he next draws the figure* 2:

*Children sing the two tones:*

*Teacher covers numbers with chalk:*

*"How can we tell which one is* DO *? To find out where* DO *lives we have to use a key. It is called a* clef *which we add to the line and that tells us where* DO *lives.* RE *lives upstairs."*

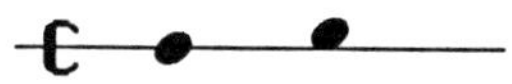

*Children sing the notes from the staff:*

*For drills in* Staff Notation, *use* Intonation Exercises 1 *and* 2, *Chapter One.*

*Lessons in this chapter could also include transcription drills.*
*For example:* *Teacher places staff notation fragments on the board and children are asked to identify them by writing correct numbers beneath the notes:*

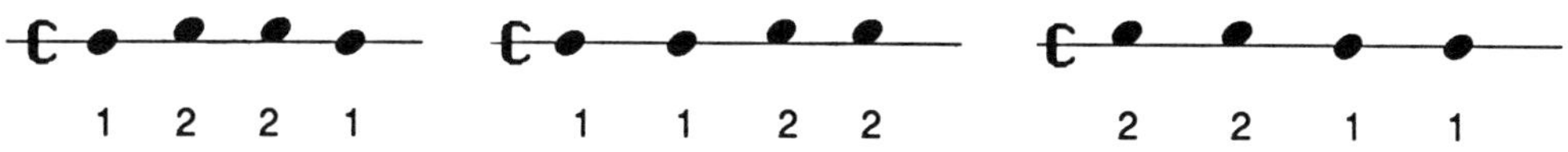


| All children must take an active part in each lesson |
|---|

# Creative Activity

<u>Musical Conversation - Step 3</u> *Game of QUESTIONS and ANSWERS continued with names and rhythmic groupings of notes*

*Teacher writes pentachord on board twice, once ascending and once descending:*

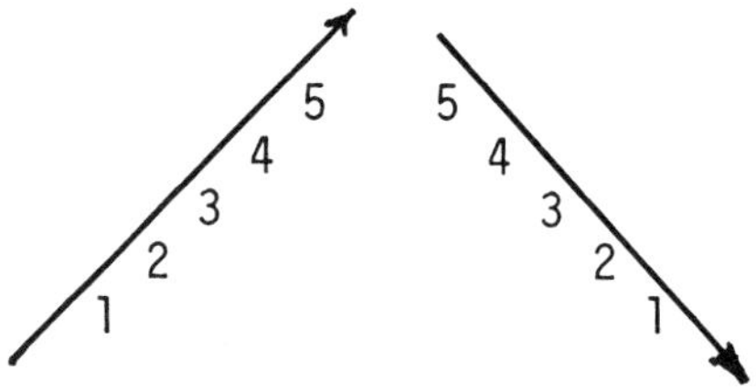


*Rule of the game is: when the question goes up, the answer comes down. For example:*

| *QUESTION* | *ANSWER* |
|---|---|
| 1 2 | 2 1 |
| 1 2 3 | 3 2 1 |
| 1 2 3 4 5 | 5 4 3 2 1 |

*Next step: variety of answers.*
*Teacher sings question while making* Rhythm Gesture II

*Children answer in a jumbled chorus of several possible answers. Teacher points out that many musical answers are possible to a musical question.*

*Now children ask the same question several times. Teacher gives a different answer each time and writes each one on the board:*

*QUESTION (Children)* *ANSWER (Teacher)*

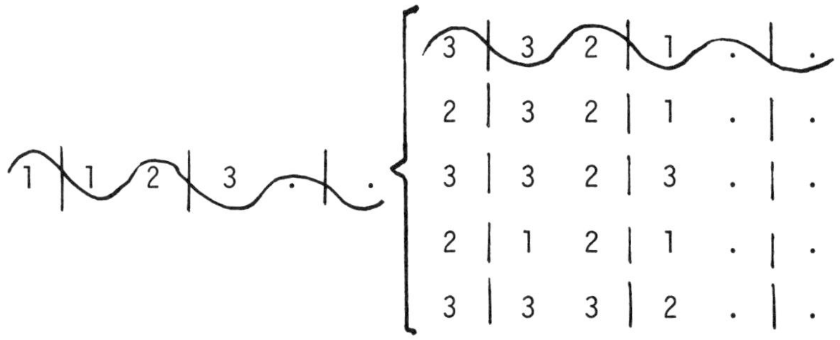


*"Can you think of a different answer? Which one do you like best?"*

# *Songs*

*Melodic application of rhythm patterns*

## Song 14 (1 = G)

*A text will be offered for this song in Chapter Six.*

(a + c) || 1 | 1 2 | 3 3 | 3 . | .
3 | 3 4 | 5 5 | 5 . | .
5 | 5 4 | 3 3 | 3 . | .
3 | 3 2 | 1 1 | 1 . | . ||

## Song 15 (1 = A)

a) || 2 | 1 1 | 1
New b) 2 | 1 . | 1
c) 2 | 1 . | . ||

By the end of Chapter Five the children should feel at ease singing a variety of melodic and rhythmic designs.

The teacher will resort to imitation only when a totally new problem is presented. At this stage the children are passing from imitation to reflection. During this period of transition, the teacher will find the exercises graded in such a fashion that the children can use them with a minimum of direction and almost without assistance.

The best aid a teacher can give the class is a well-prepared lesson.

# Chapter Six

## Vocal Training

Timbre, Rhythm, Pitch, Legato - Continued

*Review* Vocal Exercise 1

*1 = Bb C D*

|| 1 ———————— ||
Nu ————————

*Give higher pitches to Bluebirds and lower pitches to Robins and Sparrows.*

Vocal Exercise 6

*1 = G Eb Ab*

|| 2 1 2 3 4 5 . .
Nu Nu Nu Nu Nu Nu ———

5 5 4 3 2 1 . . ||
Nu Nu Nu Nu Nu Nu ———

*This uses tones of Major Pentachord. Children should be familiar with this melody.*

*Practise this exercise slowly and rhythmically.*

*Keep <u>Nnnn</u> sounding between the up and down pulses.*

*Each line of the vocalise is sung on a single breath. Teacher gives signal for inhaling.*

> Special drills in deep breathing are not necessary at this stage of child's development. If teacher says: "Do not stop until you come to the end," this will suggest that the child should take enough air into the lungs to finish the phrase. Too much air in the lungs is difficult for a child to control.

# Intonation

*All exercises on* Diagram 3
*All intonation work in this chapter is based on* 1 2 3 4 5.
*Teacher should use these drills with greater freedom than was the case in earlier chapters.*
*Pointing must be deliberate and precise.*
*Frequently renew pitches of* DO *and* SOL *during the drills by testing with pitchpipe.*

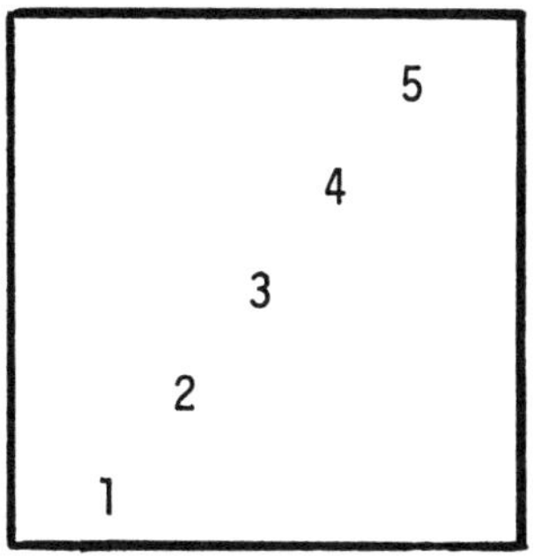


Diagram 3

Intonation Exercise 12 *(1 = G )*

| Descending | Ascending |
|---|---|
| 5 4 3 2 1 | 1 2 3 4 5 |
| 5 4 3 2 1 | . 2 3 4 5 |
| 5 4 3 2 | 2 3 4 5 |
| 5 4 3 2 | . 3 4 5 |
| 5 4 3 | 3 4 5 |
| 5 4 3 | . 4 5 |
| 5 4 | 4 5 |
| 5 4 | . 5 |

*The Pentachord is sung descending and ascending. Alternate lines contain dot (.). As before, the dots are "think" tones. When practising horizontally, the dot can be considered a "holding" tone and children do not take a breath.*

Intonation Exercise 13 *(1 = $A^b$ or A)*

| | | | | | | | | | |
|---|---|---|---|---|---|---|---|---|---|
| 1 | 2 | 3 | 4 | 5 | 5 | 4 | 3 | 2 | 1 |
| 12 | | 12 | 34 | 5 | 54 | | 54 | 32 | 1 |
| 12 | | 34 | 34 | 5 | 54 | | 32 | 32 | 1 |

*Intervals of the Pentachord are used freely with interior tones repeated. Children should think ahead before each line so as to obtain a musical phrase rather than a hesitant spelling out process.*

Intonation Exercise 14 *(1 = $A^b$ )*

| | |
|---|---|
| 1 2 3 4 5 | 5 4 3 2 1 |
| 1 1 2 1 2 | 2 1 2 1 1 |
| 1 2 1 2 2 | 1 2 2 2 1 |

*Intervals of the Pentachord with special attention given to stepwise progression* DO - RE.

DO NOT SING WITH THE CHILDREN. DO NOT GIVE THEM THE TONE THEY ARE SEEKING.

# Rhythm

## Rhythm Patterns - Series 4

*A new rhythm is here added to the basic rhythm patterns studied in the previous chapter. The new pattern at d) presents long notes in the middle as well as the end of a pattern.*

*Study first with* Metrical Language *and* Metrical Gesture, *then with* Rhythm Gestures I *and* II.

a) b) c) New d)

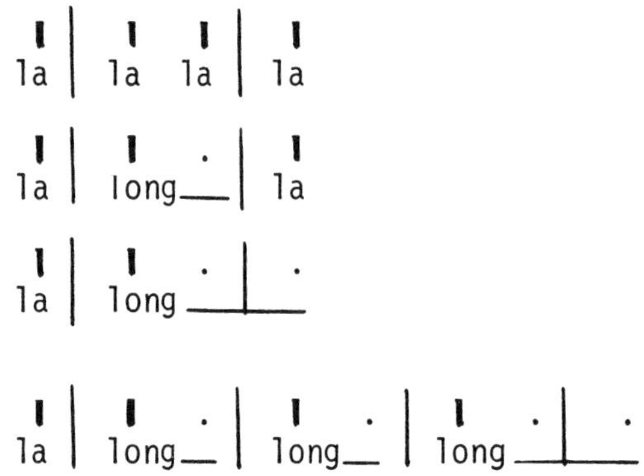


When children render the rhythms, do not let them "bump" on the dots of the long notes.

## Combining Rhythm Patterns

*In Chapter Four, two short rhythm patterns were combined to make a longer pattern. New combinations are discovered here.*

*A (a + b)*

*(Known) B (a + c)*

*C (b + c)*

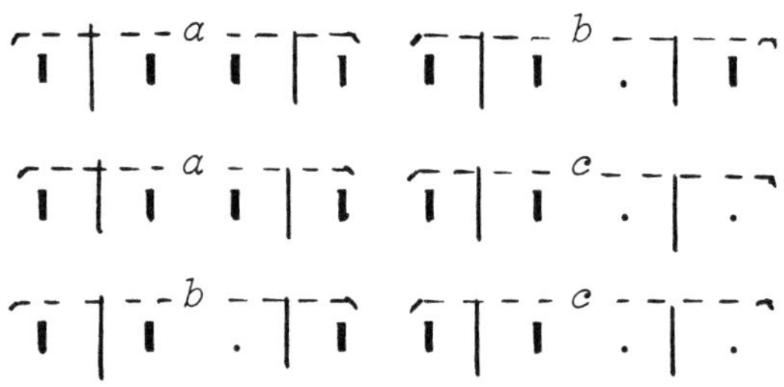


## Melodic Application

*B (a + c)*

*C (b + c)*

*New d)*

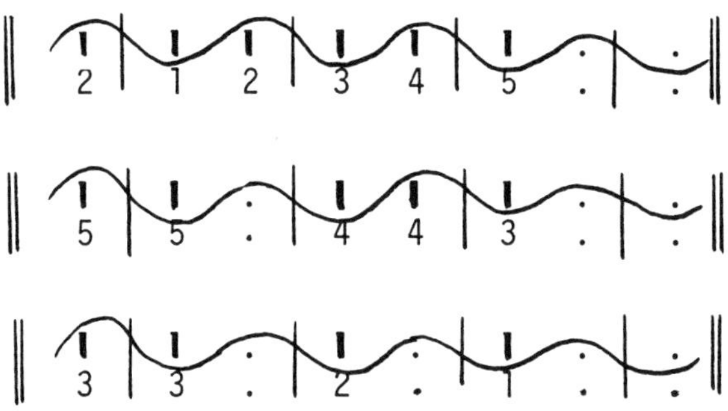


Rhythm patterns should always be in full view of children

# *Notation* The two-line staff with DO, RE and MI

*Review* DO *and* RE *on* Staff Notation 1

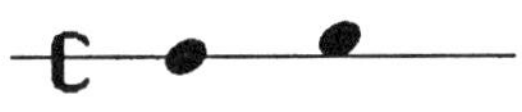

DO RE

**Intonation Exercise 1** *(1 = $A^b$)*

```
--------------------------------->
| 1  2                  2  1 |
| 1 2 1   1 2 2   1 2   1 2 1 1 |
```

**Intonation Exercise 2** *(1 = $A^b$)*

```
a) ---------->   b) ---------->
| 1 1 1 2 1 |   1 2 1 1 1 |
| 1 2 2 2 1 |   1 2 1 1 2 |
| 1 2 2 1 1 |   2 1 2 1 1 |
c) ---------------------------->
```

*Presenting* MI *on staff*

*Teacher draws staff line on board and adds clef and numbers* 1 *and* 2 *for* DO *and* RE *as before:*

*"How can we show* MI *(3)on staff? By adding another line:"*

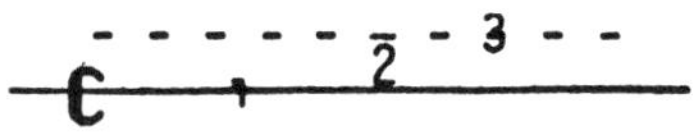


*Teacher makes "snowball" of all three numbers:*

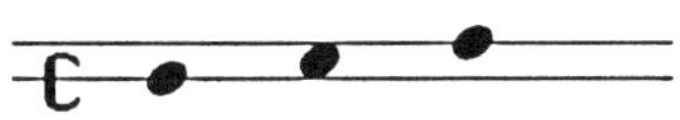

*Children read* DO RE MI *on staff following teacher's pointer, up and down.*

*On the new staff review* Intonation Exercises 3 *and* 4. *Teacher proceeds using pointer as with number diagrams.*

**Staff Notation 2**

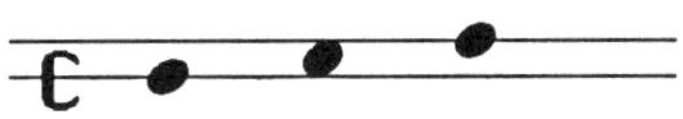

**Intonation Exercise 3**
*(1 = Ab)*

```
a) ---------->   b) ------------->
| 1  2    3   | 3   2    1 |
| 1 2  3 3 3  | 3 2   1 1 1 |
| 1 1  1 2 3  | 3 3   3 2 1 |
c) ------------------------------>
```

**Intonation Exercise 4**
*(1 = Ab)*

```
------------------------->
| 1 2 3   3 2 1     |
| 1 2 3   . 2 1     |

| 1 2 3   3 2       |
| 1 2 3   3 2 3 2   |
| 1 2 3   3 2 3     |

| 1 2 3   . 3 2     |
| 1 2 3   . 3 2 2 1 |
```

## Creative Activity

Musical Conversation - Step 3 *(Cont'd)*

*In Chapter Five, the same question, i.e.,*  *was asked several times by the children. To each question, the teacher made a different response.*

*In this chapter, the same question is asked, this time by the teacher, and the children are invited to respond, one at a time. Four or five children will be called upon to make a response and each response should be different. If the responses are written on the board or projected on a screen, all the children may participate in the musical dialogue as the teacher designates different individuals or groupings to lead this question-and-answer segment of the lesson.*

*QUESTION*

(?)

*POSSIBLE ANSWERS*

3 | 3 3 | 2 . | . ||

3 | 2 3 | 2 . | . ||

2 | 1 2 | 1 . | . ||

2 | 3 2 | 1 . | . ||

Rhythm Gesture I

*or*

Rhythm Gesture II

*At first, the possible answers may be in full view of the class (on board or screen) so that the child called on can make a choice. After a few repetitions, however, the answers need not be shown as the children should be able to think up their own answers.*

> This game lays the foundation for musical composition. It should stimulate interest on the part of the children to say something in music.

# Dictations

**Ear Tests** *Teacher sings a fragment on* Nu. *Children identify tones by singing the note-names while making corresponding arm or finger gesture, or by pointing to correct notes on* Diagram 3.

| | | |
|---|---|---|
| 1 2 3 2 3 | 1 2 3 4 5 5 | 1 2 1 2 3 4 5 |
| 1 2 3 4 3 | 2 2 1 1 2 3 | 5 4 5 4 3 2 1 |

**Eye Tests** *Teacher presents melodic fragment silently by:*

*a) pointing to corresponding numbers on* Diagram 3; *or,*
*b) using* Finger Notation; *or,*
*c) using* Measuring Gesture.

| | | |
|---|---|---|
| 1 2 3 4 3 | 1 2 3 4 5 | 1 2 3 3 2 2 3 |
| 5 4 5 4 3 2 1 | | 3 3 3 2 3 2 1 |
| 1 1 2 2 2 3 | | |

*On* Staff Notation 2 *with pointer:*

| | | |
|---|---|---|
| 1 2 3 3 | 2 2 3 | 1 2 1 2 3 |
| 3 3 3 2 | 3 2 1 | 2 2 1 2 2 1 |

**Rhythmic Dictation**

1. *With* Rhythm Patterns - Series 4 *in view of class, teacher sings a melodic fragment based on a combination of two rhythms. Class is asked to identify the two rhythms.*

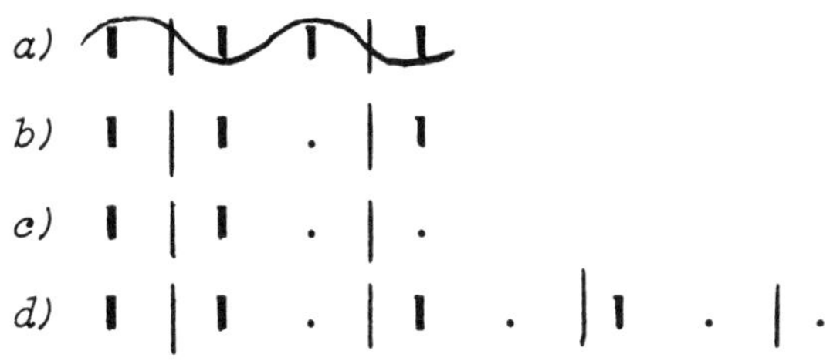


*Teacher:*

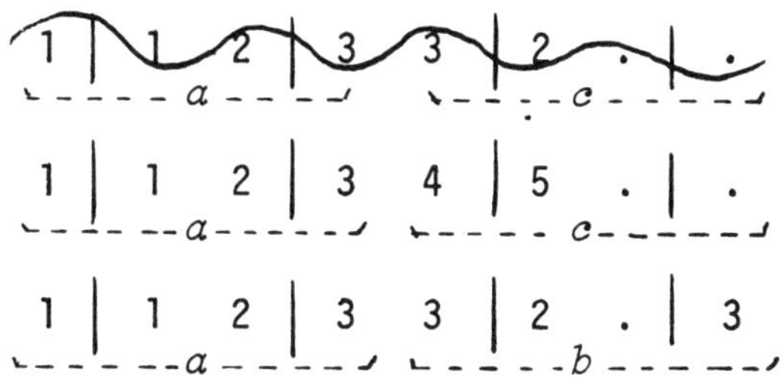


2. *Teacher writes a rhythm pattern combination on board, e.g.,*

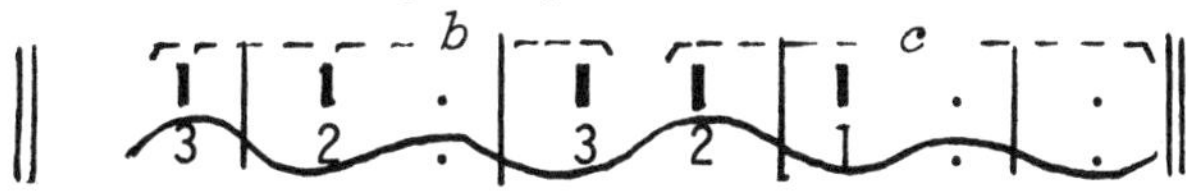


*Teacher then sings a melody based on this pattern and children are asked to fit the melody into the pattern at the board. A child comes to the board and adds the correct numbers and the rhythmic curve. Bluebirds repeat making* Rhythm Gesture 2; *Robins do same; Sparrows make gesture while Bluebirds and Robins sing melody.*

## Songs

Songs 16 and 17 *apply in musical form the intervals and rhythm patterns learned in this chapter.*

### Song 16 *(1 = G)*

*a)* || 1 | 1 2 | 3
*b)* 3 | 2 . | 3
*c)* 2 | 1 . | . ||

### Song 17 *(1 = G)*

*A (a + b)* || 1 | 1 2 | 3 3 | 2 . | 1
*B (a + c)* 1 | 1 2 | 3 4 | 5 . | .
*A (a + b)* 5 | 5 4 | 3 3 | 2 . | 3
*B (a + c)* 3 | 4 3 | 2 2 | 1 . | . ||

Words and Melody

*Accent is on the first syllable. Students should sing second syllable softly.*

*Do not teach by imitation. Children can read the tune. If they cannot read the word, teacher will sing the word* A - men, *after they have discovered the tune.*

|| 1 | 2 . | . ||
A- men ____

### Before I Go to Sleep *(1 = G)* Song 14 *with words*

|| 1 | 1 2 | 3 3 | 3 . | .
Be- fore I go to sleep ____
O let my an- gel come ____

3 | 3 4 | 5 5 | 5 . | .
I pray you, Lord, to keep ____
To guard us all at home ____

5 | 5 4 | 3 3 | 3 . | .
My soul all thro' this night ____
And when I wake I'll say: ____

3 | 3 2 | 1 1 | 1 . | . ||
Un- til the morn- ing light. ____
Lord, bless us all this day. ____

# Chapter Seven

## Vocal Training

*Review* Vocal Exercise 1

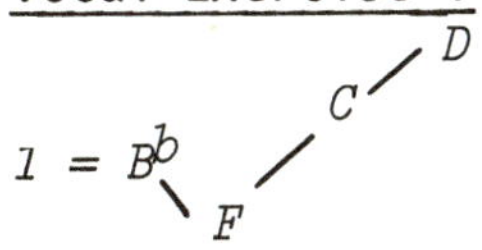

*Review* Vocal Exercise 6

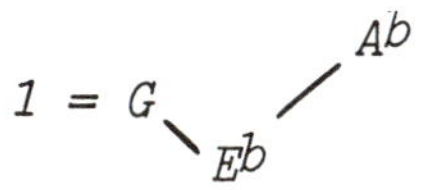


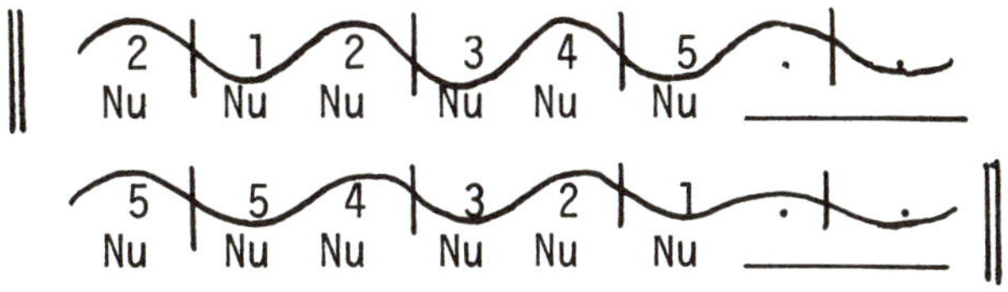


In the review of vocal exercises, work for smoothness and beauty of tone quality. Be sure chins are low and teeth unclenched. Feel cheeks to be sure they are soft and not tense.

Vocal Exercise 7. *Introduce this exercise after work has begun on the interval* DO - MI.

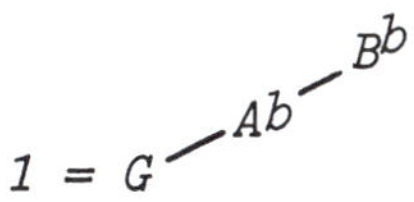


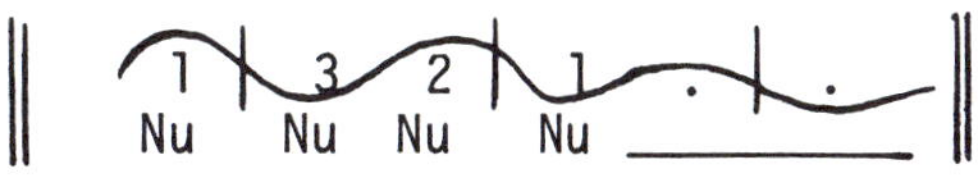


Generate enthusiasm for achieving beauty of tone as a goal worth striving for.

# Intonation

*Review* Intonation Exercises 13 *and* 14.

*Use* Diagram 3

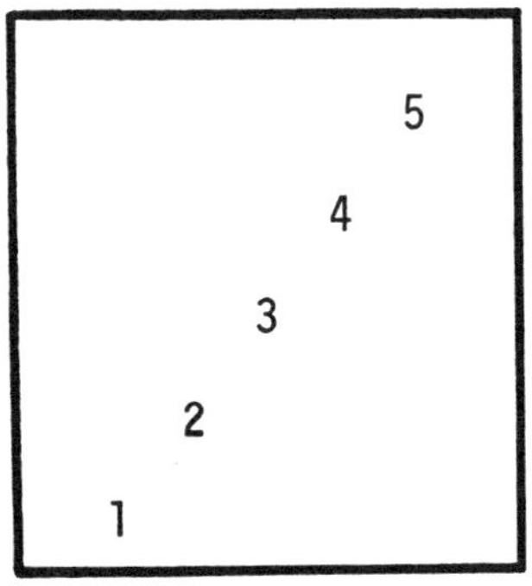


Diagram 3

## Intonation Exercise 15 *(1 = A♭)*

| 1 2 3 4 5 5 4 3 2 1 |
| 1 2 3 3 2 3 2 1 2 3 |
| 3 2 2 3 2 3 2 2 3 3 |
| 3 2 3 2 3 3 2 3 2 1 |

Free use of intervals of pentachord 12345. Special attention to RE - MI.

## Intonation Exercise 16 *(1 = A)*

*First drills on skip :* DO - MI. *Note carefully direction of arrows. Do not renew pitch at beginning of each line.*

*a)* → *b)* → *c)* →
| 1 2 3 | 3 2 1 | 1 2 3 3 2 1 |
| 1 2 3 | 3 2 1 | 1 3 3 1 |
| 1 . | 3 . |

## *Presenting* Intonation Exercise 16

*First Day: Drill on a) by pointing to diagram* 1 2 3. *Repeat* 1 2 3. *Then start again at* 1 *and quickly withdraw pointer. At this point children have in fact sung the interval* MI - DO.

*Second Day: Drill on b) by pointing to diagram* 3 2 1. *Repeat* 3 2 1. *Begin again at* 3 *and quickly withdraw pointer. Children have in fact sung the interval* DO - MI.

*Third Day: Drill on c).*

*For variety present skip* 1 - 3, 3 - 1, *with* Measuring Gesture, Finger Notation *and* Staff Notation 2.

Staff Notation 2 

# Notation

1. DO - MI on staff and place of FA (4)

*Place* DO - MI *on staff in* Number Notation

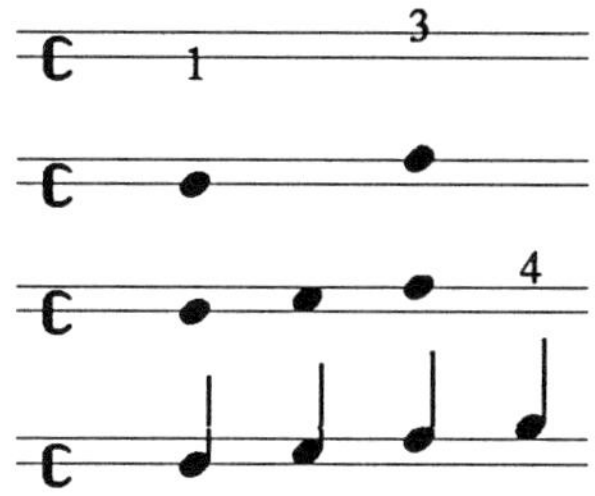


*Cover the numbers as "snowballs". Give eye and ear tests. (Verify with pitch pipe.)*

*Fill in scale and add* FA (4). *Let children suggest where it should go.*

*Cover number as "snowball." With pointer ask Bluebirds to sing up and down staff. Then Robins. (1 = G)*

2. Staff Notation 3 *One- and two-pulse notes.*

*Teacher shows children that the one-pulse rhythm stroke is the same as the* quarter note. *For each single stroke, or* quarter note, *the child says* la.

*Teacher shows children that a stroke and a dot equal two pulses. The* half note *also equals two pulses. For each* half note, *the child says* long.

*Using* Metrical Language *and* Metrical Gesture I, *children sing the following rhythm patterns from* Series 4.

*a)*

*Repeat several times.*

*b)*

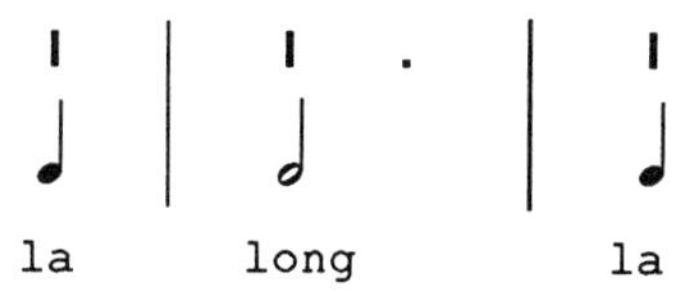


*Repeat several times.*

# Rhythm

Review Rhythm Gestures I *and* II, *using recordings especially prepared for this purpose. When recording is not available, children should sing for each other in alternating groups as follows:*

*Bluebirds sing melody while Robins and Sparrows make gesture.*

*Robins sing melody while Bluebirds and Sparrows make gesture.*

Song 14 *(Chapter Five) or* Song 17 *(Chapter Six) may be used.*

*Review* Rhythm Patterns - Series 4
*Combinations and melodic applications.*

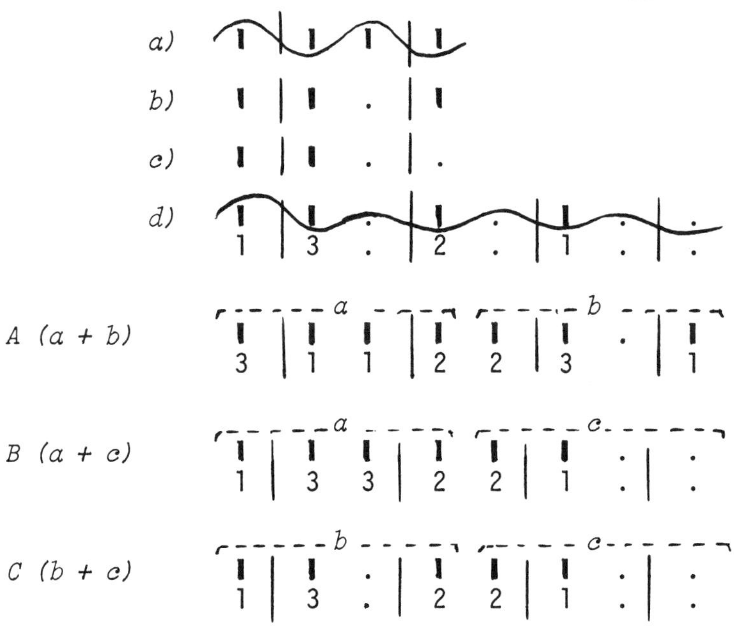

*Melodic applications use skips* DO - MI, MI - DO. *Sing each pattern using* Metrical Language *while making* Metrical Gesture I. *Bluebirds sing melody at A on note names while Robins and Sparrows make* Rhythm Gesture II. *All sing melody on* Nu *while making same gesture. Another day drill on B. A third day, drill on C, or d.*

# Dictations

## Tonal Dictation

*Review* Eye *and* Ear Tests *of Chapter Six.*

*Use:* Diagram 3
Finger Notation
Measuring Gesture
Staff Notation 2
*Single-line quotations from songs studied thus far.*

*For drills on interval* DO - MI :

1 2 3  3 1  1 3  3 2 1
3 1  1 2 3  3 1  1 2 1

## Rhythmic Dictation

*With* Rhythm Patterns - Series 4 *in full view of class, teacher dictates melodic application A by singing melody on* Nu *and making* Rhythm Gesture II

*A (a + b)* 

*Children must identify the combination of a + b.*
*A child is invited to the board and first writes the strokes with finger, then with chalk. Another child adds bar lines. **
*A third child adds melody and the fourth adds the rhythmic curve.*

*Bluebirds sing line while making* Rhythm Gesture II.
*Robins repeat.*

* *Add bar line before last note and count back by two's.*

| Do not dictate rhythm combinations on one tone. Always use a melody. |
|---|

# Creative Activity

1. Musical Conversation - Step 3 continued.

   a) *Review conversation on* 1 2 3 *of last chapter. Invite a child to ask the question; invite another child to give the answer.*

   *"Remember, when the question goes up, the answer comes down."*

   b) *Teacher makes the question longer using pentachord* 1 2 3 4 5. *Teacher writes several possible answers on the board and asks a child to select one of them. Teacher repeats question and child answers. Teacher repeats the question and Bluebirds answer; then Robins. Sparrows merely make* Rhythm Gesture II

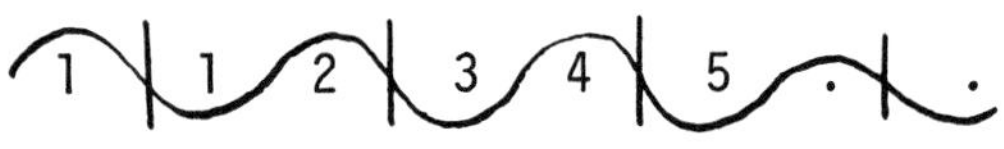


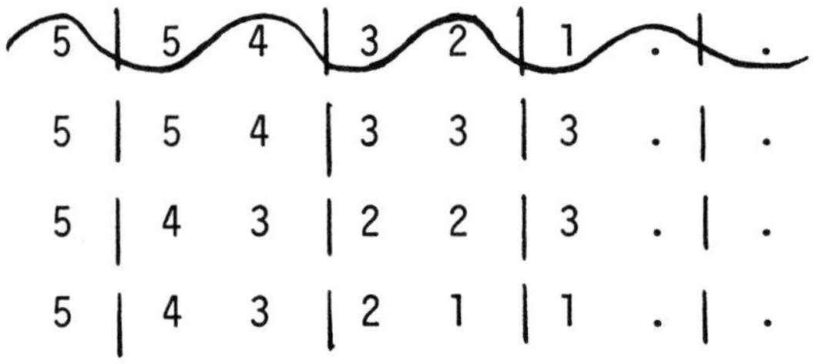


2. Composition. *Children have seen how two short patterns can be combined to make a longer pattern. Here the children learn how the longer pattern can be repeated in its entirety to make a pattern that is longer still. For example:*

*Pattern B is made up of a + c*

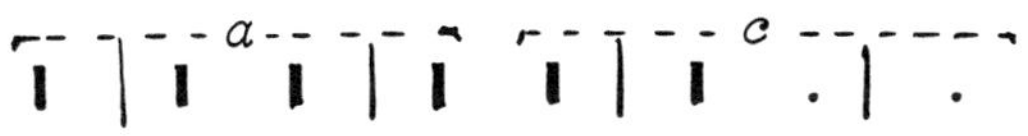


*If we repeat B we can make a more complete melody -*

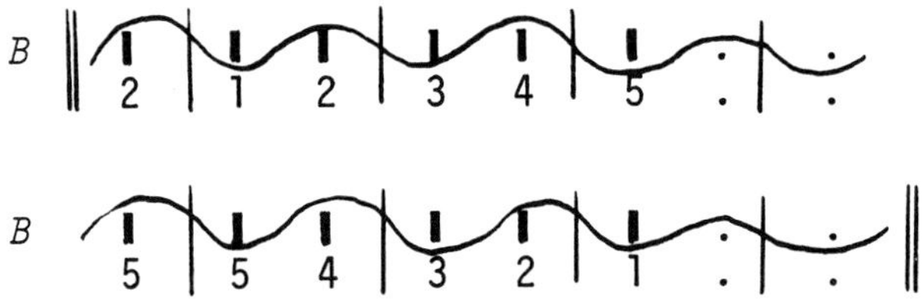


*Take another example. Pattern C is made up of b + c*

*If we double C we can make a more complete melody:*

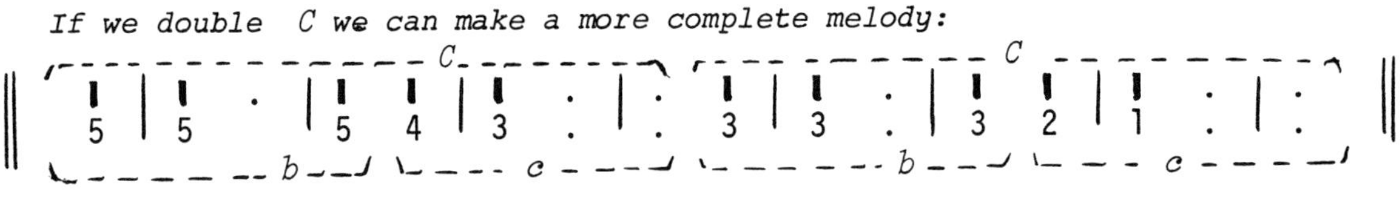

# Songs

*Note that* Song 18 *uses skip* DO - MI (1 - 3). *This song should not be taught until the skip is learned.*

**Song 18** *(1 = G)*

‖ 3 | 1 2 | 3 2 | 3 . | .
3 | 1 2 | 3 4 | 5 . | .
5 | 5 4 | 3 2 | 3 . | .
2 | 1 3 | 2 2 | 1 . | . ‖

*N.B.*

**Song 19** *(1 = G)*

‖ 2 | 1 2 | 3 4 | 3 . | .
4 | 3 . | 3 . | 2 . | .
2 | 3 4 | 5 5 | 5 . | .
5 | 4 3 | 2 2 | 1 . | . ‖

**Words and Melody**
*(1 = G)*

‖ 5 | 5 4 | 3 . | 3 . | . ‖
Al- le- lu- ia_____

‖ 1 | 2 3 | 1 . | . ‖
Al- le- lu- ia_____

# Chapter Eight

## Vocal Training

*Review exercise of the previous chapter. Strive for legato, i.e., smooth linking of tones, and timbre, i.e., uniform controlled quality.*

*Review*
Vocal Exercise 1

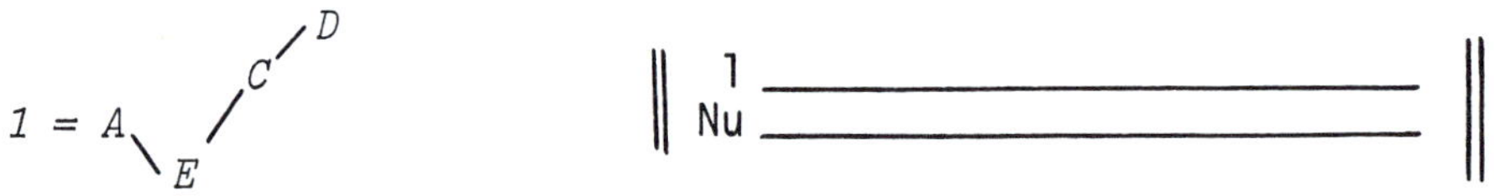


*Review*
Vocal Exercise 6

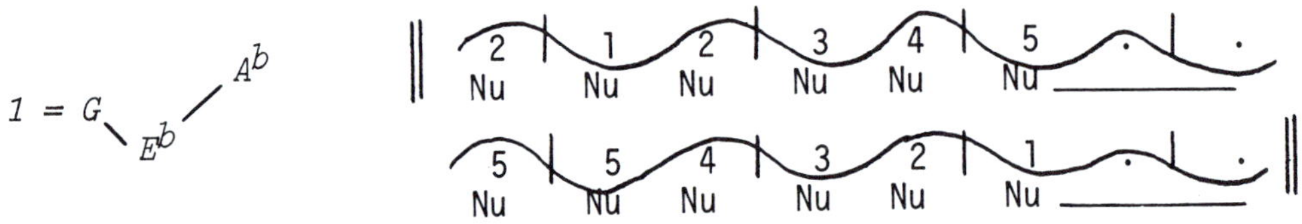


*Review*
Vocal Exercise 7

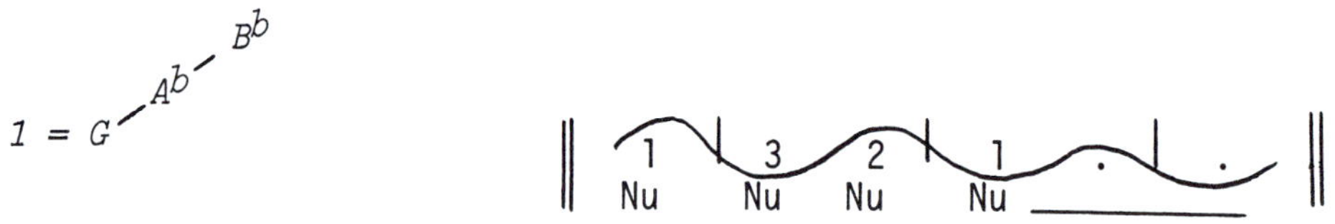


*In* Voc. Ex. 7, DO - MI *must be rendered with precision avoiding all traces of "scooping" between the two tones. This exactness will be enhanced by the correctness of the rhythmic gesture.*

> Bluebirds on higher pitches.
> Robins on lower pitches.
> Sparrows - a few trials on lower pitches.

# Intonation

*Follow same process as in Chapter Two when* Diagrams 2 *and* 3 *were presented, that is, teach each new tone first to the ear while making correct corresponding* Measuring (Melodic) Gesture.
*In this chapter teacher sings new tone several times on syllable* Nu - 56565, *assigns the new number to the tone, and tells its name:* LA.

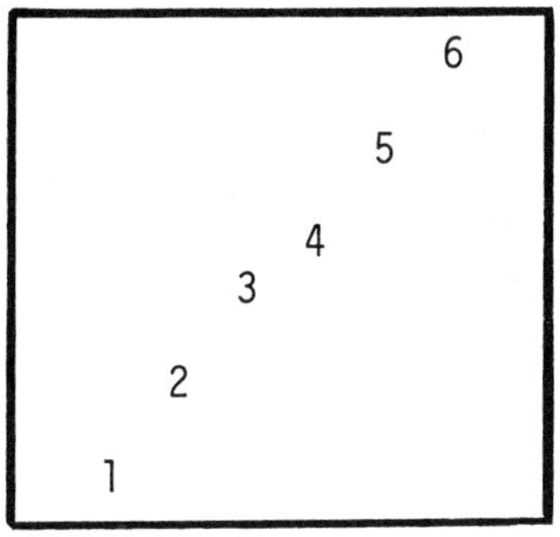


Diagram 4

Intonation Exercise 17 *(1 = F)*

| 1 2 3 4 5   5 5 5   5 6 5   5 4 3 2 1 |
| 1 2 3 4 5 6 5   5 6 5 6 5 5   5 6 5 4 3 2 1 |

*Teach on* Diagram 4. *Allow a brief moment of silence where spaces between the numbers occur. A minimum of imitation should be expected. Let children discover how to show* LA *on their fingers and with the* Measuring Gesture.

6 LA

Intonation Exercise 18 *(1 = F or G)*

| 1 2 3 4 5 6 5   5 6 6   6 6 5   5 6 5 4 3 2 1 |
| 1 2 3 4 5 6   6 6 6   6 5 6   5 6 5 4 3 2 1 |

*Teach from* Diagram 4; *then horizontally from overhead projector or chart. Give special attention to pauses on* LA *and repetitions of that tone.*

LA

Intonation Exercise 19 *(1 = F or G)*

| 1 2 3 4 5   5 4 3 2 1 |
| 1 2 3 4   4 3 |
| 1 2 3 4   . 3 |
| 1 2 3 4   4 3 4 3 |
| 1 2 3 4   . 3 4 3 2 |
| 1 2 3 4   . 3 2 |
| 1 2 3 4   . 3 2 1 |

*Teach from* Diagram 4. *Drill stresses half-step* MI - FA. *Each line that has a dot is sung on one breath. Each line that does not have a dot will allow a breath between number groups.*

*Review* Intonation Exercises 5, 6, 7, *and* 8 *on* Staff Notation 4.

# Rhythm

*Review* Rhythm Gestures I *and* II. *Rhythmic gestures should by now be growing more and more precise, supple, light, and floating. The arm and body movements must never cause a retard - a slowing down - of the melody. On the contrary, rhythm gestures should lead the way. It is well, therefore, to study the melody well before adding the gestures.*

*Review* Rhythm Patterns - Series 4. *Teacher makes a "word" out of each simple pattern. Children memorize these "words" as single entities. Then teacher writes them out as a single line.*

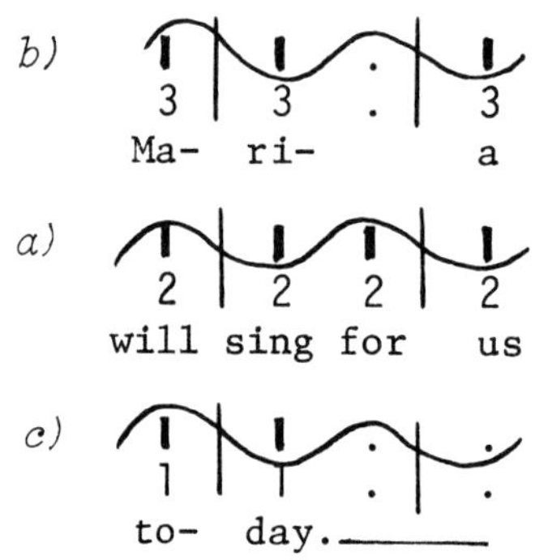


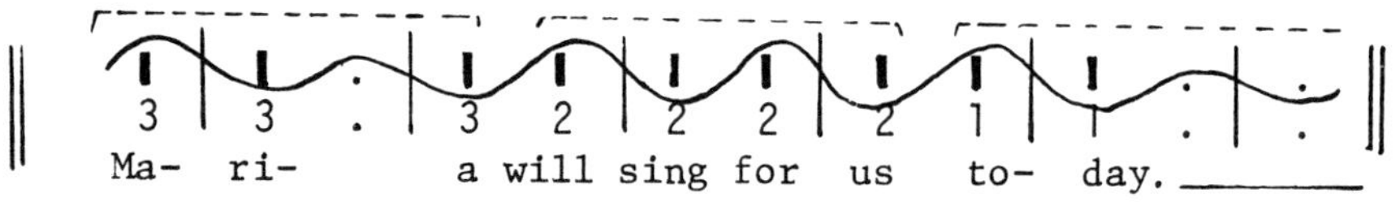


*Continue with drills on* Rhythm Patterns - Series 4. *Each pattern must be rendered accurately with* Metrical Gesture, Metrical Language, *and on different pitches. When the rhythm gestures are applied to a rhythm pattern, they must accommodate the long notes. This is sometimes difficult. Consider the following melodic applications to the rhythm patterns being studied.*

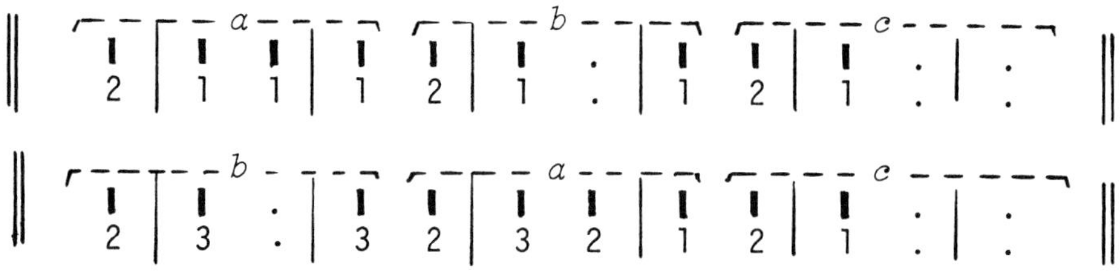

# *Notation*

1. Staff Notation 4. Extension of staff to include SOL *and* LA.

*Teacher draws staff of two lines, adds* DO Clef, *writes numbers of tones already seen on staff.*

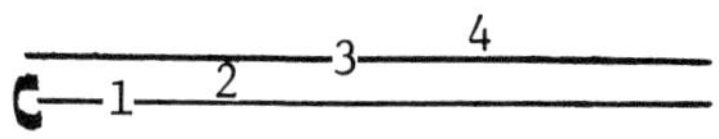


*Children sing tones up and down as teacher points to them. (1 = F)*

*Teacher adds third line and asks children where* SOL (5) *should go. Teacher adds number* 5 *on third line. "Where shall we put* LA?" *Teacher adds number* 6 *above staff. Children sing up and down as teacher points to numbers* 1 2 3 4 5 6, 6 5 4 3 2 1, *several times. (1 = F)*

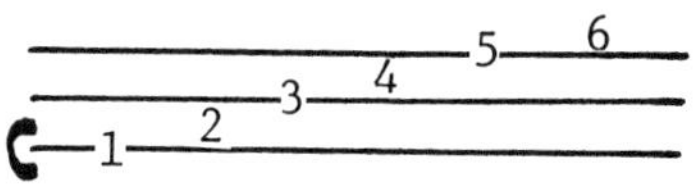


*Teacher covers numbers as "snowballs" to make* Staff Notation 4. *Children sing up and down several times as above. (1 = F)*

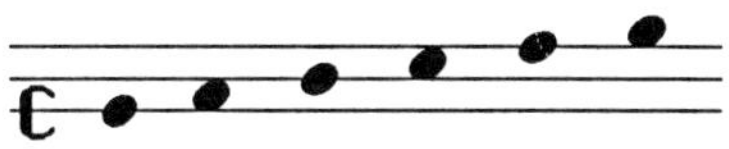

*For drills on the new staff, review* Intonation Exercises 5 (P. 38), 6, 7 *and* 8 (P. 46).

| Exercises in visualization and memorization should be given as frequently as possible from the three-line staff in order to strengthen the child's perception of the staff notation signs. |
|---|

2. *Review* Staff Notation 3.

*Teacher places a rhythmic pattern on board to be transcribed to staff notation. Measure bars should be made longer than usual so as to contain the notes that will be added by children. A child is invited to add correct one- and two-pulse notes.*

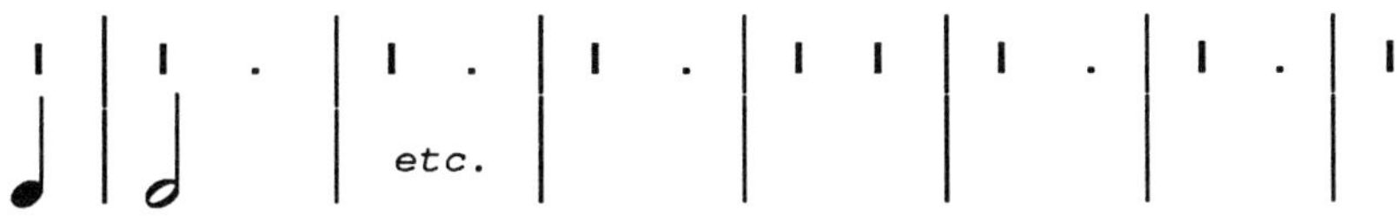


*After notes have been added, children sing rhythm with* Metrical Language "la, long..." *while making simple* Metrical Gesture I.

# Creative Activity

## Musical Conversation - Step 3 continued and developed

*To awaken the imagination of the children, teacher might set the scene as follows:*

> *"Let us suppose we became acquainted with a small family of birds, say, Canaries. You know how they are always singing and talking to each other. Let us listen."*

*In advance, teacher has placed a simple melody of four lines on board, for example,* Song 14 *in Chapter Five, and assigns four children to represent Mr. and Mrs. Canary, and two young Canaries. Teacher assigns different line to each member of the family. As they sing, the rest of the class listens to the conversation. By imagining themselves listening to the conversation of the birds, they will readily understand the idea of musical dialogue being proposed here. They will then want to make up their own conversation of question and answer. Let them do so.*

*After a few attempts, question and response dialogues should be accompanied by rhythm gestures to give more musical meaning to conversations.*

*A few rules must be imposed or conversation will get out of hand.*

1. *Children sing on neutral syllable* Nu.
2. *If question goes up, answer comes down. (See preceding chapters.)*
3. *If answer ends on* DO, *the conversation is ended.*

*Q.* 1 | 1 2 | 3 . | . *A.* 3 | 3 2 | 1 . | .

*Q.* 1 | 1 2 | 3 4 | 5 . | . *A.* 5 | 5 4 | 3 2 | 1 . | .

4. *If response does not end on* DO *the conversation can be continued.*

*Q.* 1 | 1 2 | 3 . | . *1st Ans.* 3 | 3 3 | 2 . | .

*2nd Q.* 2 | 3 4 | 5 . | . *2nd Ans.* 5 | 5 4 | 3 . | .

*3rd Q.* 2 | 3 4 | 5 5 | 5 . | .

*Last Ans.* 5 | 5 4 | 3 2 | 1 . | . ||

> Teacher must invite <u>all</u> children to participate, otherwise a few will dominate the time given to this part of the lesson and the less gifted will not have a chance to enjoy the game.

# Dictations

> Frequently give simple dictations to encourage less gifted children.

Tonal Dictation - Diagram 4 *Special emphasis is given here to the new tone* LA.

Ear Tests

| 1 2 3 4 5 6 5 5 6 5 6 5 | 1 2 3 4 5 6 5 5 5 6 6 5
| 1 2 3 4 5 6 6 6 6 6 5 6 | 1 2 3 3 4 4 3 1 2 3 4 3 4 3

Eye Tests *With pointer,* Measuring Gesture, Finger Notation, *and for visual memory tests, i.e., child views test for an instant then turns around to sing fragment from memory.*

| 1 2 3 4 5 6 5 5 6 5 6 5 | 1 1 2 3 4 5 5 6 6 5 4 3
| 1 3 3 2 1 3 3 2 1 3 | 1 2 3 3 3 1
| 1 1 1 2 3 1 2 3 1 3 | 3 2 1 1 3

Staff Notation 4 - Ear *and* Eye tests

Rhythmic Dictation *With* Rhythmic Patterns - Series 4 *in full view of class, teacher dictates new combinations of a), b) and c). Each example may be sung on* Nu *or note names with* Metrical Gesture I *or* Rhythm Gesture II. *Only melodic applications of rhythms studied should be used. For example:*

*B (a + c)*

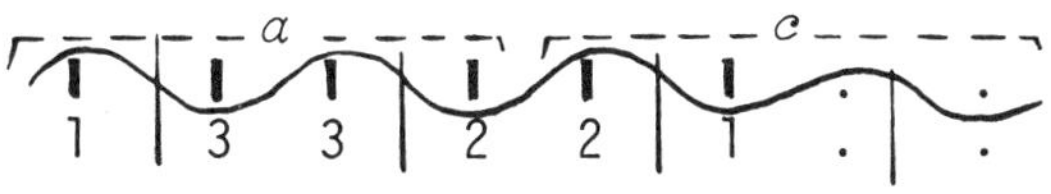


*C (b + c)*

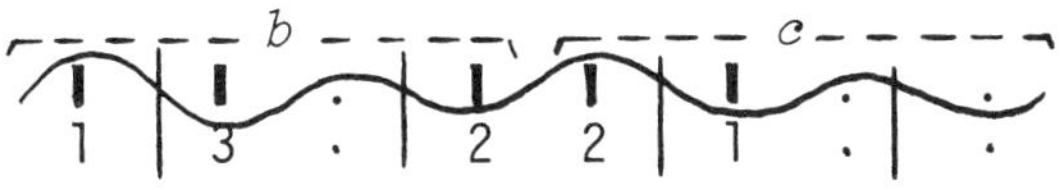


*d)*

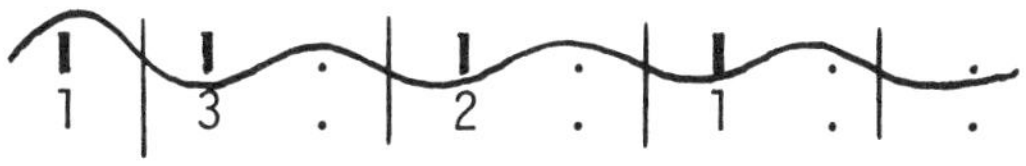


*Children must identify correct combinations and proceed as in Chapter Seven.*

*Visual memory tests may be given here as in* Eye Tests *above. Additional melodic applications are suggested below for these tests.*

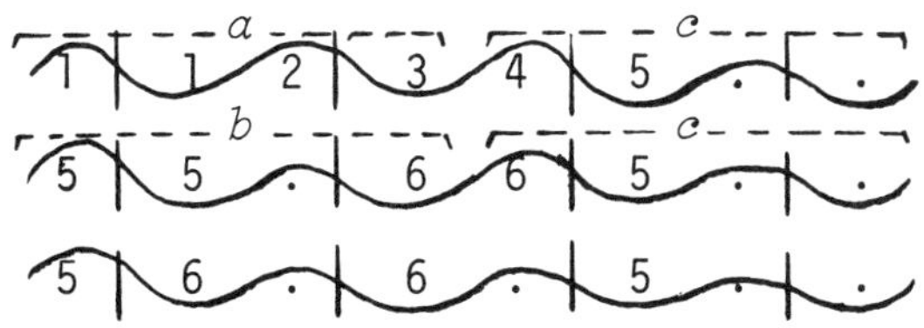

## Songs

Songs 20 *and* 21 *are presented as means of assimilating intonation and rhythm skills offered in this chapter.*

**Song 20** *(1 = G)*

|| 1 | 1 2 | 3 4 | 5 . | .
5 | 5 6 | 5 6 | 5 . | .
5 | 6 . | 5 4 | 3 . | .
2 | 1 . | 2 . | 1 . | . ||

**Song 21** *(1 = G)*

|| 1 | 1 2 | 3 4 | 5 . | .
5 | 6 . | 6 . | 5 . | .
5 | 5 6 | 5 4 | 3 . | .
4 | 3 . | 2 . | 1 . | . ||

**Words and Melody**
*(1 = G)*

*Another melody is offered for "A-men." instead of*

|| 2 | 1 . | . ||
A- men _____

*or*

|| 1 | 2 . | . ||
A- men _____

*the new melody is*

|| 6 | 5 . | 6 . | . ||
A- men _____

*Because of problem of singing two different tones on one syllable, children sing melody first on note names; then on* Nu*; finally, on word.*

|| 6 | 5 . | 6 . | . ||
LA SOL ____ LA ____
Nu Nu ____ Nu ____
Nu Nu ________
A- men ________

*Review:* "The Flowers Awake"
"Before I Go to Sleep"
"Hail, Holy Queen"

## We Thank You, God, for Everything (1 = G)

2 | 1 1 | 1 2 | 3 3 | 3 . | .
We thank you, God, for flow- ers sweet;

4 | 3 3 | 3 4 | 5 5 | 5 . | .
We thank you for the food we eat:

5 | 5 5 | 5 5 | 6 6 | 5 . | .
We thank you for the birds that sing;

4 | 5 5 | 5 4 | 3 2 | 1 . | .
We thank you, God, for ev- 'ry - thing.

Measuring Gesture for "LA"

Dictation with Finger Notation

Posture of repose for "A-men"

# Chapter Nine

| | 1 | 2 | 3 | 4 | 5 |
|---|---|---|---|---|---|
| Stand<br>**Vocal Training** | Greeting and opening song: *The Flowers Awake*<br>*Alleluia Amen* sung by Bluebirds and Robins<br>Sparrows make gesture in silence<br>Voc. Ex. 1 Bluebirds 1 = C<br>Robins 1 = A<br>Sparrows 1 = F Practise with individuals | | Greeting<br>*Ball Game* with Sparrows who respond on same tones<br>Voc. Ex. 6 Bluebirds 1 = Ab<br>Robins 1 = F<br>Invite pupils to sing alone to establish confidence | Robins 1 = G | Greeting and opening song:<br>*I Saw a Ship*<br>Deep breath<br>Strong Nnnnn<br>Test Sparrows for promotion |
| Sit<br>**Intonation** | Int. Diagram 4<br>Int. Ex. 20<br>Special study of FA-MI<br>(diagram: 1 2 3 4 5 6) | **Review:** Int. Ex. 6, 7, 8 of Chapter Four on Staff Notation 4: | **Review:** Int. Ex. 20 on Diag. 4<br>**Present:**<br>**Int. Diagram 5**<br>**Int. Ex. 21**<br>(diagram: 5 6 7 1̇) | Measuring Gesture and Finger Notation for TI DO | **Review:** Int. 21<br>Listen for accurate pitch at TI - DO |
| **Dictations** Ear Tests / Eye Tests | With Int. Diagram 4 in view<br>1234 43<br>1234 32<br>Red end of pointer<br>1234 343<br>12345 43 | With Staff Notation 4 in view<br>1234 43<br>1234 32<br>1234 343<br>12345 43 | 1̇765<br>1̇1̇765<br>On fingers: 1̇1̇ 1̇1̇ 1̇765 765 55 | **KEEP DIAGRAM 5 IN FULL VIEW OF CLASS**<br>1̇765 55<br>55 5671̇<br>With Meas. Gest.<br>55 5671̇ 5671̇ 1̇1̇ | 5565 65<br>5671̇ 1̇1̇<br>On board and erase:<br>1̇765 5671̇ 1̇1̇765 5671̇ |
| Stand<br>**Rhythm** | **Present:** Rhythm Gesture III — Ternary Rhythm<br>Prepare gesture in segments:<br>Up-down — swing over — up-down<br>Make continuous gesture | Down-pulse is twice as long as up-pulse<br>Do not rush second pulse of measure<br>Play recording or sing song in ternary rhythm beginning with up-pulse | | Rhythm Gesture III →<br>Song 23<br>**Review:** Rhythm Gesture II with *Before I Go to Sleep* | |
| Sit<br>**Notation** | **Transcribe:** Staff Notation 5 to Number Notation<br>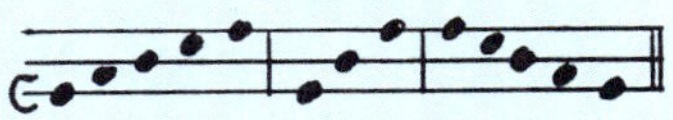 | **Review:** Time values of staff notes<br>**Transcribe:** R. P. Series 5 to Staff Notation | Sing on one tone or with Melodic application | **Transcribe:** Rhythm ex. to Staff Notation using | **Transcribe:** R. P. Series 5 to rhythm strokes:<br>a)<br>b)<br>c) |
| Stand<br>**Vocal Training** | Voc. Ex. 6 Bluebirds 1 = Ab<br>Robins 1 = G<br>Sparrows make gesture in silence | | Voc. Ex. 7 →<br>Bluebirds 1 = Ab | Bluebirds 1 = Bb →<br>Robins 1 = Ab<br>note skip 1 - 3 | Test individual voices |
| Sit<br>**Creative Activity** | Musical Conversation Step 3<br>Reverse statement:<br>3 3 2 1 . . | Encourage ending on SOL, MI and RE (5 3 2)<br>Avoid ending on FA and LA (4 6) | Try not to "end" conversation on DO | Statement: 2 1 2 3 4 5 . .<br>Pupils add at least 3 responses before ending on DO (1) | |
| **Rhythm** | **Present:** Rhythm Patterns Series 5 →<br>a)<br>b)<br>c) | Special work on c) → | Metrical Gesture and Language | R. P. Series 4 with Metrical Gesture 1 on tones of Int. Diagram 5 | R. P. Series 5 with Melodic application |
| Stand<br>**Songs** | **Review:** Song 21<br>*Hail, Mary* | Melody only on note names of *I Saw a Ship*<br>*Before I Go to Sleep* | Song 23<br>*I Saw a Ship* with words<br>5 5 4 3 . 3 . .<br>Al -le- lu- ia. → | Song 22 → | *I Saw a Ship* |

# Chapter Nine

## Vocal Training

In each lesson, practise vocalises with individuals so that they will become used to singing alone.

*Review* Vocal Exercise 1

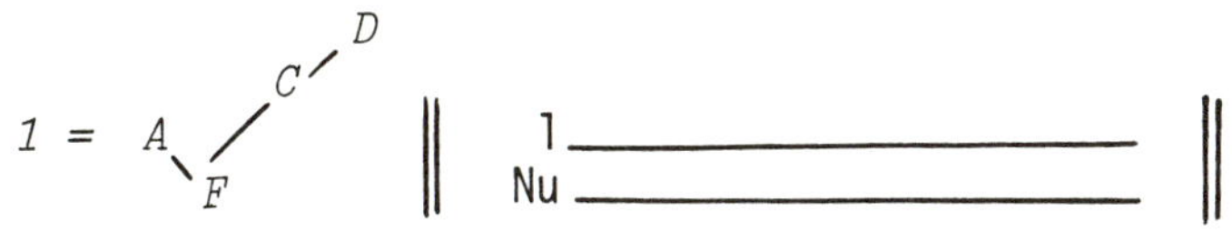


*Review* Vocal Exercise 6

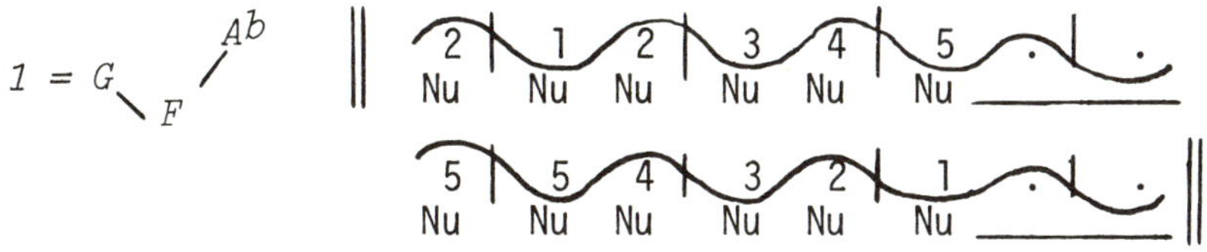


*Review* Vocal Exercise 7

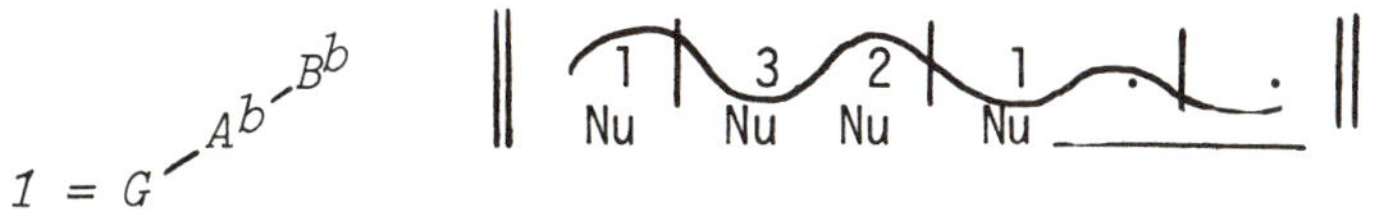


## Intonation

Continuation of the study of FA - MI and MI - FA.
Stopping and starting in middle of pentachord.

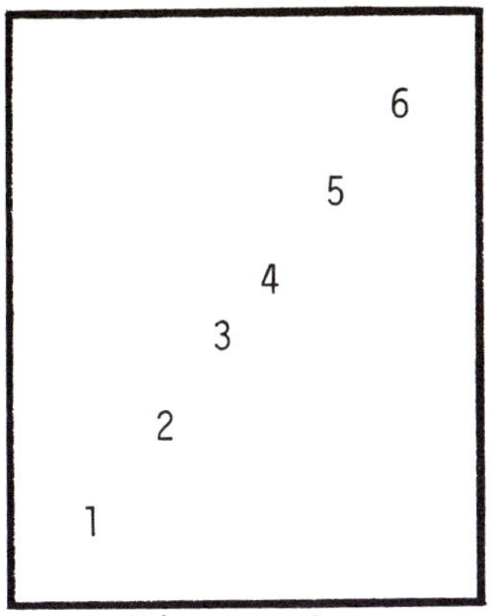

Diagram 4

*Present* Intonation Exercise 20 *on* Diagram 4 *and* Staff Notation 4.

*Practise in two ways:*
- *Considering the dot(.) as a "think" note of the previous tone;*
- *Considering the dot(.) as a "hold" note of the previous tone. Sing entire line on one breath.*

Intonation Exercise 20 *(1 = G )*

| | | | | | | | | | | | |
|---|---|---|---|---|---|---|---|---|---|---|---|
| 1 | 2 | 3 | 4 | 5 | 6 | 6 | 5 | 4 | 3 | 2 | 1 |
| 1 | 2 | 3 | 4 | 5 | 6 | . | 5 | 4 | 3 | | |
| | | 3 | 4 | 5 | 6 | . | 5 | 4 | 3 | | |
| | | 3 | 4 | 5 | 6 | . | 5 | 4 | 3 | 2 | |
| | 2 | 3 | 4 | 5 | 6 | . | 5 | 4 | 3 | 2 | 1 |

Staff Notation 4

*Review* Intonation Exercises 6, 7, *and* 8 *of Chapter Four using* Staff Notation 4.

*Presenting* Diagram 5 *for* Intonation Exercise 21

*This diagram is based on what is already known, that is,* Diagram 3. *Teacher sings pentachord*

1 2 3 4 5 *(1 = C)*

7 TI $\dot{1}$ DO

*The low pitch for* DO *is suggested because it is the teacher who will first sing the upper tetrachord.*

*Teacher says: "Attention, now! Starting with* SOL *you count the number of tones I shall sing."*

*Teacher sings (on syllable* Nu*),* SOL LA TI DO, *while making the large* Measuring Gesture *for each tone.*

*Children repeat while counting the steps.*

*(If teacher cannot sing that high, the tones should be played on the pitch pipe:* G A B C.*)*

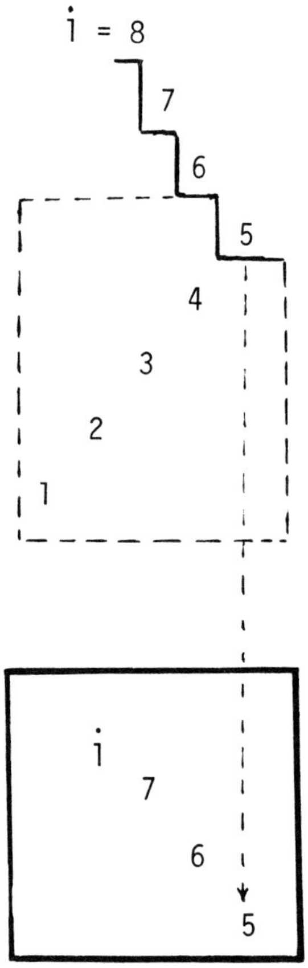


Diagram 5

*Teacher draws steps on* Diagram 3 *starting at* SOL *and adds figures* 6 7 8 *as shown.*

*Children repeat upper tetrachord on* Nu *while making large* Measuring Gesture.

*Teacher gives names to new notes:* TI *(pronounced as TEE)*
DO *(pronounced as DOUGH)*

Diagram 5 *is then placed in a square on the blackboard.*

*Teacher says: "You will notice that at* 8 *we begin again on* DO *but the tone is higher. Because we can hear the same sounds we call the tones by the same name and show them by the same number - except for the dot on* 1 *when we sing the high* DO = $\dot{1}$."

*Note: The numbers of the upper tetrachord are shown slanting in a different direction so as to distinguish them readily from those of the lower tetrachord.*

Finger Notation *for* TI *and* DO *will be discovered readily.*

7 TI

$\dot{1}$ DO

| Sing new tones several times on fingers and with arm gestures. |
|---|

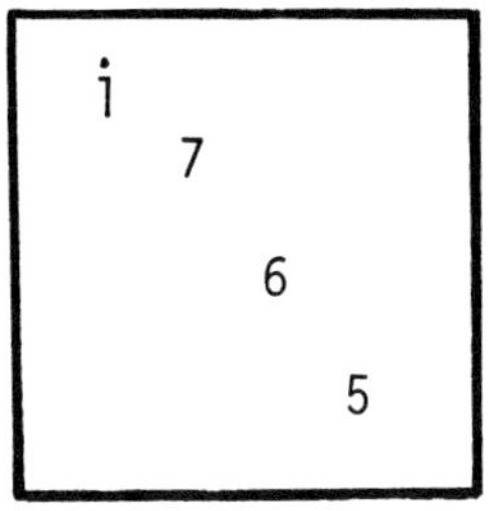


Diagram 5

Intonation Exercise 21 *(1 = C)*

a) → b) →

|   1̇ 7 6 5 | 5 6 7 1̇ |
| 1̇ 1̇ 7 6 5 | 5 5 6 7 1̇ |
| 1̇ 1̇ 7 6 5 5 5 | 5 5 6 7 1̇ 1̇ 1̇ |

c) →

Insist from the outset on a true pitch for the interval of a semitone at DO - TI or TI - DO.

# Notation

1. *Review* Intonation Exercises 9, 10, 16, *and* 20, *from* Staff Notation 5 *giving special attention to the skips* 1 - 3, 3 - 1, *in* Int. Ex. 16.

Staff Notation 5

2. *Review* Staff Notation 3 *as in Chapter Eight.* I = ♩ I . = 𝅗𝅥

*Teacher transcribes rhythm strokes to staff notation equivalents. Children sing rhythms on syllable* Nu *while making simple* Metrical Gesture 1.

3. *NEW. Transcribe* Rhythm Patterns Series 5 *of this chapter from* Staff Notation.

*Teacher places staff notation equivalents of each rhythm pattern on board.*

*A child is invited to come to board and add correct rhythm strokes beneath notes.*

*Teacher adds measure bars and rhythm curve. All sing with* Metrical Language. *Repeat with* Rhythm Gesture III *while singing on one tone.*

# Rhythm

## *Presenting* Rhythm Gesture III

*This new gesture is designed to give the children a feeling for ternary rhythm, which is different from the binary rhythm studied up to now because the down-gesture is twice as long as the up-gesture.*

PREPARATION. *With both arms stretched out at shoulder level to the left, the children make one single binary gesture, that is, up and down. Then with both arms stretched out at shoulder level to the right, they repeat the single up and down of the binary rhythm gesture.*

Rhythm Gesture III

ARM MOVEMENTS. *Children assume preparatory position with arms outstretched to the left. They make one binary rhythm as above. Then, without stopping, they prolong the down movement by swinging both arms to the right. STOP. Repeat gesture but beginning at the right side so as to finish at the left. STOP. This gesture should describe an arc in a curving graceful movement.*

*As soon as the children can render single units of the ternary rhythm, always beginning on the up-pulse, they may link them together in longer units.*

FOOT MOVEMENTS. *These will be difficult to describe and so should be allowed to happen without specific direction. By following the drawings one can feel the transfer of body weight as the arms swing from one side to the other.*

MUSICAL ACCOMPANIMENT. *As soon as gesture seems to have the quality of natural waltzing movement, a song may be sung by the teacher or a recording played while the children make the appropriate gestures. Tunes chosen to accompany the gestures should have a strong up-pulse and be composed in ternary rhythm. Examples of such tunes include the following:*

*"Lullabye" by Brahms*
*"Away in a Manger" - Christmas Carol*
*"Let All Things Now Living" - English Folk Melody*
*"Prelude in A" - Chopin (Op. 10)*

Rhythm Patterns - Series 5.

a) b) c)

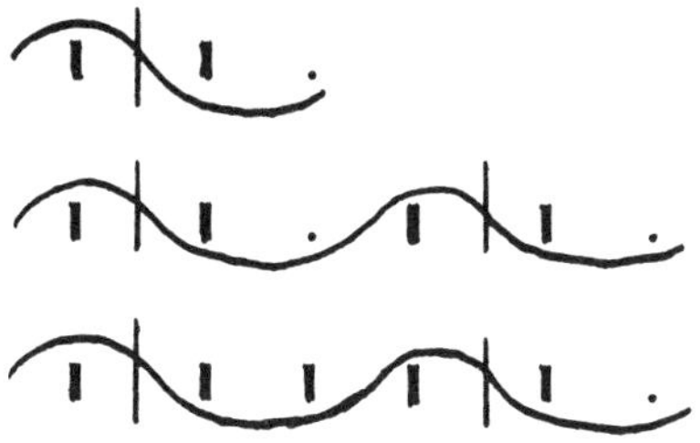

*Melodic Application*

a) b) c)

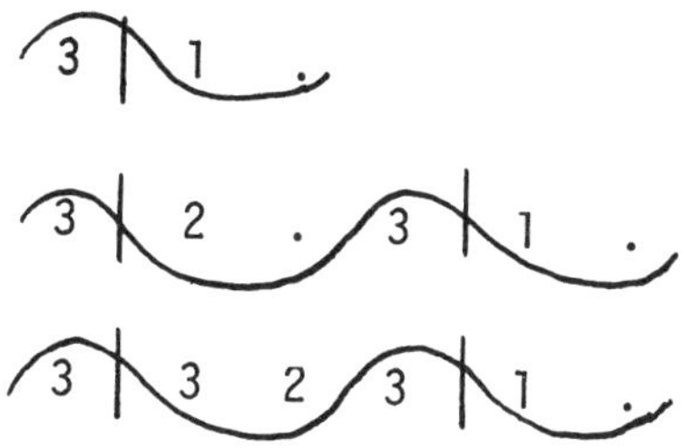


*Pattern "a" represents a single ternary rhythm: one pulse for the up-gesture, two pulses for the down-gesture. Teacher writes rhythm on board. Children sing with* Metrical Language.

a)

*Pattern "b" is constructed by placing two "a" patterns together. Children sing each line separately as follows:*

Metrical Gesture I *and* Metrical Language
Metrical Gesture I *on* Nu
Metrical Gesture I *with note names*
Rhythm Gesture III *with note names*

b)

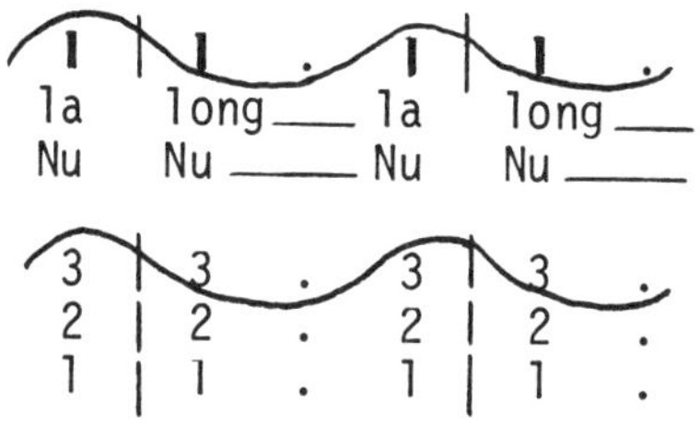


*Pattern "c" is constructed by adding a note to the rhythm of the down-pulse. Practise each line separately as above.*

c)

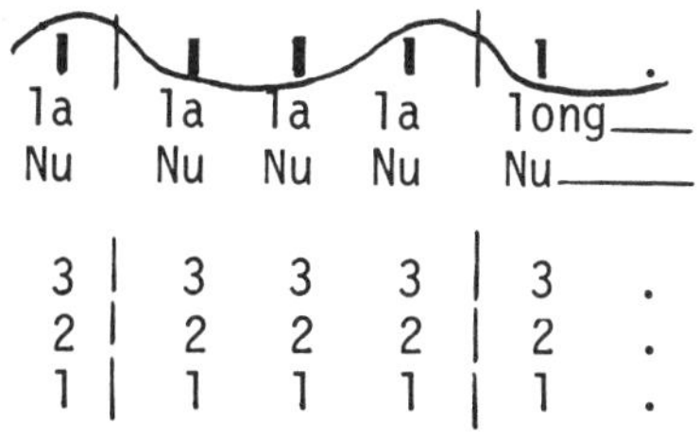

# Creative Activity

*Review songs studied thus far as dialogues between singing groups or rows, for example,* Song 20 *and* Song 21 *in Chapter Eight.*

## Musical Conversation - Step 3 continued

*Reversing direction of statement and response.*

*For example:*

*Descending statement*

3 | 3 2 | 1 . | .

*Ascending Response*

2 | 3 4 | 5 . | .
1 | 1 2 | 3 . | .
2 | 3 4 | 3 . | .

*No one of the responses finishes the conversation. Yet another fragment of melody is needed to bring the conversation to a close on* DO.

*Encourage the use of* SOL, MI *or* RE *at the end of responses that aim to continue the conversation. Avoid endings on* FA *and* LA *for now. These will be used later.*

*In order to link the statement and response rhythmically, use* Rhythm Gesture I *or* II *during the "conversations."*

*Examples:*

*Statement:* 3 | 3 2 | 1 . | .

*First response:* 2 | 3 4 | 5 . | .
*Second response:* 5 | 5 4 | 3 . | .
*Final response:* 4 | 3 2 | 1 . | . ||

*Statement:* 2 | 1 2 | 3 4 | 5 . | .

*First response:* 5 | 5 6 | 5 4 | 3 . | .
*Second response:* 4 | 3 4 | 5 6 | 5 . | .
*Final response:* 4 | 3 2 | 1 2 | 1 . | . ||

# Dictations

**Tonal Dictation**

| |
|---|
| 1̇ |
| 7 |
| 6 |
| 5 |

Diagram 5

Staff Notation 4

*Use tests at:* *a) for* Finger Notation
*b) for* Measuring Gesture
*c) with* Diagram 5
*d) with* Staff Notation 4 *on syllable* Nu
*e) with* Diagram 5 *on syllable* Nu

**Ear Tests**

*a)* 1̇ 7 6 5 / 1̇ 1 7 6 5 |
*b)* 1̇ 7 6 5 5 5. / 5 5 5 6 7 1̇ |
*c)* 1̇ 7 6 5 5 5 / 5 5 5 6 7 1̇ |
*d)* 1 2 3 4 4 3 / 1 2 3 4 3 2

*e)* 5 5 6 5 6 5 / 5 6 7 1̇ 1̇ 1̇

**Eye Tests**

*a)* 1̇ 1̇ 1̇ 7 6 5 / 1̇ 1̇ 7 6 5 5 5 |
*b)* 5 5 5 6 7 1̇ / 5 6 7 1̇ 1̇ 1̇ |
*c)* 1̇ 7 6 5 5 6 7 1̇ / 1̇ 1̇ 7 6 5 5 6 7 1̇

*d)* 1 2 3 4 3 4 3 / 1 2 3 4 5 4 3 |
*e)* 1̇ 7 6 5 5 5 / 5 6 5 6 7 1̇

**Rhythmic Dictation**

*With* Rhythm Patterns - Series 4 *(Chapter Six) in full view of the class, teacher dictates melodic application of tones studied in* Intonation Exercise 21.

*C (b + c)*
*B (a + c)*
*d)*
*b)*

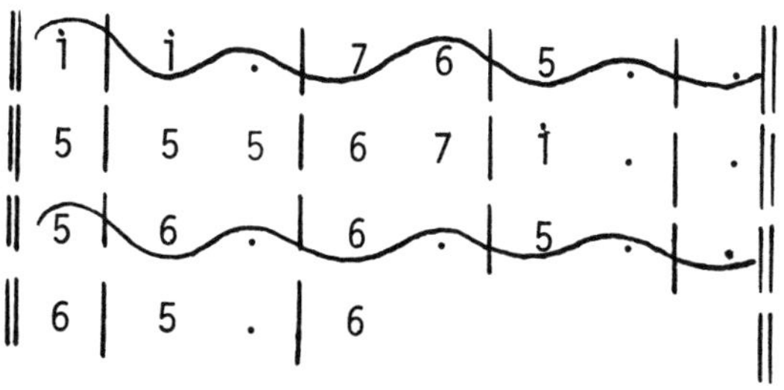

# *Songs*

**Song 22** *(1̇ = C)*

‖ 1̇ | 1̇ 1̇ | 1̇ 1̇ | 1̇ . | .
1̇ | 1̇ . | 7 6 | 5 . | .
5 | 5 6 | 5 6 | 5 . | .
5 | 5 . | 6 7 | 1̇ . | . ‖

**Song 23** *(1 = F or F#)*

‖ 5 | 5 . 6 | 5 .
5 | 5 . 4 | 3 .
3 | 3 . 4 | 3 .
3 | 3 . 2 | 1 . ‖

**I Saw a Ship A-Sailing** *(1 = F or F#)* *Mother Goose*

‖ 3 | 1 . 2 | 3 . 4 | 5 . 6 | 5 .
I saw a ship a- sail- ing,__

5 | 5 . 6 | 5 . 4 | 3 . 3 | 2 .
A- sail- ing on the o- pen sea,__

3 | 1 . 2 | 3 . 4 | 5 . 6 | 5 .
And oh! it was all lad- en__

5 | 5 . 4 | 3 . 1 | 3 . 2 | 1 . ‖
With man- y pret- ty things for me.__

*Note slurs (two syllables on one vowel) at the end of the first and third lines. Note also the skips* 3 - 1 *and* 1 - 3.

# Chapter Ten

## Vocal Training

*Encourage individuals to sing alone - a few at each lesson. Otherwise, vocalise children in groups beginning with Bluebirds.*

Vocal Exercise 1. *Begin every lesson with these single tones, all attention being given to placing the voice in the resonating areas of the head to produce a beautiful vocal quality on the highest and the lowest tones.*

*(1 = A, F, C, D)*

|| 1 ______
Nu ______ ||

Vocal Exercise 8. *The upper tetrachord of the major scale. Special attention must be given to the small interval* $\dot{1}$ 7. *Listen for accurate pitch. These two tones are usually sung too far apart.*

*($\dot{1}$ = D or $E^b$ )*

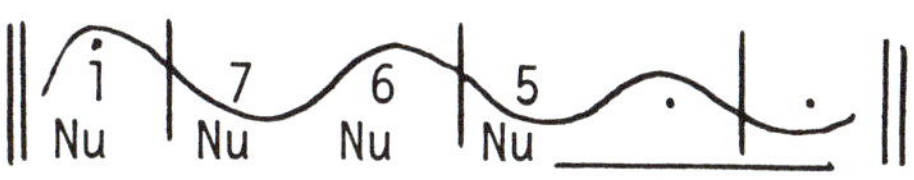


Work for true pitch during the vocal exercise. Attention to this will enhance the success of future work.

*For the first time the vocal exercise begins on a high pitch. The upper tone must be attacked neatly and with a good tone. The arm gesture for the highest pitch is useful here.*

*Prepare the vocal exercise by singing the two outer tones separately as in* Vocal Exercise 1. *Select the same tones that will be used in singing the* Vocal Exercise 8.

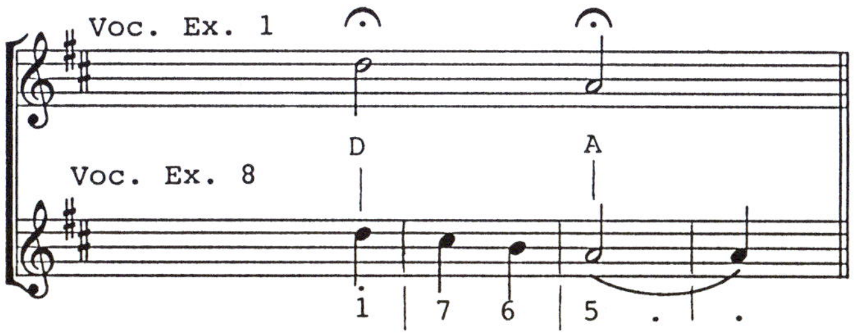


Bluebirds should sing Vocal Exercise 8 rhythmically as a model for the Robins and Sparrows.

# Intonation

*Use* Diagram 5 *for* Intonation Exercises 22, 23, 24, *and* 25.

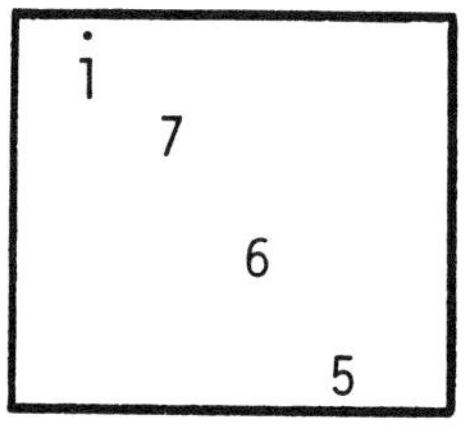


Diagram 5

Intonation Exercise 22. *The purpose of this exercise is to enable the pupils to stop short on any tone of the tetrachord. Practise the exercise vertically on the diagram and then horizontally from the chart. Sing along arrow a); then along arrow b).*

*(1̇ = D)*

```
 a) ---------->  b) ---------->
| 1̇ 7 6 5     |  5 6 7 1̇  |
| 1̇ 7 6       |  5 6 7    |
| 1̇ 7         |  5 6      |
| 1̇ 7 6 5     |  5 6 7 1̇  |
```

[ Insist on precision in stops and starts. ]

Intonation Exercise 23. *Stop and repeat last tone sung. Teach on the diagram first. Then teach horizontally from the chart.*

*(1̇ = D)*

```
 a) ------------------------->  b) ------------------------->
| 1̇ 7 6 5   5 5 5   |  5 6 7 1̇   1̇ 1̇ 1̇  |
| 1̇ 7 6     6 6 6   |  5 6 7     7 7 7  |
| 1̇ 7       7 7 7   |  5 6       6 6 6  |
| 1̇ 7 6 5   5 5 5   |  5 6 7 1̇   1̇ 1̇ 1̇  |
```

Intonation Exercise 24. *Stop, repeat, then continue in the same melodic direction. Teach on diagram; on fingers; then horizontally from the chart.*

*(1̇ = D)*

```
  ------------------------------------------>
| 1̇ 7 6 5   5 5 5   5 6 7 1̇   1̇ 1̇ 1̇ |
| 1̇ 7 6     6 6 5   5 6 6      6 7 1̇ |
| 1̇ 7       7 6 5   5 6        6 7 1̇ |
| 1̇ 7 6 5                    5 6 7 1̇ |
```

Intonation Exercise 25. *This exercise links the top tetrachord with the lower pentachord. Introduce it with* Finger Notation.

*(1̇ = D)*

```
  ------------------------------------------>
| 1̇ 7 6 5   5 4 3   3 4 5   5 6 7 1̇ |
```

Do not try to teach all the above exercises in one lesson.

# Rhythm

*Review* Rhythm Gesture III. *Insist on having the arms lift the the whole body on the "up " pulse of the rhythm. Then, be sure the feet are in the correct position. Finally, work with the arms and feet together. When* Rhythm Gesture III *is well done it has the character of a walzing movement.*

Rhythm Patterns - Series 6. *Pattern b) follows a) which has set the pace: brisk, lively. Teach these patterns using* Metrical Gesture I *and* Metrical Language. *Later, use* Rhythm Gesture III.

*Melodic Application*

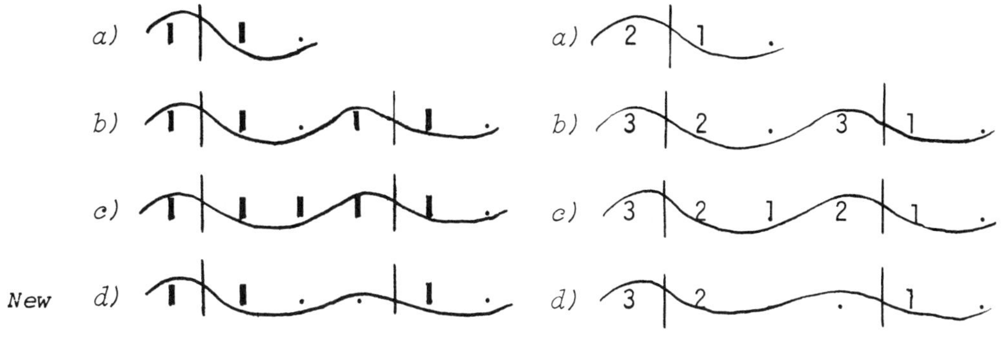


Combining patterns for melodic application:

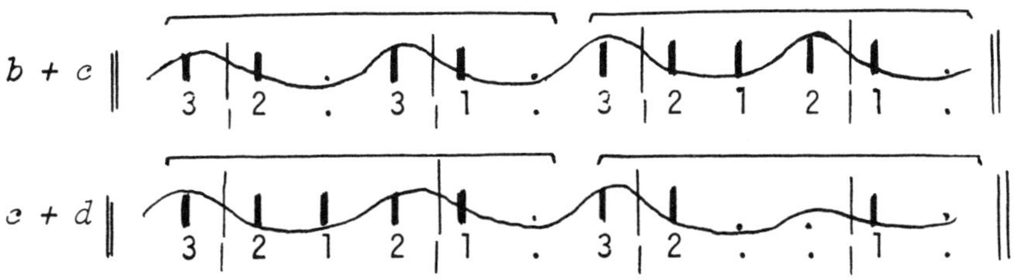

# Notation

This lesson reviews two-pulse note values studied earlier and adds three-pulse note values. All of these note values are found within the ternary measure.

*By comparing the signs used to denote length, the teacher will demonstrate the time value of the notes as follows:*

*Short note:* I = ♩

*Long note :* I . = 𝅗𝅥

*Note that is longer still:* I . . = 𝅗𝅥.

Staff Notation 6.

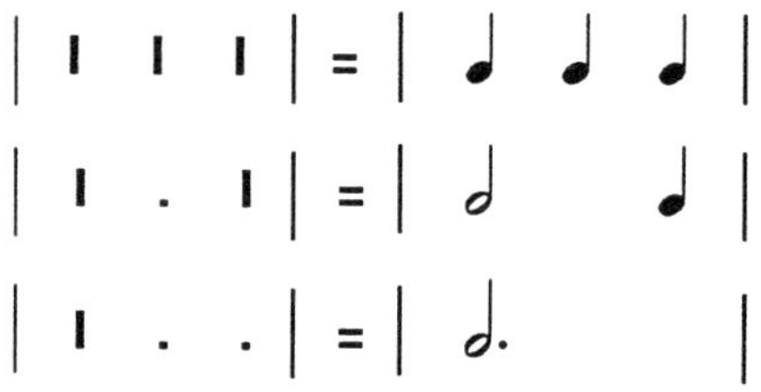

Combining pitch and time values for a song in Staff Notation.

*Step 1.* *Review* Intonation Exercise 16 *on* Staff Notation 4.

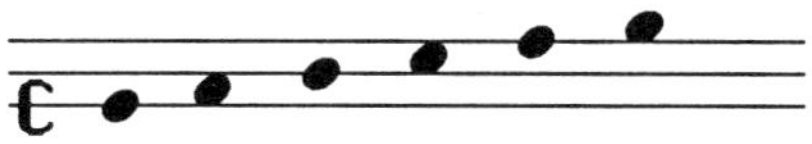

*a)* | 1 2 3 | 1 2 3 | 1 .
*b)* | 3 2 1 | 3 2 1 | 3 .
*c)* | 1 2 3 3 2 1 | 1 3 3 1 |

*Step 2. Read the following line on* DO *with* Metrical Gesture I *and* Metrical Language.

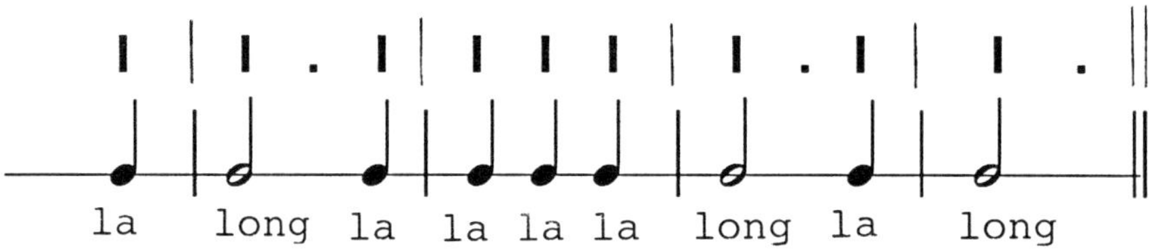


*Step 3. Sing the line given below naming the tones and making* Metrical Gesture I; *also while making* Rhythm Gesture III.

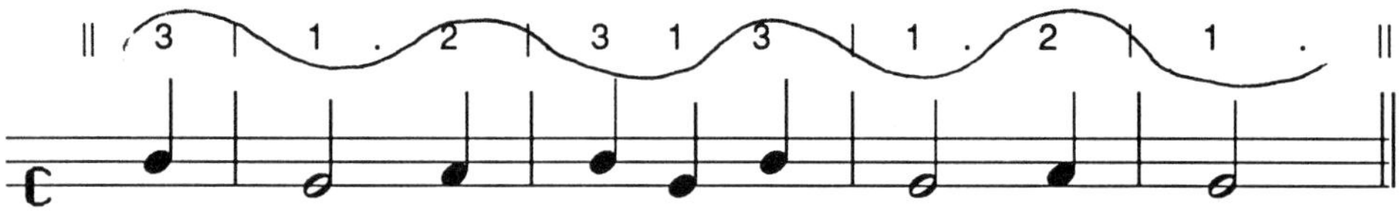

## *Creative Activity* Musical Conversations Using Tones of the Upper Tetrachord

*All the exercises of this chapter can serve as themes for improvisation.*

Intonation Diagram 5, Rhythm Patterns - Series 6, *should be in full view of the students to guide them in answering a melodic or a rhythmic question.*

*For example:*

*Question:* $\dot{1}$ | $\dot{1}$ 7 6 | 5 . *Answer:* 5 | 5 6 7 | $\dot{1}$ .

$\dot{1}$ | $\dot{1}$ . 7 | 6 . 5 | 6 . 7 | $\dot{1}$ .

5 | 5 6 7 | $\dot{1}$ . $\dot{1}$ | $\dot{1}$ . 7 | $\dot{1}$ .

Attentive listening
(dictation) Grade I

# Dictations

Ear Tests (1̇ = C or D) *Dictations are given on the syllable* Nu.

| 1̇ 7 6 5  5 5 5 | 1̇ 7 6  6 6 6 | 1̇ 7 6  6 6 5 | 1̇ 7 6 5  5 4 3

| 1̇ 1̇  1̇ 7 6 | 5 6  6 6 6 | 5 6 7  7 7 1̇ | 3 4 3  3 2 3 1

| 1 2 3  3 2 3 | 3 4 5  5 6 7 1̇ |

Eye Tests (1̇ = C or D) *Dictations are given with pointer at the diagram on the board; with finger and/or arm gestures; by visual memory, i.e., teacher writes on the board and erases from left to right, or children observe, then turn away and sing from memory.*

|| 1̇ | 1̇ . 7 | 1̇ .
1̇ | 1̇ 7 6 | 5 . ||

|| 5 | 5 . 6 | 5 .
5 | 5 6 7 | 1̇ . ||

Rhythm Tests (1 = G) *Teacher sings on* Nu *while making* Rhythm Gesture III.

|| 3 | 2 . 3 | 1 . ||

|| 3 | 2 1 2 | 1 . ||

Staff Notation Tests on Diagram 4 (1 = G) *Tests are given with the pointer at the diagram.*

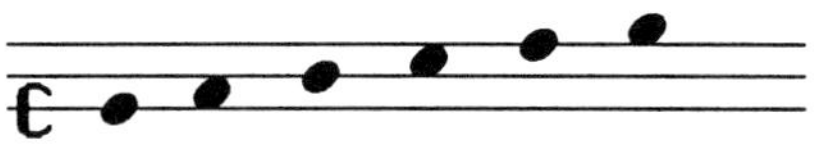

1 2 1  3 4 5 6 5

5 6 5 4 3  1 2 1

*"Look-and-Remember Test"*

## *Songs*

*These will be prepared melodically from* Diagram 5, *and rhythmically from* Rhythm Patterns - Series 6, *of this chapter.*

*Sing first with* Metrical Gesture I, *then with the rhythm gesture as indicated.*

### Song 24

*Continue the practise of giving the songs the form of a musical dialogue as described in a previous chapter. Use* Rhythm Gesture III.

*($\dot{1}$ = D)*

‖ $\dot{1}$ | $\dot{1}$ . $\dot{1}$ | $\dot{1}$ .
$\dot{1}$ | $\dot{1}$ 7 6 | 5 .
5 | 5 . 6 | 5 .
5 | 5 6 7 | $\dot{1}$ . ‖

Children making the best gestures are invited to the front of the room to make the gestures while others sing from their places.

### Song 25

*Binary rhythm. Use* Rhythm Gesture II. *Proceed by visual observation and memory, line after line, or else by auditory memory:*

*($\dot{1}$ = C)*

> *Robins sing a line of the song as they read it from a chart or the blackboard;*
> *Bluebirds, having turned their backs to the chart or blackboard, repeat the line from memory.*

‖ $\dot{1}$ | $\dot{1}$ 7 | 6 6 | 5 . | .
5 | 6 . | 6 . | 5 . | .
5 | 5 4 | 3 4 | 5 . | .
5 | 6 . | 7 . | $\dot{1}$ . | . ‖

### O Come, O Come, Emmanuel *($\dot{1}$ = D) Advent Prayer Part 1*

*The word "Advent" means "coming." The season of the year known as Advent is therefore a time of preparation for the coming of the Savior at Christmas.*

*The teacher recites the text of the prayer rhythmically and the children imitate. Then the two tones of the hymn, namely,* 6 *and* 5, *are prepared as follows on* Diagram 5:
*Teacher ($\dot{1}$=D):* $\dot{1}$ 7 6 5 5 6
*Children:* 5 6 5

‖: 6 | 6 6 | 6 6 | 6 6 | 5 . | . :‖
*Bluebirds:* O come, O come Em- ma- nu- el, ______
And ran- som cap- tive Is- ra- el, ______

6 | 5 . | 6 . | . ‖
*All:* a- men. ______

# Chapter Eleven

## Vocal Training

*Review:*
Vocal Exercise 1
*(1 = A, F, C, D)*

‖ 1 ________ ‖
Nu ________

Vocal Exercise 9. *Similar to* Voc. Ex. 8 *except that it presents the upper tetrachord coming down and going up. As noted previously, the danger point for pitch is the small interval* 1̇ 7.

*(1̇ = D)*

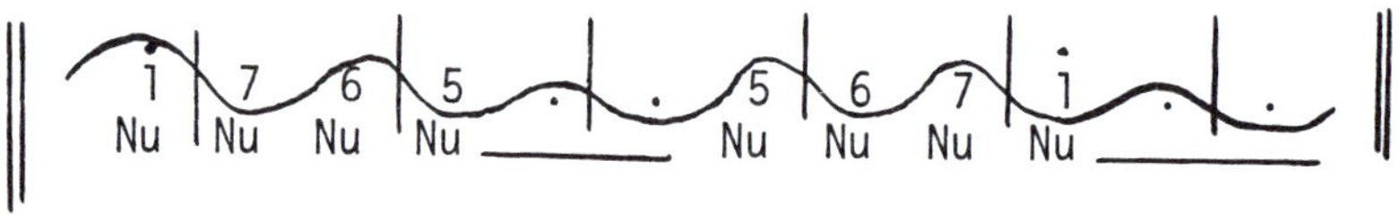


*Practise this exercise at a rather high pitch with care to place the tone in the resonating cavities.*

*Sing slowly but with a steady pulse using* Rhythm Gesture I *or* II

*Notice especially the step* 1̇ - 7 *and* 7 - 1̇. *Be sure that the half step is true.*

*Prepare* Vocal Exercise 9 *each time with a long* DO (1̇) *attacking the pitch with the arm and hand fully extended upward while singing the syllable* Nu.

> Vocal Training in this lesson should include:
>
> a) Practise with small groups beginning with the *Bluebirds*. Sparrows listen.
>
> b) Use of Rhythm Gesture I or II.
>
> c) Practise without Rhythm Gestures but singing in such a way as to convey a sense of the rhythm in the vocal rendition of the exercise.
>
> d) Careful attention to resonance of Nnnn between the up and the down of the rhythmic wave.

# Intonation

Intonation Exercises 26 *and* 27 *will help to establish the interval* 1̇ 7, *provided the pitch is carefully checked.*

1. *Use* Diagram 5.

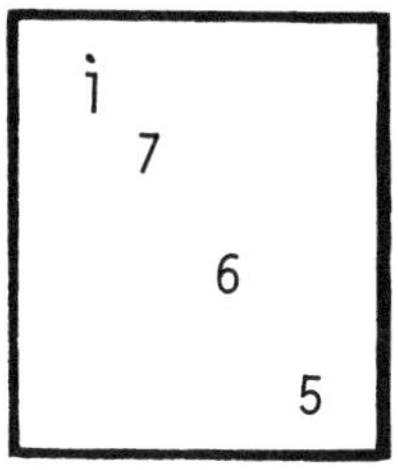


**Intonation Exercise 26.** *Stop at various tones. Repeat last tone. Continue in contrary motion:*

*a) -starting from top of tetrachord*
*b) -starting from bottom*

*(1̇ = D) Preparation:* 1̇765

```
a) ---------------------------->  b) ---------------------------->
| 1̇ 7 6 5   5 5 5   5 6 7 1̇ | 5 6 7 1̇   1̇ 1̇ 1̇   1̇ 7 6 5 |
| 1̇ 7 6     6 6 6     6 7 1̇ | 5 6 7     7 7 7     7 6 5 |
| 1̇ 7       7 7 7       7 1̇ | 5 6 6     6 6 6     6 6 5 | 5671̇
```

**Intonation Exercise 27.**

*Drill as follows:*
1. *Repeat tone on which direction changes*
2. *Do not repeat tone on which direction changes. Instead, think on the dot.*

```
---------------------------->
| 1̇  7  6  5    5  6  7  1̇ |
| 1̇  7  6  5    .  6  7  1̇ |
| 1̇  7  6          6  7  1̇ |
| 1̇  7  6          .  7  1̇ |
| 1̇  7                7  1̇ |
| 1̇  7                .  1̇ |
```

2. *Repeat both exercises using* Staff Notation 7.

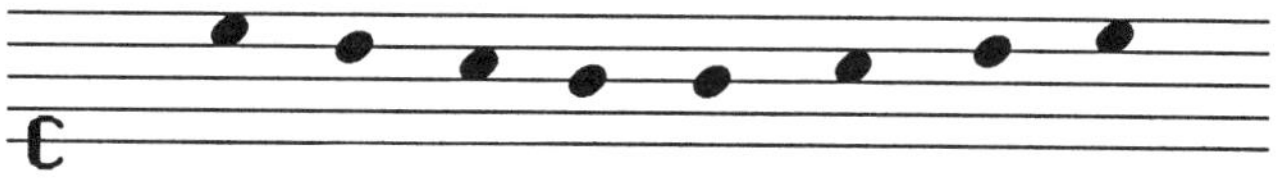

3. *Present both intonation exercises also with* Finger Notation *and* Arm Measuring Gesture.

The hand movement from 1̇ to 7 should be very slight thus indicating but a slight drop of pitch from DO to TI. The arm remains extended for 1̇ and 7. The elbow bends for 6 (LA) and the hand rests on the forehead for 5 (SOL).

## Rhythm

*Continue study of* Rhythm Gesture III - *first without singing, then with melodic application. If possible, pupils should listen to a recording - tape or disc - of a slow waltz melody that begins on an up-pulse. They will try to follow the "up" and "down" pulses of the rhythm while remaining seated. When it is evident that the children feel the rhythmic movement, they may stand and repeat the gesture to the accompaniment of the recording.* *

N.B. Children must feel a strong lift on the UP-PULSE to the full extent of their reach when making this gesture as it is the characteristic element of the gesture that ought not to be missed.

Rhythm Patterns - Series 6 *(Cont'd). Review with* Metrical Gesture I *and* Metrical Language. *Following this, apply* Rhythm Gesture III *while singing. All of these patterns are known except Pattern e). Children should try to identify rhythm patterns sung by teacher.*

*a)*

*b)*

*c)*

*d)*

*New* *e)*

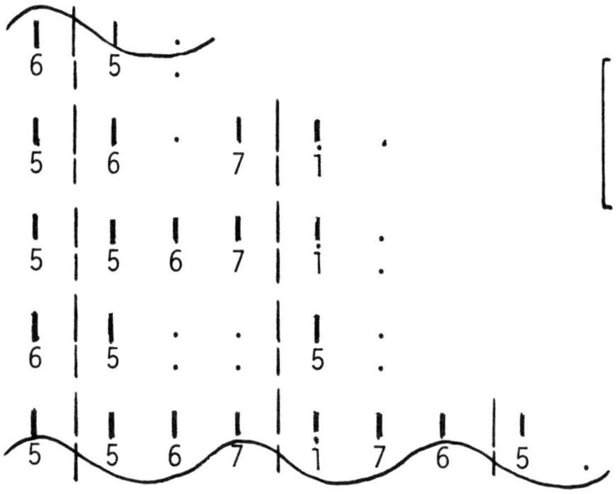

Each pattern is studied separately. Then they are combined to form longer phrases as shown below.

Combining patterns for melodic application. *Use tones of the upper tetrachord, that is:* i̇ (8) 7 6 5

*A (a + a + a)*

*B (c + a)*

*C (a + c)*

*Also possible:* *D (c + c)*

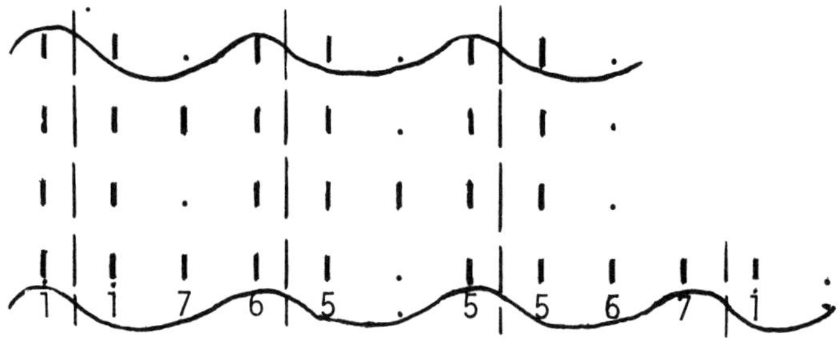

* A small disc has been made for this exercise and is available from the Ward Center.

## *Notation*

The five-line staff completed. Two upper lines are added to the three lines already known. In this way, the upper tetrachord is accommodated on the staff.

*Draw two dotted lines and place* TI *and* DO (7 $\dot{1}$) *in their respective places on the staff.*

*Fill in the top two notes of the scale to complete the upper tetrachord.*

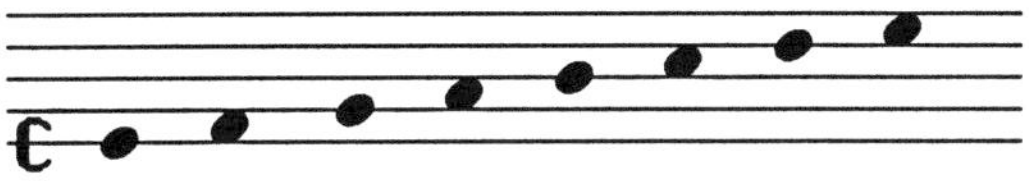

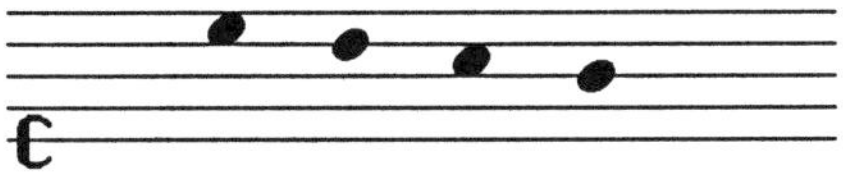

*Review* Intonation Exercises 21 *and* 22 *on* Staff Notation 7.

Staff Notation 7

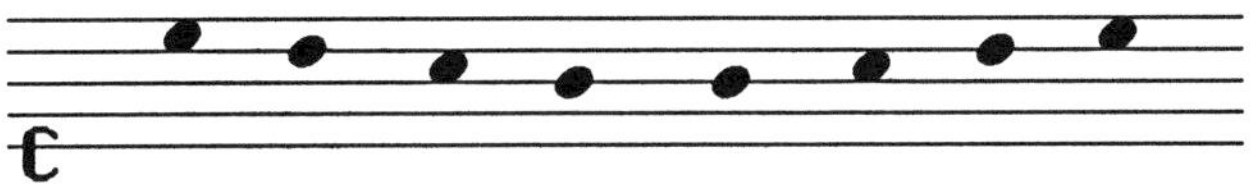

Intonation Exercise 21

*(1 = D)*

| | a) | b) |
|---|---|---|
| | $\dot{1}$ 7 6 5 | 5 6 7 $\dot{1}$ |
| | $\dot{1}$ $\dot{1}$ 7 6 5 | 5 5 6 7 $\dot{1}$ |
| c) | $\dot{1}$ $\dot{1}$ 7 6 5 5 5 | 5 5 6 7 $\dot{1}$ $\dot{1}$ $\dot{1}$ |

Intonation Exercise 22

*(1 = D)*

| a) | b) |
|---|---|
| $\dot{1}$ 7 6 5 | 5 6 7 $\dot{1}$ |
| $\dot{1}$ 7 6 | 5 6 7 |
| $\dot{1}$ 7 | 5 6 |
| $\dot{1}$ 7 6 5 | 5 6 7 $\dot{1}$ |

*Use lines from* Song 27 *as transcription exercises.*

## Creative Activity

The rhythm patterns of this chapter provide basic structures on which children can build their compositions.

*Keep* Rhythm Patterns *b), c), d), and e) in full view of the class. Continue "composing" musical dialogues or conversations between children.*

1. *Improvise on tones of the upper tetrachord (*i̇ 7 6 5*) and* Rhythm Patterns - Series 6, *while making* Rhythm Gesture III.

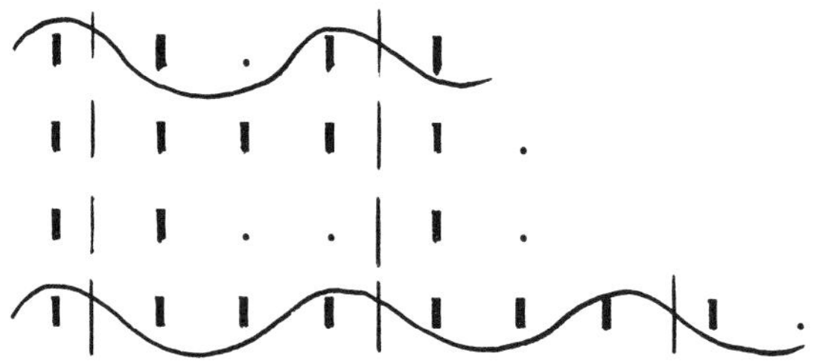


2. *Combine patterns in the form of a dialogue.*

3. *Suggest familiar verbal phrases in the rhythm of the patterns given. Examples:*

*b)* ‖ i̇ | 7 . 6 | 5 . ‖
How old__ are you?__

*c)* ‖ 5 | 5 6 7 | i̇ . ‖
Look up at the sky.__

*d)* ‖ 5 | 6 . . | 5 . ‖
Good morn- ing.__

*e)* ‖ i̇ | i̇ 7 6 | 5 6 7 | i̇ . ‖
And what is the name of your dog?__

N.B. Teacher sings the model and children try to invent original phrases for the given patterns. Examples:
*e)* The cow has jumped over the moon.
O where is the little dog gone?
And what is your big brother's name?

# Dictations

Tests derived from chapter exercises.

Ear Tests *(1̇ = C or D) Dictations are given on the syllable* Nu.

| 1̇ 7 6 5  5 6 7 1̇ | 1̇ 7 6 5  6 6 5 | 1̇ 7 6 5  6 7 1̇ | 1̇ 7 6 5 4 3 |

| 1̇ 7 6 6  6 7 1̇ |  5 6 6  6 6 5 | 1̇ 7 6  7 1̇ | 3 3 2 1 2 2 |

| 5 4 3 2 3 1 |

| 1 1 3 3 2 1 |

Eye Tests *1. Lines shown below are written on the board or prepared on an acetate for overhead projection. Children identify lines that are sung by the teacher. When a line is correctly identified, all repeat it.*

*a)* 1̇ | 1̇ 7 6 | 5 .

*b)* 1̇ | 1̇ 7 6 | 6 .

*c)* 1̇ | 1̇ . 7 | 1̇ .

*d)* 5 | 6 . 7 | 1̇ .

2. *On* Staff Notation 7 *with a pointer.*

| 1̇ 7 6 5  5 5 5 | 5 6 7 1̇  1̇ 1̇ 1̇ |

| 1̇ 7 6  6 5 | 5 6 5 5  6 7 1̇ |

3. *The teacher writes the following line on the board and allows a moment for study then erases the line starting from left to right. Individual students try to sing the line from memory with the proper rhythm gesture.*

‖ 5 | 5 . | 6 7 | 1̇ . | . ‖

## *Songs*

Melodic application of rhythm patterns.

### Song 26

*Melodic application of patterns b) and d).*

(1̇ = D)

b) ‖ 1̇ | 1̇ . 7 | 6 .
d) 6 | 5 . . | 5 .
b) 5 | 6 . 5 | 6 .
d) 7 | 1̇ . . | 1̇ . ‖

*When the melody has become familiar, re-write it on two lines instead of on four. Thus:*

(b + d) ‖ 1̇ | 1̇ . 7 | 6 . 6 | 5 . . | 5 .
(b + d) 5 | 6 . 5 | 6 . 7 | 1̇ . . | 1̇ . ‖

### Song 27

*Notice that the first and third lines consist of two patterns joined together and that the second line is the new pattern e) studied in this chapter.*

*The first line may be used for melodic and rhythmic dictation as well as for transcribing to staff notation.*

(1̇ = C or D)

(a + b) ‖ 1̇ | 1̇ . 7 | 6 . 6 | 5 .
e) 5 | 5 6 7 | 1̇ 7 6 | 5 .
(a + b) 5 | 6 . 7 | 1̇ . 7 | 1̇ . ‖

### Rejoice, Rejoice, O Israel *Advent Prayer Part 2*

*Teach this song as a continuation of* "O Come, O Come, Emmanuel," *in Chapter Ten.*
*Divide class into two groups:*
*I - the people of God praying for a Redeemer;*
*II - the Angels answering.*
*Sing each day during Advent as a prayer.*

*Preparation:* 1̇ 7 6 5 *(1̇ = D)*

(1̇ = D)

I ‖ 6 | 6 6 | 6 6 | 6 6 | 5 . | .
Re- joice, re- joice, O Is- ra- el,

II - 6 | 6 6 | 6 6 | 6 6 | 5 . | .
Thy Sa- vior comes, Em- man- u - el,

I & II - 5 | 5 4 | 3 . | 3 . | . ‖
Al- le- lu- ia.

# Chapter Twelve

## Vocal Training

> Continue to work with individuals. Listen for clear tonal emission and smooth progressions from one tone to the next.

*Review* Vocal Exercise 1

*1 = A / F, C, D*

‖ 1 ———————— ‖
‖ Nu ———————— ‖

*Review* Vocal Exercise 9 *(1̇ = D)*

‖ 1̇ 7 6 5 . . 5 6 7 1̇ . . ‖
‖ Nu Nu Nu Nu ——— Nu Nu Nu Nu ——— ‖

## Intonation

*These exercises are designed to develop greater flexibility in use of step-wise progressions in the upper tetrachord.*

| | | | |
|---|---|---|---|
| 1̇ | | | |
| | 7 | | |
| | | 6 | |
| | | | 5 |

Diagram 5

Intonation Exercise 28 *(1̇ = D)*

| | | | |
|---|---|---|---|
| 1̇ 7 6 5 | 5 6 5 | 5 6 7 1̇ | 7 1̇ |
| 1̇ 7 6 5 | 6 6 | 6 5 6 7 | 1̇ 1̇ |
| 1̇ 7 6 5 | 6 6 | 6 7 6 7 | 1̇ 1̇ |
| 1̇ 7 6 5 | 6 5 | 5 6 7 1̇ | 7 1̇ |

Intonation Exercise 29 *(1̇ = D)*

| | | |
|---|---|---|
| 1̇ 7 | 1̇ 7 6 | 5 6 5 6 5 |
| 6 5 | 6 5 6 | 6 5 6 7 1̇ |
| 1̇ 7 | 6 6 5 | 5 6 6 5 6 |
| 6 5 | 6 6 5 | 6 7 1̇ 7 1̇ |

Intonation Exercise 30 *(1̇ = D)* *Discovering the skip* 5 - 1̇. 1̇ - 5. *Teach in same way as for discovering the skip of* 1 - 3, 3 - 1, *in Chapter Three.*

*a)*

| |
|---|
| 1̇ 7 6 5 |
| 1̇ 7 6 5 |
| 1̇ |

*b)*

| |
|---|
| 5 6 7 1̇ |
| 5 6 7 1̇ |
| 5 |

*c)*

| | |
|---|---|
| 1̇ 7 6 5 | 5 6 7 1̇ |
| 1̇ 5 | 5 1̇ |

*Review* Staff Notation 7 *with* Int. Ex. 23 *and* 24, *Chapter Ten.*

# Rhythm

*Drill each line with* Metrical Gesture, Metrical Language, Rhythm Gesture III, *singing on one tone, melodic improvisation, and dictation.*

*Sing patterns in the form of a dialogue between the Bluebirds and Robins or between two individuals.*

*Review* Rhythm Patterns - Series 6 *

a) I | I .

b) I | I . I | I .

c) I | I I I | I .

d) I | I . . | I .

e) I | I I I | I I I | I .

A) I | I . I | I . I | I .

*New* f) I | I . . | . .

* *Suggest improvising verbal phrases as in Lesson Eleven, P. 98, such as: "Hel-lo" to pattern a) on* $\dot{1}$ | 5 .; *"Keep smil-ing" to d) on* 5 | $\dot{1}$ . . | 5 . *etc.*

*Melodic application* ($\dot{1}$ = *D*)

c) $\dot{1}$ | $\dot{1}$ 7 6 | 5 .

b) 5 | 6 . 7 | $\dot{1}$ .

e) $\dot{1}$ | $\dot{1}$ 7 6 | 5 6 7 | $\dot{1}$ .

A) 5 | 6 . 5 | 6 . 7 | $\dot{1}$ .

> Consider Rhythm Patterns as "rhythm words" and note how single patterns are joined into phrases. Later, these combinations will grow into "rhythm sentences."

## *Notation*

Staff Notation 8: The Tie

The Tie *binds together two notes at the same pitch so that instead of two separate notes, the tied notes become one long note. In order to show how a two-pulse note and a one-pulse note are tied together, the children make the gesture in the air as the teacher writes them on the board in this order:*

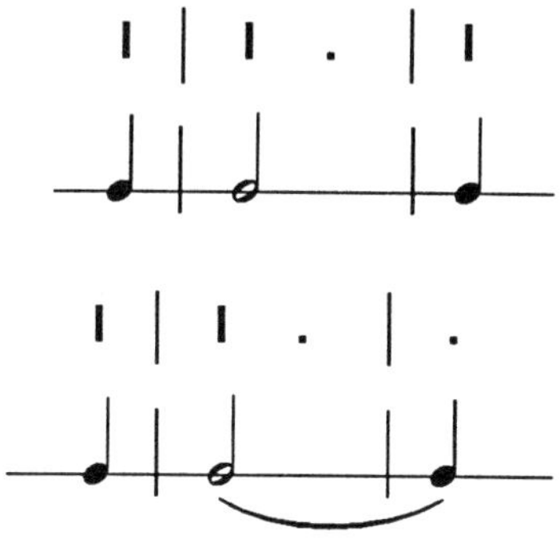

*Rhythm Pattern*
*Bar lines and pitch line*
*Two-pulse note and one-pulse notes*
*Tie*

*N. B. One-pulse rhythm stroke becomes dot as tie is added.*

*Apply this procedure to all exercises in transcription.*

*We can also show a three-pulse note of one measure tied to a two-pulse note of the next measure.*

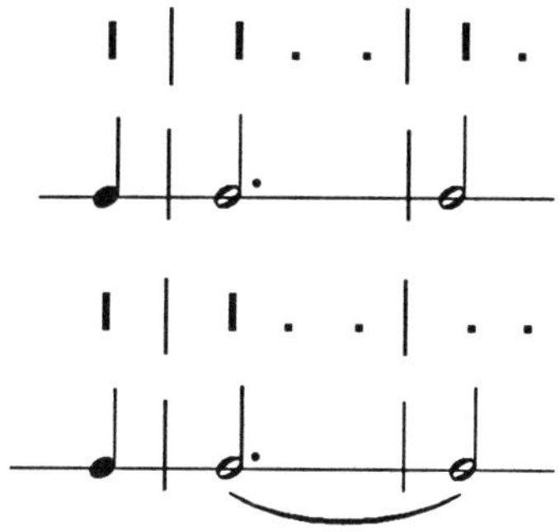

*Repeat as above.*

*Note "ties" in songs of this chapter.*

### Exercises in Transcription

1. *Teacher writes a rhythm pattern on board and fills in staff notation equivalents by adding the staff notes beneath rhythm lines, e.g., :*

R. P. 2 *(a + b)*
*Chapter Three*

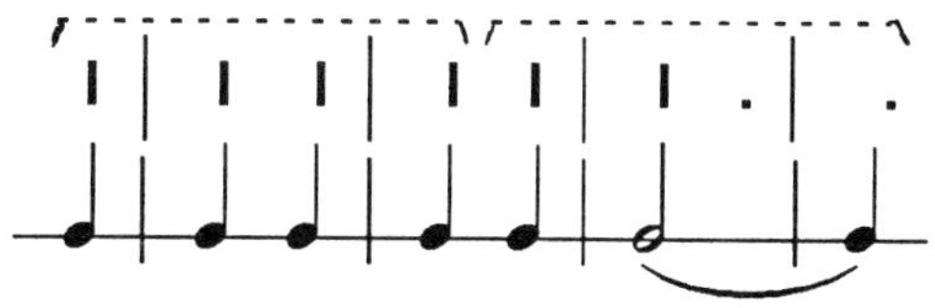

2. *Teacher now writes on board the rhythm only of Line 4 -* Song 29. *A child is invited to come to board to add notes and tie. When completed, Bluebirds sing while Robins and Sparrows make* Rhythm Gesture III.

3. *Select lines from songs of previous chapters for transcription drills.*

# *Dictations*

Suggested plan for dividing dictation drills into five groups for the five lessons of this chapter.

| | Ear Tests | Eye Tests | Rhythmic Dictation |
|---|---|---|---|
| *LESSON 1* | $\dot{1}$ 7 6 5 6 6 5<br>5 6 6 7 6 7 $\dot{1}$ | $\dot{1}$ 7 6 5 6 6<br>6 6 6 5 6 7 $\dot{1}$ | *c*<br>‖ 6 \| 5 6 7 \| $\dot{1}$ . ‖ |
| *LESSON 2* | $\dot{1}$ 7 $\dot{1}$ 7 6 5<br>6 6 5 6 7 $\dot{1}$ | $\dot{1}$ 7 6 6 5 6 5<br>‖ 6 \| 6 5 \| 6 7 \| $\dot{1}$ . \| . ‖ | *c* *d*<br>‖ 6 \| 5 6 7 \| $\dot{1}$ . 7 \| $\dot{1}$ . . \| $\dot{1}$ . ‖ |
| *LESSON 3* | $\dot{1}$ 7 6 5 5 $\dot{1}$<br>$\dot{1}$ 7 6 5 5 6 5 $\dot{1}$ | $\dot{1}$ 7 6 5 $\dot{1}$ 7 $\dot{1}$<br>5 6 5 $\dot{1}$ 7 6 5 | *e*<br>‖ $\dot{1}$ \| $\dot{1}$ 7 6 \| 5 6 7 \| $\dot{1}$ . ‖ |
| *LESSON 4* | 5 6 7 $\dot{1}$ $\dot{1}$ 5<br>$\dot{1}$ 5 5 $\dot{1}$ 7 6 5 | *On* Staff Notation 4<br>1 2 3 4 5 6 | *A*<br>*b* *a*<br>‖ $\dot{1}$ \| $\dot{1}$ . 7 \| 6 . 5 \| $\dot{1}$ . ‖ |
| *LESSON 5* | 5 6 7 $\dot{1}$ 5 5 $\dot{1}$<br>5 $\dot{1}$ 5 5 6 5 $\dot{1}$ | *On* Staff Notation 7<br>5 6 7 $\dot{1}$ $\dot{1}$ 5 | *A*<br>‖ 5 \| $\dot{1}$ . 7 \| 6 . 7 \| $\dot{1}$ . ‖ |

# *Creative Activity*

Musical Conversations *are now made with rhythm gestures:*

*Two children stand and face each other. Teacher announces "Gesture II" or "Gesture III." One child sings an opening phrase and the other answers. When one of them ends on* DO, *the conversation is ended. To avoid rhythmic errors, the teacher tells the children beforehand to sing their last note on a down-pulse.*

## Songs

The rhythm of the songs without words is derived from joining known patterns together to make longer rhythm "words" or phrases. The tones for the melodies are taken from the intonation exercises studied thus far.

**Song 28** *($\dot{1}$ = C)*

‖ $\dot{1}$ | $\dot{1}$ 7 | 6 6 | 5 . | .
5 | 6 . | 6 . | 5 . | .
5 | 5 4 | 3 4 | 5 . | .
5 | 6 . | 7 . | $\dot{1}$ . | . ‖

**Song 29** *($\dot{1}$ = C)*

‖ $\dot{1}$ | $\dot{1}$ 7 6 | 5 .
5 | 6 . 6 | 5 .
5 | 5 6 7 | $\dot{1}$ .
7 | $\dot{1}$ . . | . . ‖

Song 30 *and* Song 31 *can be prepared by reviewing tones studied on* Intonation Diagram 4 *and* Staff Notation 4, *Chapters Eight and Nine. Teacher then points to notes of song being studied and invites children to identify pitch and pulse values of notes.*

*"A note on the staff tells you two facts: a) How long do you hold it,*
*b) How high or low it is in pitch."*

*Following this study, children sing melody while making* Metrical Gesture. *Bluebirds sing melody while Robins and Sparrows make* Rhythm Gesture III *for* Song 30, *and* Rhythm Gesture II *for* Song 31.

**Song 30** *(1 = A$^b$)*

**Song 31** *(1 = A$^b$)*

A
CHRISTMAS
CAROL

*(1 = A)*

| | 1 | 1 | 1 | 1 | 1 | 1 | 1 | 1 | 1 | 2 | 3 | 1 . . |
|---|---|---|---|---|---|---|---|---|---|---|---|---|
| 1. | A | child | is | born | in | Beth- | le- | hem, | al- | le- | lu- | ia! ______ |
| 2. | O | come, | a- | dore | as | An- | gels | sing, | al- | le- | lu- | ia! ______ |
| 3. | Then | sing | we | high, | then | sing | we | low: | al- | le- | lu- | ia! ______ |

| | 3 | 3 | 3 | 3 | 3 | 3 | 3 | 3 |
|---|---|---|---|---|---|---|---|---|
| 1. | Glad | ti- | dings | for | Je- | ru- | sa- | lem, |
| 2. | And | give | our | hearts | to | Christ, | our | King, |
| 3. | *Be-* | *ne-* | *di-* | *ca-* | *mus* | *Do-* | *mi-* | *no.* |

| | 3 | 2 1 | 2 3 | 2 . . | 1 | 2 | 3 | 1 . . |
|---|---|---|---|---|---|---|---|---|
| 1 - 3. | al- | le- | lu- | ia, ______ | al- | le- | lu- | ia. ______ |

*First practise the two Alleluias. Note that the Alleluia at the beginning of the third line contains a "slur," that is, two different tones sung on one syllable:*

| 3 | 2 1 | 2 3 | 2 |
|---|---|---|---|
| Al- | le- | lu- | a |

*Children study words. Teacher explains "Benedicamus Domino" - Latin for "Let us bless the Lord."*

*Children sing words with* Rhythm Gesture II.

*Bluebirds sings entire melody with rhythm gesture. Robins and Sparrows join in singing at the Alleluia.*

# Chapter Thirteen

## Vocal Training

Insist on strong <u>Nnnn</u> to introduce "oo" sound in Nu. Children must be critical of sounds they make. Are they smooth? Rough?

Control of breath is what sustains the tone. Quiet deep breathing is better than filling the lungs so as to create a tension in the neck or throat.

*Review* <u>Vocal Exercise 1</u>

*i = A♭ F C E♭*

‖ i ———— Nu ———— ‖

*Review* <u>Vocal Exercises 4, 5</u> *and* <u>6.</u> *Sing all three exercises from same* DO, *for example*

*1 = G, A♭ or A*

*Require each group of children to sing all three exercises in sequence. Bluebirds may be given slightly higher note as a starting point.*

<u>Vocal Exercise 4</u>

‖ 2 1 2 1 . . ‖
Nu Nu Nu Nu ____

<u>Vocal Exercise 5</u>

‖ 2 1 2 3 2 1 . . ‖
Nu Nu Nu Nu Nu Nu

<u>Vocal Exercise 6</u>

‖ 2 1 2 3 4 5 . .
Nu Nu Nu Nu Nu Nu

5 5 4 3 2 1 . . ‖
Nu Nu Nu Nu Nu Nu

*NEW* <u>Vocal Exercise 10</u> *Begins on top note of tetrachord and ends on same note. Clear resonant tones should be possible at this time. The* Measuring Gesture *for high* DO *will be helpful in achieving a good attack.*

*Bluebirds will provide a good model for others. Teacher must not neglect Robins and Sparrows.*

‖ i | i 7 | 6 5 | i . | . ‖
Nu Nu Nu Nu Nu Nu ____

# Intonation

*In the chapters studied thus far, the lower part of the scale -* DO *up to* LA *- was covered in detail. Then the same was done for the upper part of the scale -* SOL *up to* DO. *In this chapter, the two segments of the scale are joined, thus forming the complete scale, or family of* DO.

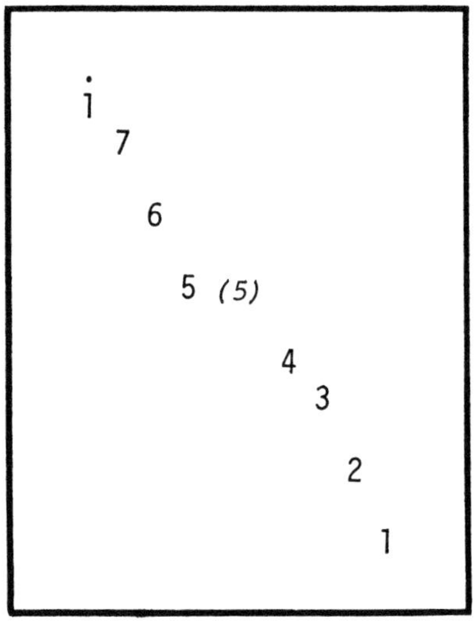


Diagram 6

Intonation Exercise 31 *Use* Diagram 6

*When drilling on first line, stop at* 5, *thus giving children a chance to think of this tone as a conclusion, then as a starting point. The second line does not repeat the tone of junction (*5*) but lengthens it by a dot during which the children "think"* SOL *(*5*).*

(1̇ = $E^b$)

| 1̇ 7 6 5 5 4 3 2 1 |
| 1̇ 7 6 5 . 4 3 2 1 |

| 1 2 3 4 5 5 6 7 1̇ |
| 1 2 3 4 5 . 6 7 1̇ |

Intonation Exercise 32 *Use* Diagram 6

*Junction tone* 5 *is repeated in the first line, omitted in the second. Children must "think" missing* SOL *(5).*

(1̇ = $E^b$)

| 1̇ 7 6 5 5 4 3 2 1 1 2 3 4 5 5 6 7 1̇ |
| 1̇ 7 6 5 . 4 3 2 1 1 2 3 4 . 5 6 7 1̇ |

*Teacher presents Intonation Exercises horizontally via overhead projector, in* Finger Notation, Measuring Gesture, *and from* Staff Notation 9 *as found in this chapter.*

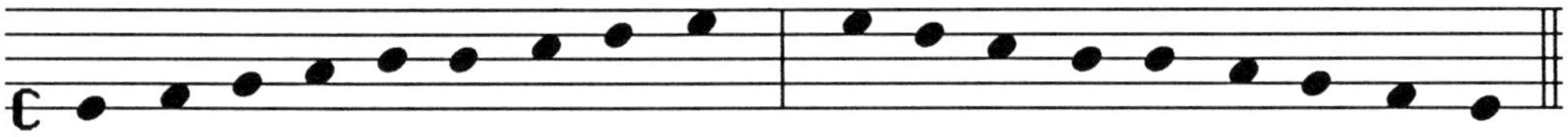

Staff Notation 9

> "Think" tones are an important part of this method. Technique of thinking tones will be developed throughout this book and those that follow.

# Rhythm

*Review* Rhythm Patterns - Series 6 *and continue to make new combinations into longer patterns or "words."*
*Practise as before with* Metrical Gesture, Metrical Language, *and* Rhythm Gesture III.
*In giving a rhythm dictation, sing pattern as a melody, occasionally adding a verbal phrase.*

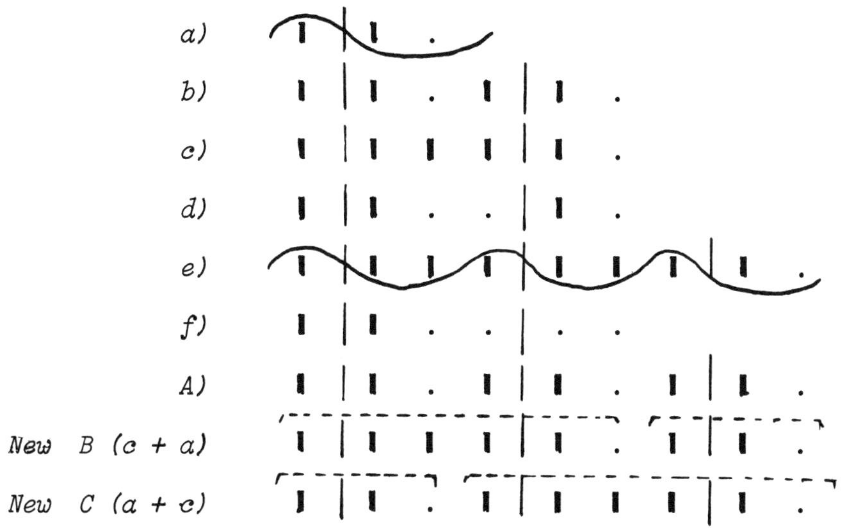


Melodic Application: *(1̇ = E♭)*

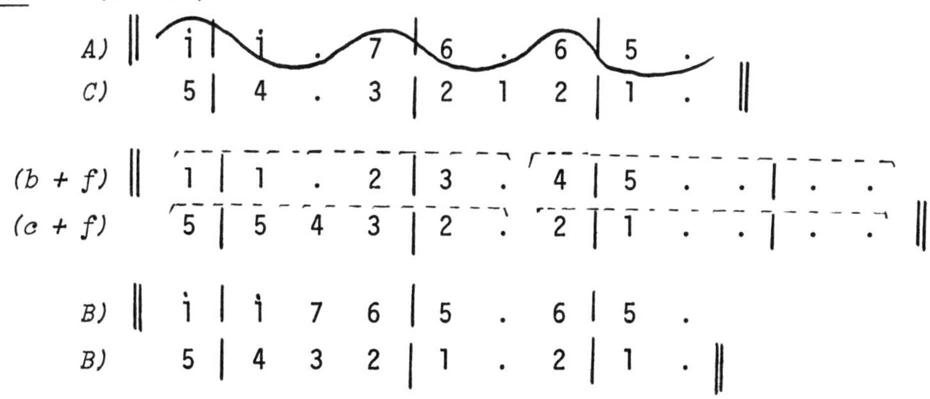


*Lines taken from the melodic application of rhythm patterns may be used for transcription exercises.*

## *Notation*

Entire scale of DO on five-line staff.

Staff Notation 9 *Lower and upper portions of scale are now combined so as to locate all tones from* 1 - i̇ *on five-line staff.*

*Practise* Intonation Exercises 31 *and* 32 *of this chapter, on* Staff Notation 9 *as well as on* Diagram 6.

*Transcribe melodic application examples of* Rhythm Patterns - Series 6.

1. *Teacher selects a line of a melody for transcription and writes it on the board in* Number Notation *with measure bars and rhythm wave. Space must be allowed for addition of staff. Notes are then added one at a time to the staff by the teacher as children suggest where each one should be placed.*

2. *Teacher reverses process by selecting another line of a melody and writing it on the board in* Staff Notation. *Teacher invites children to identify the notes by supplying the correct corresponding numbers for the notes.*

*Teacher adds rhythm wave and all sing.*

# Creative Activity

*Children may now begin to write, or compose, short musical compositions. For the time being, the work will be done by the whole class and the teacher will write the results on the board.*

*At first, to avoid rhythmic errors in the phrases suggested by the children, the teacher should propose rhythmic patterns upon which the children will compose their tunes. For example:*

*(Taken from R. P. Series 4 Chapter Seven)*

*a)* 

*b)* 

*These familiar patterns can be combined in a variety of ways. If we are composing a melody of two lines, we can either have :*

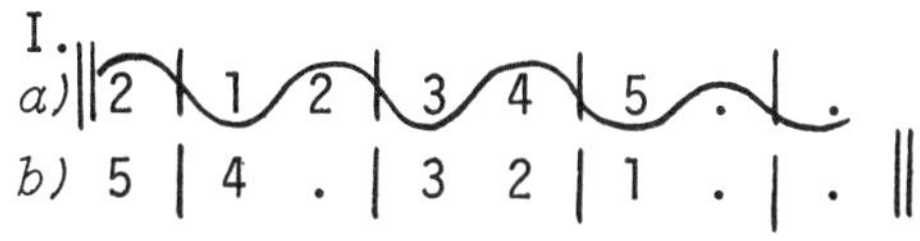


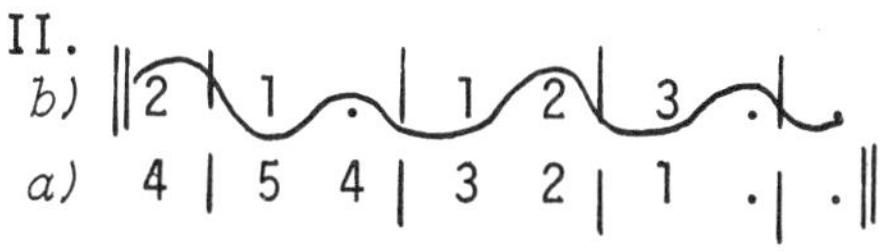


*A melody of four lines using two patterns can give us a number of different combinations:*

| a) | b) | b) | b) | a) | a) |
|---|---|---|---|---|---|
| b) | a) | b) | a) | a) | b) |
| a) | b) | b) | a) | b) | a) |
| b) | a) | a) | b) | b) | a) |

*The children do not have to use all these combinations. They choose one they want which the teacher writes on the board leaving room for the melody to be written beneath it, line by line, by the children.*

*Examples of possible combinations:*

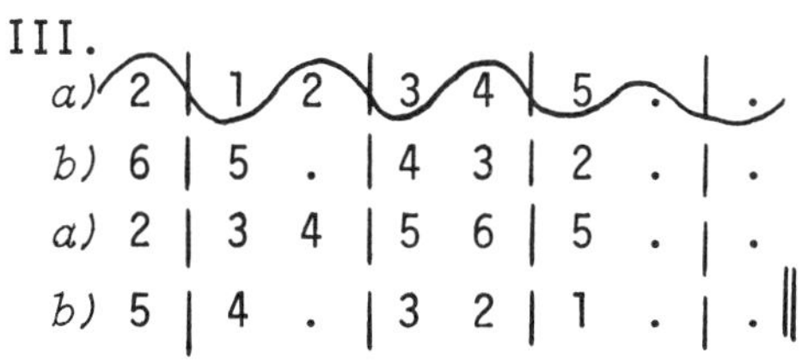


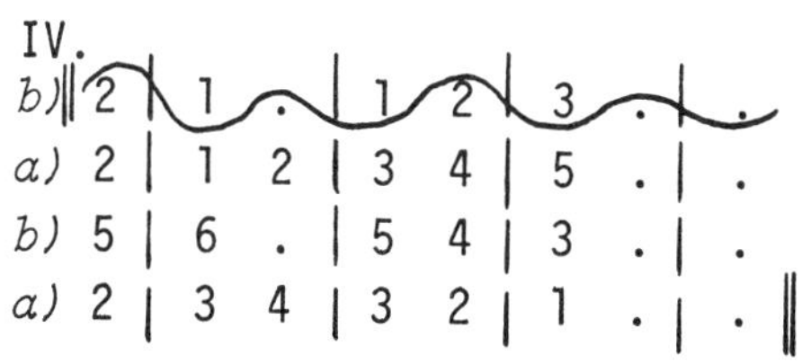


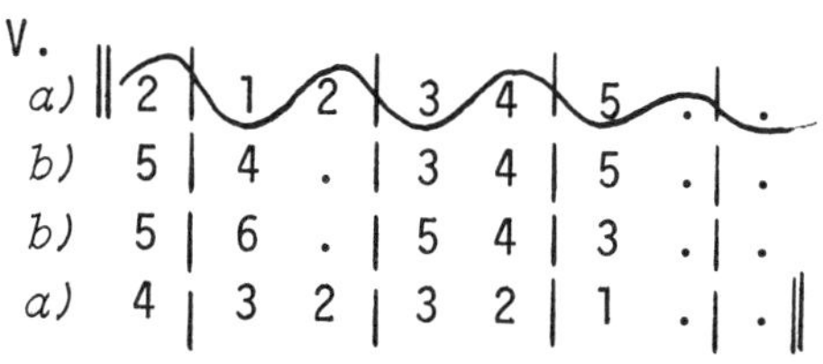


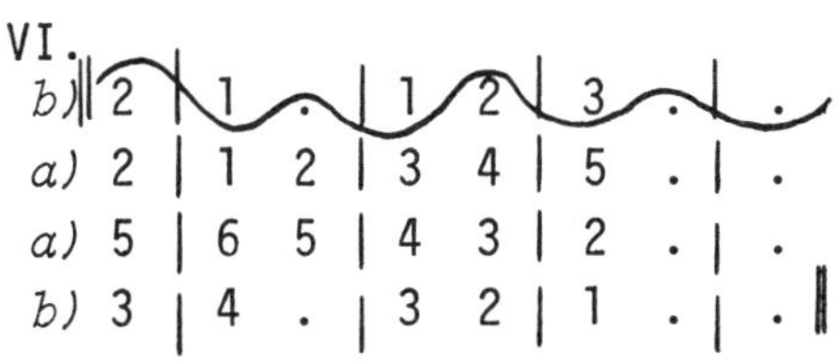

# Dictations

## Tonal Dictation

Ear Tests

| 1̇ 7 6 5 5 4 3 2 1<br>1 2 3 4 5 6 7 1̇ | 1̇ 7 6 5 6 5<br>5 6 5 4 3 2 1 | 1̇ 7 6 5 4 3<br>3 4 5 5 6 7 1̇ |
|---|---|---|

| 1 2 3 4 4 3 4 5<br>5 6 7 1̇ 1̇ 1̇ 5 | 1̇ 5 1̇ 7 6 5 4 3<br>3 2 3 1 3 2 1 |
|---|---|

Eye Tests ‖ 1̇ | 1̇ . | 7 6 | 5 . | . ‖

1̇ 7 6 5 4 3 2 1

1̇ 7 6 5 5 6 6 5

1̇ 1̇ 7 6 5 6 6 5

1̇ 5 5 6 7 1̇

*Use* Staff Notation 9 *for rapid observation and memory tests.*

## Rhythmic Dictation

*It will not be necessary to go through all the rhythmic steps used up to now in the rhythmic dictation game. It will be sufficient for the children to:*

*1. Observe which pattern is being dictated;*

*2. Repeat it accurately and rhythmically.*

*1 = F or G*
R. P. Series 4
*(On screen or blackboard)*

*1̇ = D or E♭*
R. P. Series 6
*(On screen or blackboard)*

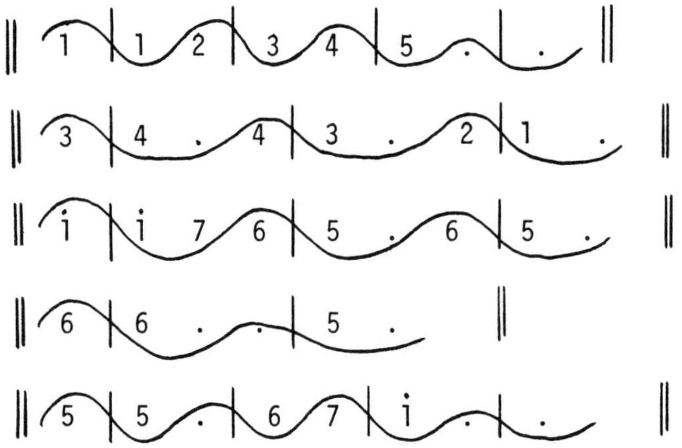

# *Songs*

**Song 32** *(1̇ = E♭)* *Prepare on* Diagram 6

‖ 1̇ | 1̇ . | 7 6 | 5 . | .<br>
5 | 5 4 | 3 2 | 1 . | .<br>
1 | 1 2 | 3 4 | 5 . | .<br>
5 | 5 . | 6 7 | 1̇ . | . ‖

**Song 33** *(1̇ = E♭)* *Prepare on* Staff Notation 9

*Teacher writes song on board in* Number Notation. *Children sing it. When melody is known, teacher draws a five-line staff beneath each line of the song. Children transcribe numbers to staff, line by line, orally. Finally they sing song from staff, one group at a time, beginning with the Bluebirds.*

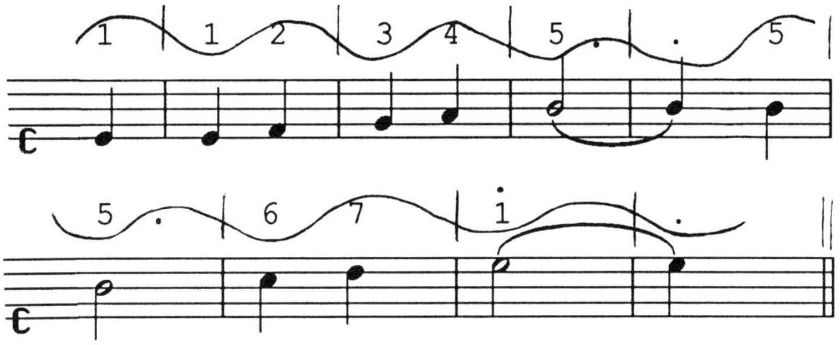


**If All the World Were Paper** *(1̇ = E♭)* *Mother Goose*

*Prepare with* Rhythm Patterns – Series 6 *and* Intonation Diagram 6

*b + d* ‖ 3 | 1 . 2 | 3 . 4 | 3 . . | 2 .<br>
If all__ the world__ were pa- per__

*b + f* 2 | 3 . 4 | 5 . 6 | 5 . . | . .<br>
And all__ the sea__ were ink, ______

*b + d* 5 | 1̇ . 7 | 6 . 5 | 6 . 6 | 5 .<br>
If all__ the trees__ were bread__ and cheese__

*b + f* 3 | 5 . 4 | 3 . 2 | 1 . . | . . ‖<br>
What would__ we have__ to drink? ______

# Chapter Fourteen

## Vocal Training

Invite few remaining drones (Sparrows) to listen to the accurate singing of the Bluebirds and Robins. Continue to encourage the Sparrows to match tones at a lower pitch level than that offered the others.

*Review* Vocal Exercise 1

i = A♭ (F, C, E♭)

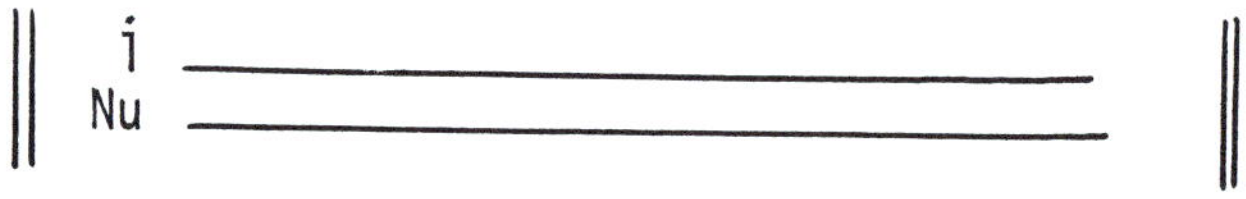


*Review* Vocal Exercise 6

1 = G (E, A)

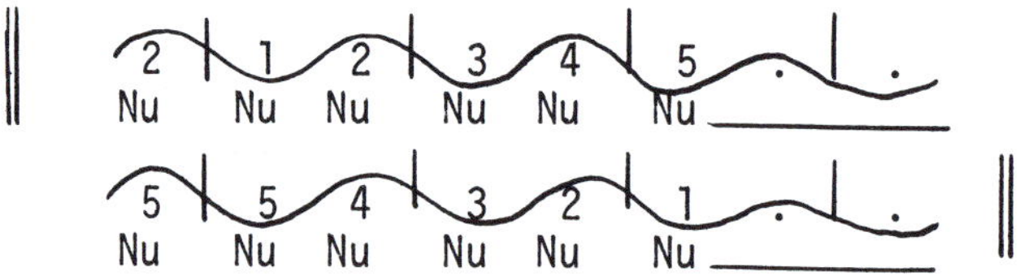


*Review* Vocal Exercise 10

i = D (E♭)

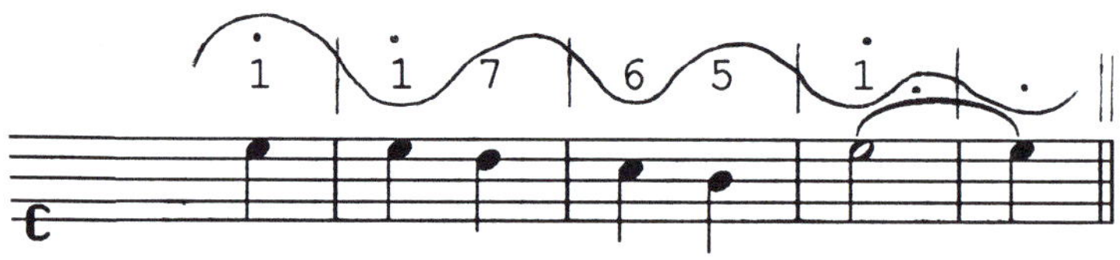

During vocal exercises children should stand erect but not rigid. Their heads should be slightly forward but chins should not be high. Lips open in shape of "oo" but without exaggeration or stiffness. There should be a feeling of space - open - inside the mouth.

# Intonation

1̇
7
6
5 *(5)*
4
3
2
1

Diagram 6

**Intonation Exercise 33** *Study of entire scale of DO family.*

| 1̇ 7 1̇ 1̇ 7 6 5 5 6 5 5 4 3 2 1 1 2 1 |
| 1 2 1 1 2 3 4 5 5 6 5 5 6 7 1̇ 1̇ 7 1̇ |

**Intonation Exercise 33a** *Rhythmic setting of scale line.*

|| 1̇ | 1̇ . | 7 6 | 5 . | .
5 | 4 . | 3 2 | 1 . | .
2 | 1 2 | 3 4 | 5 . | .
5 | 6 5 | 6 7 | 1̇ . | . ||

*Repeat* Intonation Exercise 33 *using* Staff Notation 9.

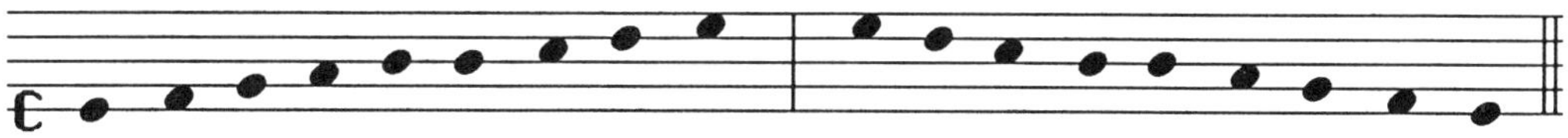

*If either overhead projector or wall chart is available,* Intonation Exercise 33 *may be shown as above so as to develop speed in horizontal reading. Immediately following this drill a transcription of the exercise to staff notation may be shown on screen. Children will try to "discover" the tones from the staff.*

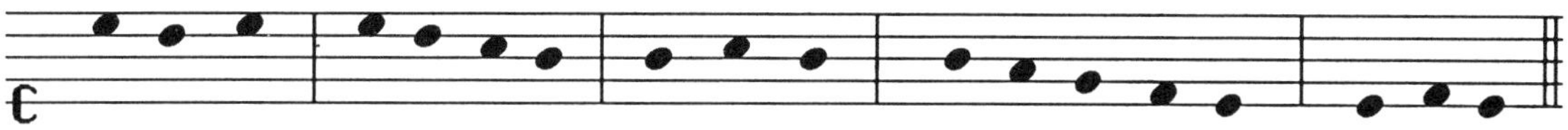

# *Rhythm*

*Review* Rhythm Patterns Series 2 *and* 3 *as a preparation for* Song 35.

Rhythm Gesture II

*From* Series 2 — a) b) c) d) A (a + b)

*From* Series 3 — (b + c)

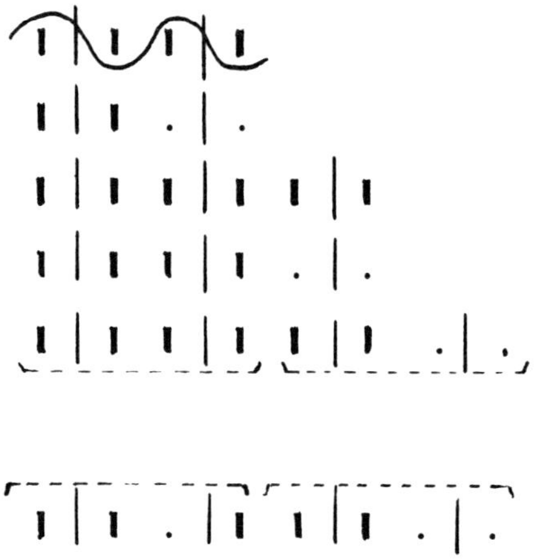

*Review* Rhythm Patterns - Series 6 *(see Chapter Thirteen) as a preparation for* Song 34.

Melodic Application:

(1 = F) ‖ 3 | 1 . 2 | 3 . 3 | 1 . 2 | 1 . ‖ (A … a)

‖ 3 | 1 . 2 | 3 2 3 | 1 . 2 | 1 . ‖ (C … a)

Game: *With rhythm patterns still in view of the class, teacher sings a short phrase using one of the patterns while making* Rhythm Gesture III. *Children identify correctly the pattern used and then repeat the phrase while making the same gesture.*

*Examples: (rhythm patterns taken from* Series 6*)*

*b)* ‖ 5 | i . 7 | i . ‖
I found__ my hat.__

*e)* ‖ i | i 7 6 | 5 6 7 | i . ‖
Did an- y- one here see the mouse?

*A)* ‖ 1 | 1 . 2 | 3 . 4 | 5 . ‖
Can John__ come out to play?__

# Notation

1.
*Review position of notes on staff by placing numbers on lines and spaces. For example, teacher places staff on board with large spaces between lines to allow for addition of numbers. Children, especially non-singers, are invited to place the numbers correctly on the staff.*

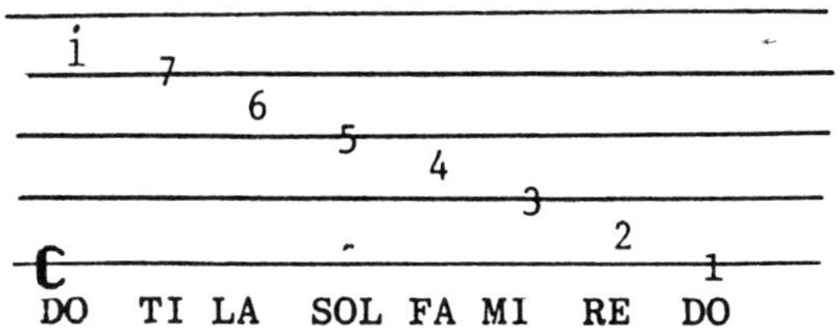


*Teacher then covers the numbers as "snowballs" and adds stems.*

*Bluebirds sing all notes of scale descending.*

*Robins repeat.*

*Sparrows listen.*

2.
*Teacher writes on board a melody in* Number Notation *above a staff of five lines.*

*Children are invited to place numbers in their correct position on staff.*

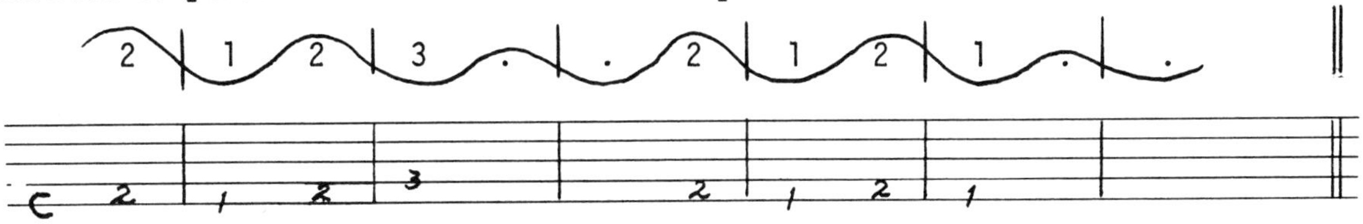


*Place numbers on staff lightly*
*Color in notes on staff*
*Find long notes*
*Find Tie*
*Add stems*
*Sing melody from staff notation*

3.
*Transcribe last line of* Song 35, *proceeding as above.*

# Creative Activity

*In Chapter Thirteen, two binary rhythm patterns were used for improvisation. In this chapter, two ternary patterns are suggested for similar-type composition. Same procedure as before: teacher places a rhythm on board and children compose a tune for it.*

R. P. Series 6

*a)* *Teacher* 

*Pupil* 1̇ | 1̇ 7 6 | 5 6 5 | 5 . . | . . ||

*b)* *Teacher* 

*Pupil* 5 | 5 . 5 | 6 . 7 | 1̇ . . | . . ||

*Several realizations of these rhythms in terms of melody are suggested below for the benefit of the teacher.*

I. *a)* || 2 | 1 2 3 | 4 3 2 | 1 . . | . .
*b)* 2 | 3 . 2 | 3 . 4 | 5 . . | . .
*a)* 5 | 5 6 7 | 1̇ 7 6 | 5 . . | . .
*b)* 4 | 3 . 4 | 3 . 2 | 1 . . | . . ||

II. *b)* || 2 | 1 . 2 | 3 . 2 | 3 . . | . .
*a)* 2 | 1 2 3 | 4 3 2 | 3 . . | . .
*b)* 2 | 3 . 4 | 5 . 6 | 5 . . | . .
*a)* 6 | 5 6 5 | 4 3 2 | 1 . . | . . ||

III. *a)* || 2 | 1 2 3 | 4 3 2 | 1 . . | . .
*b)* 2 | 3 . 2 | 3 . 4 | 5 . . | . .
*b)* 5 | 6 . 5 | 4 . 3 | 2 . . | . .
*a)* 2 | 3 4 3 | 2 1 2 | 1 . . | . . ||

IV. *b)* || 2 | 1 . 2 | 3 . 2 | 3 . . | . .
*a)* 2 | 1 2 3 | 4 3 2 | 3 . . | . .
*a)* 4 | 5 6 7 | 1̇ 7 6 | 5 . . | . .
*b)* 6 | 5 . 4 | 3 . 2 | 1 . . | . . ||

# *Dictations*

> To vary the dictation procedure, invite a child to give the class a four-note fragment, either as an ear test or as an eye test, always beginning on DO with no skips allowed.

## Tonal Dictation

Ear Tests *on* Diagram 6 *and* Staff Notation 9

| | |
|---|---|
| 1̇ 7 6 5   5 4 3 2 1 | 1 2 1   1 2 3 4 5 |
| 1̇ 7 1̇   1̇ 7 6 5 | 5 6 7 1̇   1̇ 5 5 |

| | |
|---|---|
| 1̇ 5   1̇ 1̇ 7 6 5 | 3 2   2 1   2 3 |
| 5 4 3 2   3 1 | 3 2   2 3 4 5 |

| |
|---|
| 5 4 3 2   2 3 |
| 5 1̇ 5   5 4 3 2 1 |

Eye Tests *on board or overhead projector,* Finger Notation, Measuring Gesture

*Repeat fragments from tests given above.*
*Present the following for visual observation:*

*1.* ‖ 1̇ | 1̇ . | 7 6 | 5 . | . ‖

*2.* ‖ 5 | 5 6 7 | 1̇ . 7 | 1̇ . ‖

*3.* ‖ 5 | 5 6 7 | 1̇ . 7 | 1̇ . . | . . ‖

## Rhythmic Dictation

R. P. Series 4 *1.* ‖ 5 | 4 . | 3 2 | 1 . | . ‖

R. P. Series 6 *2.* ‖ 1 | 2 3 4 | 5 . 5 | 4 3 2 | 1 . ‖

*For additional dictations, use lines from songs.*

# Songs

**Song 34** *Prepare on* Intonation Diagram 6 *and* Rhythm Patterns - Series 6
*Take breath only at end of line.*

*($\dot{1}$ = $E^b$)*

‖ $\dot{1}$ | $\dot{1}$ 7 6 | 5 . 6 | 6 . . | 5 .
5 | 6 5 4 | 3 . 2 | 1 . . | . .
2 | 1 . 2 | 3 4 5 | 6 . . | 5 .
6 | 5 6 7 | $\dot{1}$ . 7 | $\dot{1}$ . . | . . ‖

**Song 35** *Prepare on* Intonation Diagram 6 *and* Rhythm Patterns - Series 2 - 3.

*($\dot{1}$ = D)*

‖ $\dot{1}$ | $\dot{1}$ . | 7 6 | 5 . | .
5 | 4 . | 3 2 | 1 . | .
2 | 1 2 | 3 4 | 5 . | .
5 | 6 7 | $\dot{1}$ 7 | $\dot{1}$ . | . ‖

**Song 36** *Prepare on* Staff Notation 9 *and* Rhythm Patterns - Series 6.

*(1 = F)*

2 | 1 . 2 | 3 . 4 | 5 . 6 | 5 . 4 | 3 4 3 | 2 1 2 | 1 . ‖

**The World Is So Full** *($\dot{1}$ = $E^b$)* *Robert Louis Stevenson*

‖ 3 | 1 1 2 | 3 2 3 | 4 5 6 | 5 .
The world is so full of a num-ber of things

5 | $\dot{1}$ 7 6 | 5 6 5 | 4 3 2 | 1 . ‖
I'm sure we should all be as hap-py as kings.

## SUMMARY OF CHAPTERS ONE TO FOURTEEN

VOCAL TRAINING Exclusive use of the vowel sound "oo" - as in "noon" - for sustaining long tones in various registers of the voice and for maintaining good tonal quality in short melodic designs. The tones used are taken from the Intonation Exercises of the Chapters.

INTONATION The pitches of the Major Scale presented in the following order:

DO-RE
DO-RE-MI
DO-RE-MI-FA-SOL
The skips DO-MI and MI-DO
DO-RE-MI-FA-SOL-LA
DO(high)-TI-LA-SOL
The skips DO(high)-SOL and SOL-DO(high)
DO-TI-LA-SOL-FA-MI-RE-DO

RHYTHM Binary (2/4 Time) and Ternary (3/4 Time) Rhythm Patterns beginning on up-pulse.
Rhythm Gestures I, II and III, studied for coordination with rhythm patterns.

DICTATIONS Eye and Ear Tests to develop memory and acuity. Brief phrases taken from the tonal and rhythm vocabulary of the chapters.
Rhythm dictations of basic binary and ternary rhythm patterns derived from song structures.

NOTATION Various ways of showing relative pitches of the scale:

Number Notation
Finger Notation
Melodic Gesture (Hand and Forearm)
Staff Notation
- Notes of 1, 2 and 3 pulses
- The Tie
- Starting with one line and developing the full Five-Line Staff

CREATIVE ACTIVITY

Musical conversations without words
Adaptation of verbal phrases to rhythm patterns
Combining rhythm patterns to form longer structures
Composing melodies to rhythm patterns either as melodic applications or as longer song structures

SONGS Without words - as melodic designs derived from Intonation Exercises of the chapters. 32 songs in Number Notation and 4 in Staff Notation are offered.
With words - appropriate texts and melodies that can be easily grasped by children.

# Chapter Fifteen

| | 1 | 2 | 3 | 4 | 5 |
|---|---|---|---|---|---|
| **Vocal Training** | Greeting and opening song: *Hail Mary*<br>Voc. Ex. 1 Bluebirds **1 = D**<br>Robins **1 = Bb**<br>Sparrows **1 = F** | | Test each group and individuals | Opening song: *Ave Maria* | Test for promotion |
| **Intonation** | **Present:** Intonation Diag. 7 →<br>6 5 4 3 2 1<br>**Int. Ex. 34**<br>First Compass Ex.<br>Line 1 only<br>Meas. Gesture and Pointer | →<br>Int. Ex. 34 Lines 1 and 2<br>*Dialogue* Group I and Teacher using Meas. Gest. | →<br>Continue *dialogue*<br>Bluebirds sing *secret* tones<br>All make Meas. Gest. | →<br>Teacher and children take turns singing *think* tones | →<br>Lines 1, 2 and 3 by Bluebirds and Robins<br>Sparrows make gestures |
| **Rhythm** | **Present:** Rhythm Gesture IV in Binary Rhythm Arsis and Thesis (A + T)<br>Right hand and arm in rotation motion<br>Left hand and arm in rotation motion<br>Both hands and arms in rotation motion | | Arsis and Thesis in succession (A T A T)<br>Accompany gestures with song, e.g., *Mary Had a Little Lamb* or with cassette recording of down-pulse binary rhythm melody | ‖ 1 2 (3) 2 1 . ‖<br>A A T | ‖ 1 2 1 . 1 . ‖<br>A T T |
| **Dictations** | PREPARE DICTATIONS BY SINGING AGAIN TONES OF INTONATION DIAGRAM 7 | | | | |
| Ear Tests | 121 123<br>343 345 565 | 121 121 123<br>343 321 121 | 121 343<br>121 343 121 | 121 343 345<br>565 343 565 | 121 121 343<br>343 565 321 |
| Eye Tests | 2 1 2 1 2 3 4 3<br>5 5 6 5 6 5 . . | 123 343 345<br>565 565 543 | 121 343 345<br>565 343 343 | ‖ 1 2 1 . ‖<br>‖ 1 2 1 . \| 3 4 3 . ‖ | ‖ 1 1 (2) 2 1 . ‖<br>565 343 121 |
| **Vocal Training** | **Review:** Voc. Ex. 10<br>Bluebirds **i = Eb**<br>Robins **i = C** | Voc. Ex. 11 →<br>Bluebirds only **i = C**<br>Listen for accuracy at TI - DO | →<br>Bluebirds (I) **i = C**<br>Robins (II) **i = Bb** | Sparrows (III) make gesture in silence | **Review:** Voc. Ex. 10 |
| **Notation** | **Review:** Staff Notation 8<br>**Transcribe:** Lines from R.P. Series 7 | **Transcribe:** Int. Ex. 34 to Staff Notation – Segment a)<br>1 2 1 . 3 4 3 . . 5 6 5 . | **Transcribe:** Int. Ex. 34 to Staff Notation – Segment b)<br>5 6 5 . 3 4 3 . 1 2 1 . | **Transcribe:** Line 2 of Song 35 (Ch. 14) to Staff Notation →<br>5 4 . 3 2 1 . . | Line 3 of Song 35<br>2 1 2 3 4 5 . . |
| **Creative Activity** | | While making A and T gesture, groups converse with each other singing tones and bridges of Int. Ex. 34 (No skips) | | | Introduce skips in conversation |
| **Rhythm** | Study R. P. Series 7 with Metrical Gesture and Language →<br>**Dictations:** | With Rhythm Gesture IV →<br>‖ 1 2 1 . ‖ | **Review:** a) + a) with Melodic Application →<br>‖ 1 2 1 . \| 3 4 3 . ‖ | a) ‖ I I I . ‖ A T<br>b) ‖ I I (I) I I . ‖ A A T<br>‖ 1 1 (2) 2 1 . ‖<br>A A T | a) ‖ I I I . ‖<br>b) ‖ I I I I I . ‖<br>c) ‖ I I I . I . . ‖<br>‖ 1 2 1 . 1 . ‖ |
| **Songs** | **Song 37** Tones of First Compass Exercise First line | Song 37 – Complete → | | **Song 38** A A T Lines 1 and 2<br>*Ubi caritas* | Song 39 A T T Lines 3 and 4<br>*Ubi caritas*<br>*Ave Maria* |

# Chapter Fifteen

## Vocal Training

> Continue to strive for ideal of steady, clear and resonant tone during vocal exercises.

*Review* Vocal Exercise 1

$\dot{1} = B^{b}$ D / F

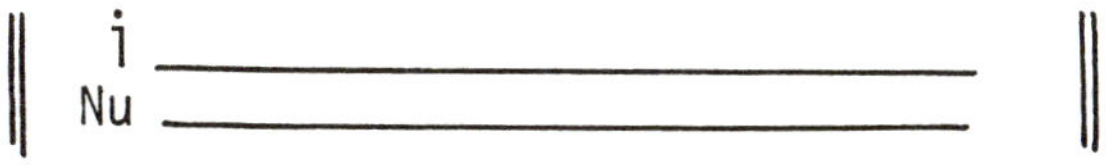


*Review* Vocal Exercise 10

$\dot{1} = E^{b}$ D

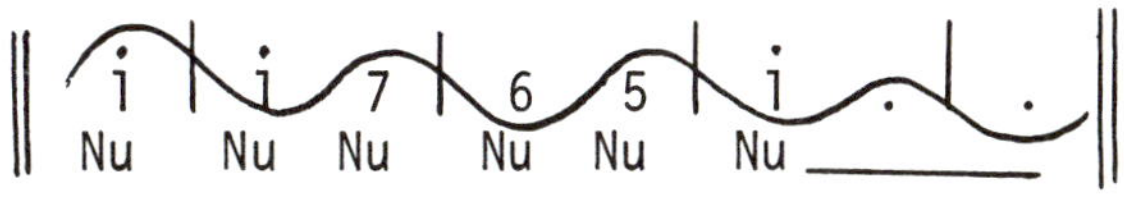


Vocal Exercise 11 *Strive for accuracy of pitch at the half step* DO - TI *and* TI - DO.

$\dot{1} = C$ $B^{b}$

u

> Constant attention to good tonal quality in all exercises is necessary to instill in children a sense of beauty in singing.

# Intonation

Diagram 7 *and* First Compass Exercise

## *Presenting* Diagram 7

*Review tones of the hexachord* DO - LA *on* Diagram 4. *Teacher explains that these tones belong to the family of* DO. *Teacher writes a large figure* 1 *on board.*

1

*"All families have grown-ups and children, for example father, mother, sister, brother, and others. It is the same in a musical family. We have first the head of the house whom we shall call the* Tonic, *No.* 1. *The other grown-ups are* MI (3) *and* SOL (5)."

*Teacher adds large* 3 *and* 5 *above* 1 *as shown at right and draws a box around the numbers.*

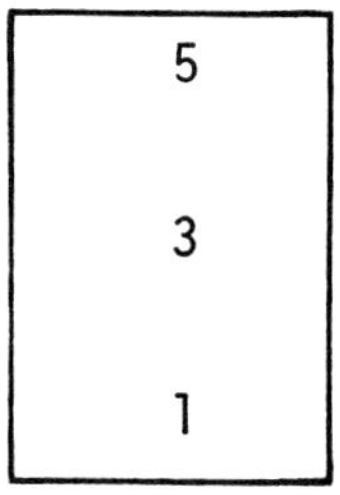


*"In the family there are also children. They are smaller and depend on grown-ups.*

RE *depends on* DO
FA *depends on* MI
LA *depends on* SOL"

*Teacher writes the dependent notes as shown in smaller numbers and connects them to the strong notes of the tonic chord line.*

Diagram 7 *is now ready for use.*

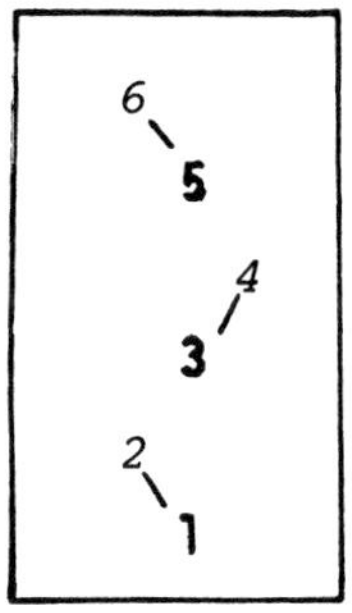


Diagram 7

## Intonation Exercise 34 - First Compass Exercise *(1 = F)*

| | bridge | | bridge | | | bridge | | bridge | |
|---|---|---|---|---|---|---|---|---|---|
| 1 2 1 | 1 2 3 | 3 4 3 | 3 4 5 | 5 6 5 | 5 6 5 | 5 4 3 | 3 4 3 | 3 2 1 | 1 2 1 |
| 1 2 1 | *1 2 3* | 3 4 3 | *3 4 5* | 5 6 5 | 5 6 5 | *5 4 3* | 3 4 3 | *3 2 1* | 1 2 1 |
| 1 2 1 | | 3 4 3 | | 5 6 5 | 5 6 5 | | 3 4 3 | | 1 2 1 |

*Presenting* First Compass Exercise *on hexachord* DO - LA.

*FIRST LINE*

*Teacher invites children to sing first line from* Diagram 7.

| *(1 = F)* | *Sing the group of* DO | 1 2 1 |
|---|---|---|
| | *Now sing the "bridge"* | 1 2 3 |
| | *The group of* MI | 3 4 3 |
| | *The "bridge"* | 3 4 5 |
| | *The group of* SOL | 5 6 5 |

*Same procedure for descent.*

*Selected children may be invited to come to the diagram and point to groups of* DO, *of* MI, *of* SOL *and the "bridges" between them.*

*SECOND LINE*

*"Now, Children, you sing the groups and I'll sing the 'bridges.' All together we shall make the* Measuring Gesture.*"*

*Repeat exercise with Bluebirds and Robins singing the groups (Sparrows remain silent but make the gesture), and a single child singing the "bridges" softly - as if telling a secret.*

*Repeat again, this time asking the children to think the "secret" notes as they make the gesture that will take them to the first tone of the next group.*

*Give children enough time to think the "secret" tones as if they were singing them from one group to the next. Teacher must adhere strictly to this slow procedure otherwise the more talented children will arrive at the next group before the others who will merely imitate what they hear.*

*Insist on a very precise* Measuring Gesture *throughout the exercise, especially during the think tones.*

*THIRD LINE*

*By the time that the second line has been practised several times with the think tones at the "bridges," the children will be able to sing the third line without difficulty. They must learn this line from memory.*

*Assimilation of the Compass Exercise will be enhanced by the dictations, improvisations, melodic applications of rhythm patterns, and the songs.*

# Rhythm

*New concept: Rhythm phrases that begin on down-pulse.*

Rhythm Patterns - Series 7 *and* Rhythm Gesture IV - Binary

*(1 = F or G)* *Melodic Application*

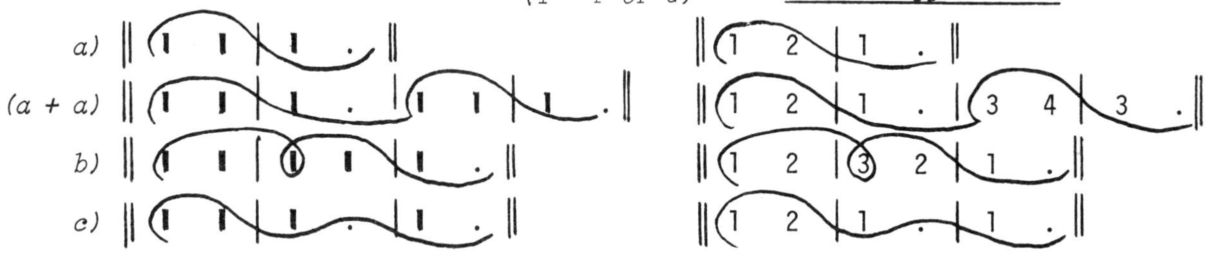


*Presenting* Rhythm Gesture IV - Binary

*Teacher announces a new rhythm gesture. Children stand.*

*Teacher extends left hand at shoulder level straight out in front.*
*Children extend right hands at shoulder level straight out in front.*
*Teacher rotates hand and arm in a counter-clockwise movement to form a circle about 8 inches in diameter.*
*Children imitate in a clockwise movement.*
*Teacher counts "one-two" for every complete circle beginning when hand is at lowest part of circle. Continue until a rhythm has been set and each row is making uniform circles.*

*Teacher extends right hand at shoulder level.*
*Children extend left hands.*
*Teacher rotates hand and arm in clockwise movement.*
*Children imitate in counter-clockwise movement.*

*Similar circles are now made with both hands and arms together while all count: "one-two" for each complete circular movement.*

ARSIS-THESIS Gesture. *Patterns a) and (a + a)*

*Teacher explains: "After each rise there is a fall. Like the airplane - after it lifts into the air, it comes in for a landing."*

*The lift is called* ARSIS *and the landing is called* THESIS.

*Children are invited to make the* ARSIS-THESIS Gesture, *first with the right hand; then with the left hand; finally, both hands together.*

*When a uniform rhythm has been established with the hand and arm movements, begin counting softly: one-two, one-two...Then accompany gesture with a song such as "Sweet Winds From the South" or "Church Bells Ringing," as given in Chapter Sixteen.*

*Presenting* Rhythm Patterns - Series 7

*Teacher writes* Rhythm Pattern *a) on board.*

*Children read rhythm with* Metrical Language *while making* Metrical Gesture. *Repeat several times.*

*Teacher adds bar-lines and points out that all the notes are contained within the bar-lines.*

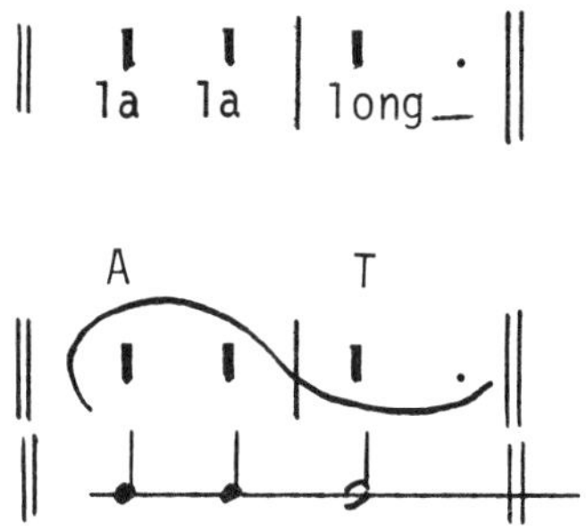


*Teacher adds rhythm curve for* Arsis - Thesis *and tells children that the new gesture will be used for melodies that begin on the down-pulse.*

*Children repeat the pattern on* DO, *then on other pitches.*

*Same procedure for* Rhythm Pattern *(a + a).*

Rhythm Pattern *b)* ARSIS-ARSIS-THESIS Gesture

*With left hand, teacher demonstrates how two* Arsis *movements can be placed one on top of another - a double lift followed by a smooth landing.*

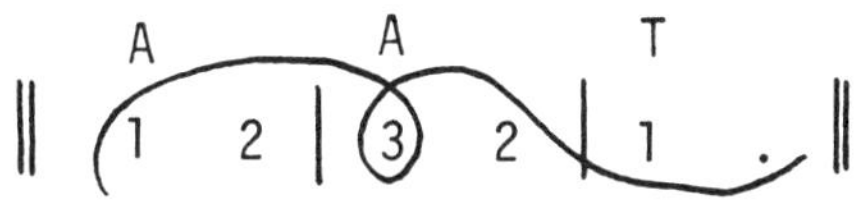


*Children repeat with right hand. Then in opposite direction with left hand. Then hands together. Take care to maintain a smooth flowing movement throughout the gesture always avoiding a "hammer-blow" on the down segment of the gesture.*

*When children can render the gesture correctly, practise* R. P. *b) as above.*

*In the vocal rendition strive for:*

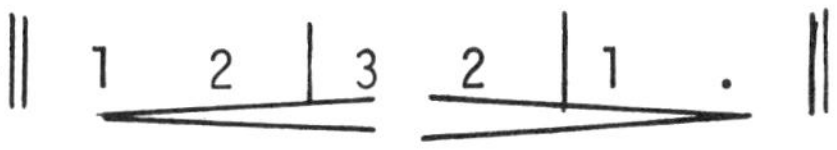


*and not:*

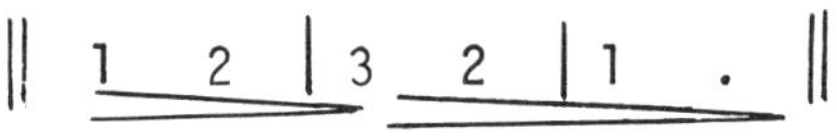

Rhythm Pattern *c)* ARSIS-THESIS-THESIS Gesture

*Practise this gesture to achieve suppleness, especially during the downward movement of the two* Thesis Gestures.

*Practise with right hand; then with left; finally, both together.*

*Now study* R. P. *c) as above.*

# Notation

*Review one-pulse, two-pulse notes, and* TIE *in binary measure structures beginning on down-pulse.*

*Review*
Staff Notation 8

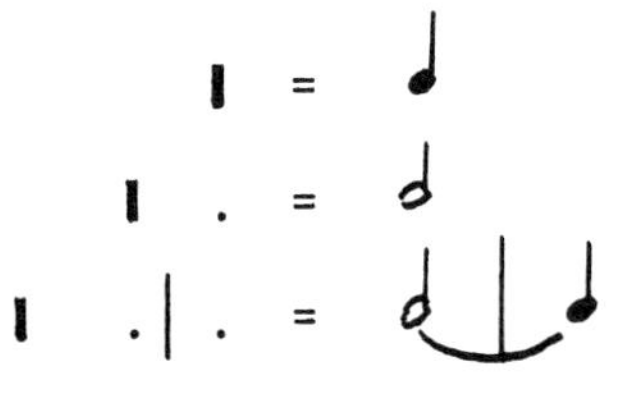

1. *Transcribe* Rhythm Patterns - Series 7 *of this chapter.*

2. *When Line 3 of* Intonation Exercise 34 *has been memorized, transcribe it to staff notation: segment a) in one lesson; segment b) in another lesson.*

1 2 | 1 . | 3 4 | 3 . | 5 6 | 5 . |

a) 

5 6 | 5 . | 3 4 | 3 . | 1 2 | 1 . ||

b) 

3. *Transcribe lines 2 and 3 of* Song 35, *Chapter Fourteen, to* Staff Notation.

# Creative Activity

Musical Conversation *Game of question and answer continues at a more rapid pace than before and involves more children.*

*The building blocks of these musical improvisations are the note-groups and "bridges" of the First Compass Exercise with* Rhythm Gesture IV - Binary.

*EXAMPLE:* *All children make gesture throughout conversation.*

*(1 = F or G)* *Teacher begins:* || 1 2 | 3 . | 3 4 | 5 . |

*1st child:* | 5 6 | 5 . | 5 4 | 3 . |

*2nd child:* | 3 4 | 5 . | 5 4 | 3 . |

*3rd child:* | 3 4 | 3 . | 3 4 | 3 . |

*4th child:* | 3 2 | 1 . | 1 2 | 1 . ||

*Teacher may prepare the conversation with a more extended question to which a child makes a more extended answer.*

# Dictations

*Children may give their responses orally, on fingers, writing in work book, on the staff, or with pointer at board.*

<u>Tonal Dictation</u> *(1 = F or G)*

| Ear Tests | Eye Tests |
|---|---|
| 1 2 1   1 2 3<br>3 4 3   3 4 5   5 6 5 | 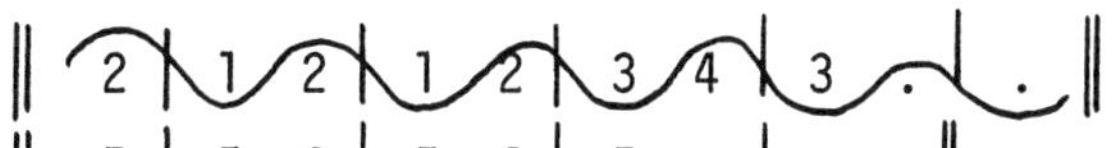<br>‖ 5 \| 5 6 \| 5 6 \| 5 . \| . ‖ |
| 1 2 1   1 2 1   1 2 3<br>3 4 3   3 2 1   1 2 1 | 1 2 3   3 4 3   3 4 5<br>5 6 5   5 6 5   5 4 3 |
| 1 2 1       3 4 3<br>1 2 1   3 4 3   1 2 1 | 1 2 1   3 4 3   3 4 5<br>5 6 5   3 4 3   3 4 3 |
| 1 2 1   3 4 3   3 4 5<br>5 6 5   3 4 3   5 6 5 | 1 2 3   3 4 3   5 6 5<br>5 6 5   3 4 3   1 2 1 |
| 1 2 1   1 2 1   3 4 3<br>3 4 3   5 6 5   3 2 1 | 1 2 1   3 4 3   1 2 3 4 3<br>3 4 3   3 2 1 2 1 |

<u>Rhythmic Dictation</u> *All examples begin on down-pulse of the measure.*

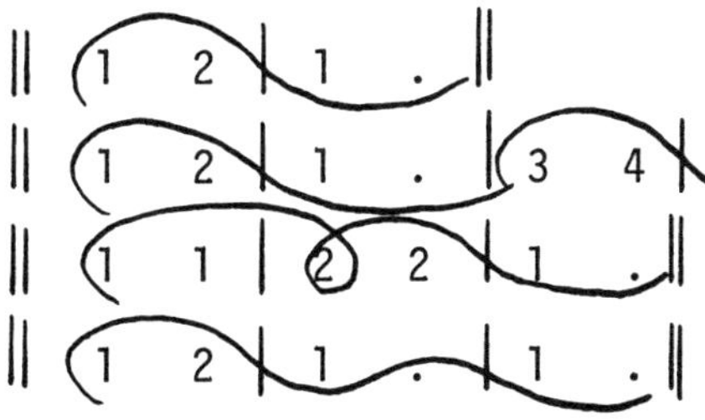


> Continue to use colored chalk for written examples on board:
> <u>yellow</u> (or white) for numbers;
> <u>red</u> for measure bars;
> <u>blue</u> for rhythm wave.

*Review procedure:*
- *Teacher dictates phrase.*
- *Children repeat with correct gesture.*
- *Children write rhythm in air; one child at board sketches rhythm with index finger, then with chalk.*
- *Another child writes numbers beneath rhythm strokes.*
- *A third child adds measure bars.*
- *Teacher (or child) adds rhythm curve.*
- *All sing, making correct gesture.*

## Songs

Melodic application of rhythm patterns and tonal groupings studied in this chapter.

### Song 37 (1 = G)

A T A T A T A T

|| 1 2 | 1 . | 1 2 | 3 . | 3 4 | 3 . | 3 4 | 5 . |

| 5 6 | 5 . | 5 4 | 3 . | 3 4 | 3 . | 3 2 | 1 . |

| 1 2 | 1 . ||

### Song 38 (1 = G)

A A T

|| 1 1 | 2 2 | 1 . |

| 3 3 | 4 4 | 3 . |

| 5 5 | 6 6 | 5 . |

| 3 3 | 4 4 | 3 . |

| 1 1 | 2 2 | 1 . ||

### Song 39 (1 = G)

A T T

|| 1 2 | 1 . | 1 . |

| 3 4 | 3 . | 3 . |

| 5 6 | 5 . | 5 . |

| 5 6 | 5 . | 5 . |

| 3 4 | 3 . | 3 . |

| 1 2 | 1 . | 1 . ||

*The new rhythm patterns studied in this chapter permit the teacher to offer short phrases as songs taken from the Gregorian Chant repertory. These are not taught by rote, but are written on the board or shown via an overhead projector. The children study the melody first, then adapt the words to it.*

### Ave Maria (1 = G) (Hail Mary)

A T T

|| 1 1 | 1 2 | 1 . ||

A- ve, Ma- ri- a.

### Ubi Caritas (1 = G) (Where love is, there is God) Melody only

Teacher: || 1 1 | 2 3 | 3 2 | 3 4 | 3 2 | 3 2 |

Class: | 1 1 | 1 2 | 2 . | . . |

Teacher: | 1 1 | 2 3 | 3 2 | 3 4 | 3 2 | 3 2 |

Class: | 1 1 | 1 2 | 1 . | . . ||

# Chapter Sixteen

## Vocal Training

*Review* Vocal Exercise 1

$\dot{1}$ = B \ G / B♭

|| $\dot{1}$ ________________ ||
|| Nu ________________ ||

*Review* Vocal Exercise 10

$\dot{1}$ = C \ G / E♭

|| $\dot{1}$ $\dot{1}$ 7 6 5 $\dot{1}$ . . ||
|| Nu Nu Nu Nu Nu Nu ________ ||

### Vocal Exercise 12

1 = G \ F / B♭

*Vocal exercises will become longer from now on. A more sustained legato should be expected. The exercises should be sung rather slowly so that tone is placed where it will have maximum resonance.*

*Practise this exercise with* Rhythm Gesture IV - Binary. *Practise also without gesture.*

> Alternate groups in singing exercises so children may listen to others and begin to form the habit of listening to their own voices.

# *Intonation*

## First Compass Exercise *Continued*

*Presenting* Diagram 8 *Upper tetrachord* SOL LA TI DO (5 6 7 1̇) *vertically*

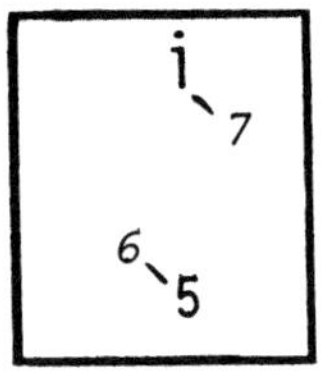


Diagram 8

**Intonation Exercise 35** *On* Diagram 8 *Upper tetrachord of scale*

*(1̇ = $E^{b}$)*

*Practise as given below over a period of three days:*

*Line 1 - Sing straight across;*
*Line 2 - Children sing large notes, teacher sings small notes;*
*Repeat Line 2 - Children sing large notes, one or two children sing small notes;*
*Line 3 - Children sing large notes only and take time to think "bridge" notes.*

| 1̇71̇ | 1̇765 | 565 | 565 | 5671̇ | 1̇71̇ |
|---|---|---|---|---|---|
| 1̇71̇ | *1̇765* | 565 | 565 | *5671̇* | 1̇71̇ |
| 1̇71̇ | | 565 | 565 | | 1̇71̇ |

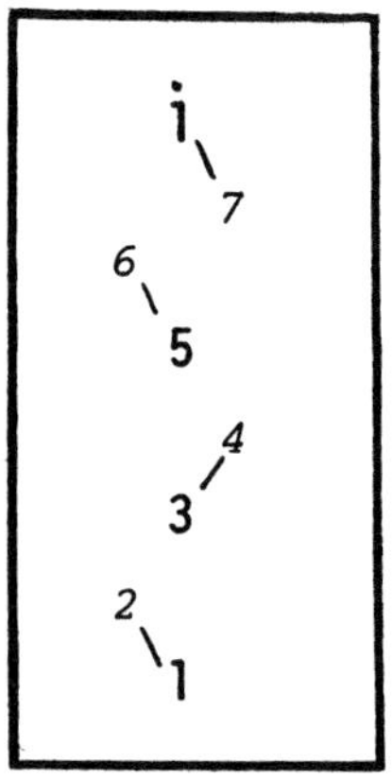


Diagram 9a

*Presenting* Diagram 9a *for*

**Intonation Exercise 36** First Compass Exercise - Complete Scale

| 121 | 123 | 343 | 345 | 565 | 5671̇ | 1̇71̇ | 1̇71̇ | 1̇765 | 565 | 543 | 343 | 321 | 121 |
|---|---|---|---|---|---|---|---|---|---|---|---|---|---|
| 121 | *123* | 343 | *345* | 565 | *5671̇* | 1̇71̇ | 1̇71̇ | *1̇765* | 565 | *543* | 343 | *321* | 121 |
| 121 | | 343 | | 565 | | 1̇71̇ | 1̇71̇ | | 565 | | 343 | | 121 |

*Child's grasp of Compass Exercises will be strengthened by drills in rhythmic application, notation, dictation, and songs.*

> Continue to use pointer for "think" tones.

# Rhythm

## Rhythm Gesture IV - Binary *Continued*

*Various combinations of* Arsis *and* Thesis *are studied in this chapter.*

*All the rhythmic patterns of this chapter are four measures long. Several combinations are possible using single lines from the songs:*

*Before studying rhythm patterns, practise the above gestures by themselves:*

- *Right arm alone*
- *Left arm alone*
- *Right and Left together*

*Teacher should announce beforehand which gesture is to be used.*

## Rhythm Patterns - Series 8

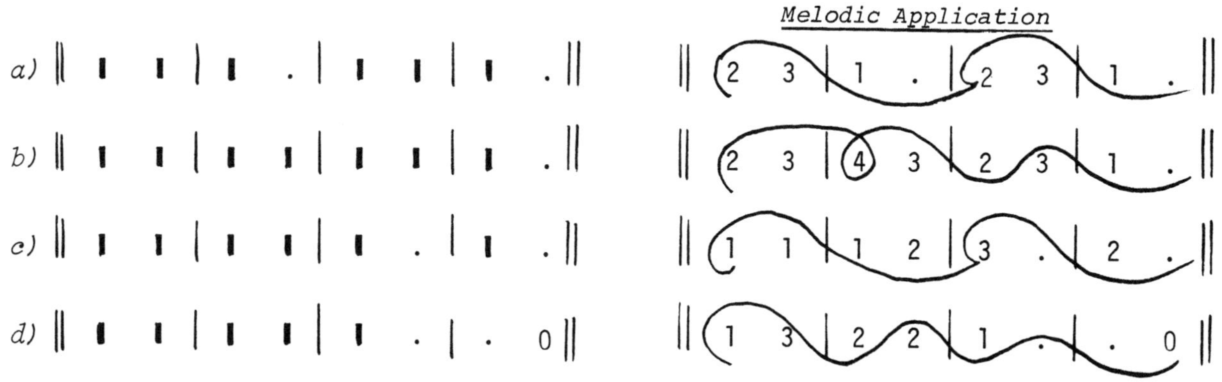


*Practise with* Metrical Gesture
Metrical Language
Rhythm Gesture IV - Binary
Melodic Application

# Notation

## Staff Notation 10 - The Rest

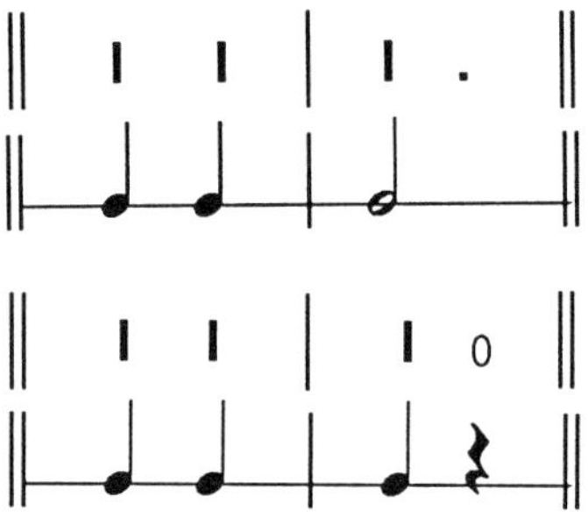

*Presenting* The Rest - *A measured silence*

*Encourage children to discover this new sign by <u>listening</u> very carefully.*

- *Teacher writes rhythm pattern on board in number and staff notation.*

- *Children sing pattern with* Metrical Language *and* Metrical Gesture.

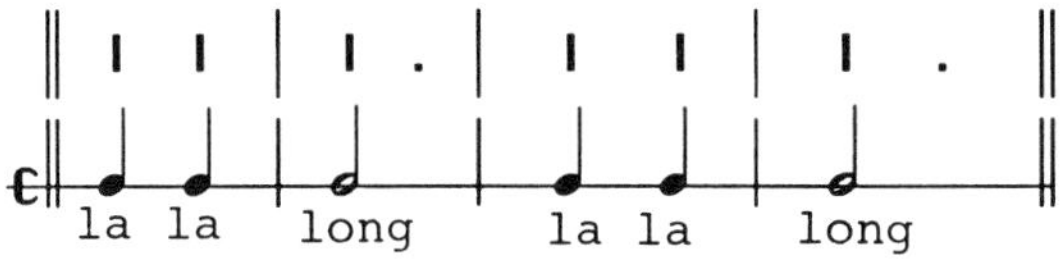


- *Teacher sings pattern again but without long notes. The second pulse of each long note is replaced by a rest.*

- *Children repeat and discover the measured silences which are the rests.*

- *Teacher writes pattern on board showing the new sign for the* Rest *both in number and staff notation.*

- *Children sing the pattern again placing index finger gently on lips for the silent pulse.*

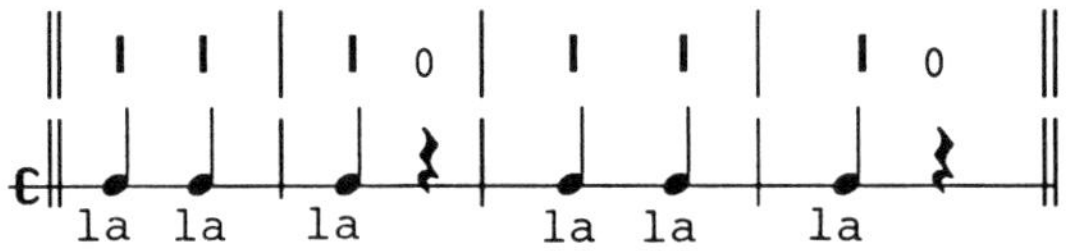

## Creative Activity

1. Musical Conversations *continued using full scale line,* Rhythm Patterns - Series 8, *and* Rhythm Gesture IV - Binary.

2. *To encourage musical composition, the teacher writes two rhythm patterns on the board, leaving space between them to insert a melody in numbers. The teacher then suggests a melody for the first line to which the children add a second line of melody. If a good tune results from the children's improvisation, the teacher writes it on the board and all sing it.*

3. *A four-line melody may now be attempted. Leaving sufficient space between each line (as in 2 above) to insert a melody, the teacher writes two rhythm patterns on the board in the form of abab as follows:*

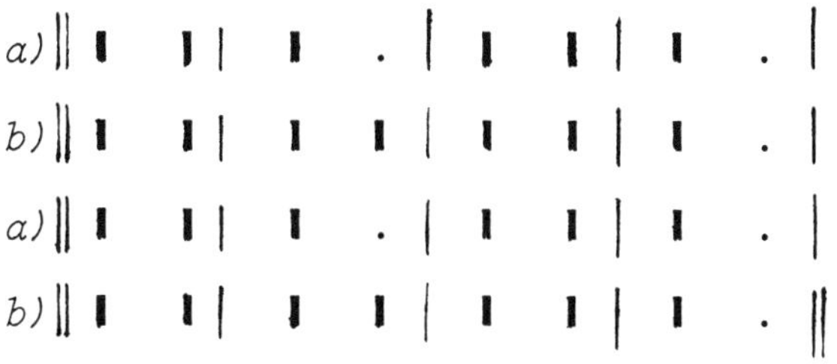


*Children are invited to supply a melody for each of the lines.*

## Dictations

**Ear Tests**

1̇71̇ 1̇765
1̇71̇ 565

121 343 565
343 565 1̇71̇

1̇71̇ 565 543
3343 565

1̇76543 343
34565 1̇71̇

1̇765 343 565
56543 121

**Eye Tests**

1̇71̇ 565 1̇71̇
565 1̇71̇ 55671̇

343 565 34565
1̇765 565 1̇71̇

*Staff Notation*

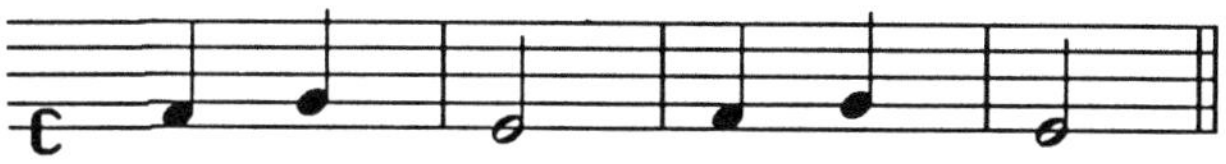

R. P. Series 8

**Rhythmic Dictation**

|| 2 3 | 1 . | 2 3 | 1 . || || 1 1 | 1 2 | 3 . | 2 . ||

|| 2 3 | 4 3 | 2 3 | 1 . || || 3 | 1 3 | 2 2 | 1 . | . ||

# Songs

**Song 40** *(1 = $G^b$)*

a) || 1 2 | 1 . | 3 4 | 3 . |
| 3 4 | 3 . | 5 6 | 5 . |
| 5 6 | 5 . | 3 4 | 3 . |
| 3 4 | 3 . | 1 2 | 1 . ||

**Song 41** *(1 = $G^b$)*

b) || 1 2 | 3 4 | 5 6 | 5 . |
| 5 6 | 5 4 | 3 2 | 3 . |
| 3 2 | 1 2 | 3 4 | 5 . |
| 5 6 | 5 4 | 3 2 | 1 . ||

**Church Bells Ringing**

*French Folk Song*

*(1 = $G^b$)*

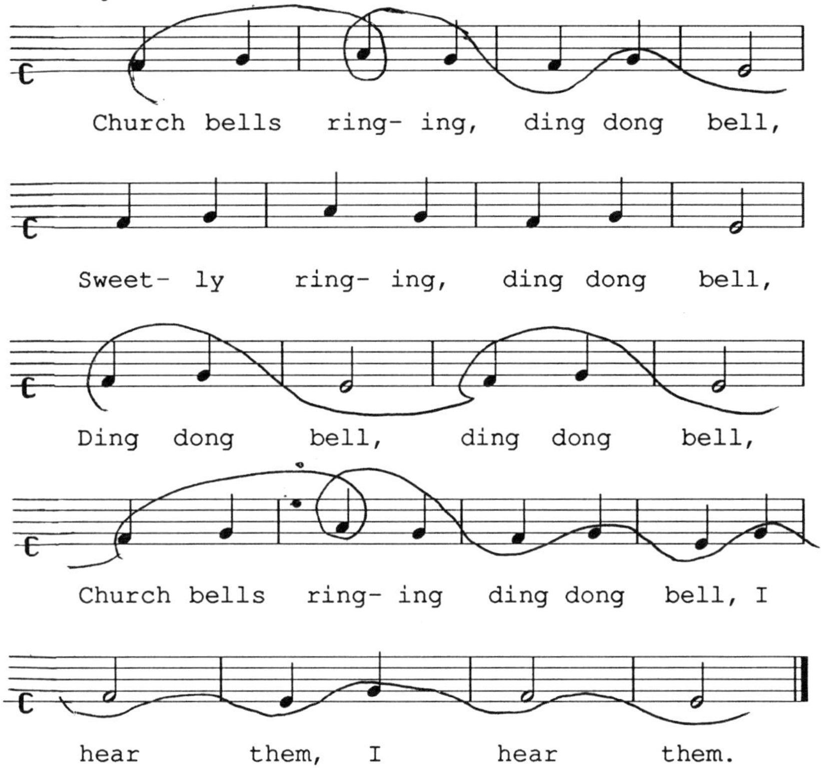

## The Father's Love

*Theme of Beethoven*

($1 = A^b$)

|| 3 3 | 4 5 | 5 4 | 3 2 |
Sweet winds from the South are blow- ing,

| 1 1 | 2 3 | 3 2 | 2 . |
Sun is shin- ing high a- bove,___

| 3 3 | 4 5 | 5 4 | 3 2 |
Riv- ers to the sea are flow- ing,

| 1 1 | 2 3 | 2 1 | 1 . ||
Joy- ful in the Fa- ther's love.___

## Benedicamus Domino

($\dot{1} = D^b, 5 = A^b$)

*(Let us bless the Lord. Thanks be to God.)*

|| 5 - - - - - - - - - - - | 5 4 | 3 . ||
*Teacher:* Be-ne-di-cá-mus Dó- mi-no.________

|| 5 5 | 5 5 | 5 4 | 3 . ||
*Class:* De- o grá- ti- as.________

# Chapter Seventeen

## Vocal Training

*Review* Vocal Exercise 1

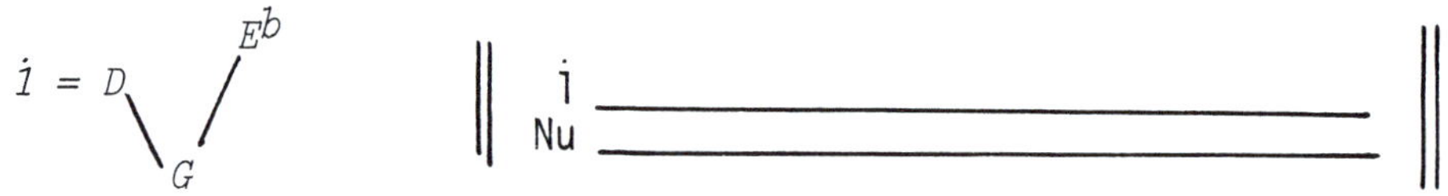


*Review* Vocal Exercise 11

*Review* Vocal Exercise 12

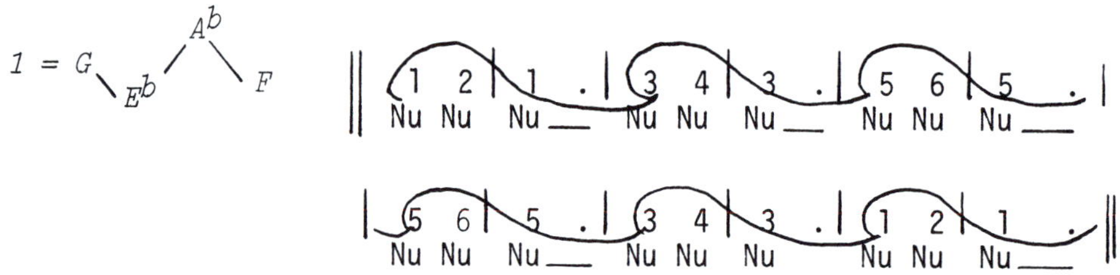


*To strengthen children's sense of accurate pitch, frequently practise* Voc. Ex. 1 *on G, B and D, that is, on the three strong tones of the G tonality. Follow this immediately with* Voc. Ex. 12, *starting on G so that* MI *and* SOL *will be the B and D heard in* Voc. Ex. 1.

*Practise with* Rhythm Gesture IV *and without gesture, listening for smooth connection between notes and groups. Work for clean attack on each note that begins a new group following a skip of a third ascending and descending.*

# Intonation

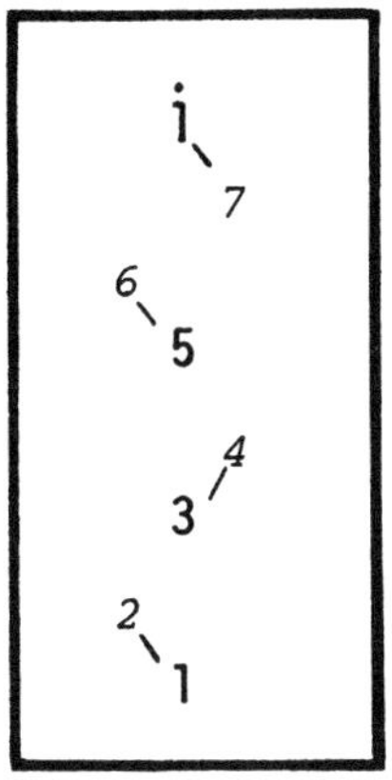


Diagram 9a

## Intonation Exercise 37 - First Compass Exercise

*Use* Diagram 9a. *Procedure:*

*Line 1 - Sing straight across;*
*Line 2 - Children sing large notes, teacher sings small notes;*
*Repeat Line 2 - Children sing large notes, one child sings small notes;*
*Repeat Line 2 - Children sing large notes, all* <u>*think*</u> *small notes.*
*Lines 3 and 4, same as Line 2.*

| | | | | | | | |
|---|---|---|---|---|---|---|---|
| 121 | 343 | 565 | 1̇71̇ | 1̇71̇ | 565 | 343 | 121 |
| 121 | *343* | 565 | 1̇71̇ | 1̇71̇ | 565 | *343* | 121 |
| 121 | 343 | *565* | 1̇71̇ | 1̇71̇ | *565* | 343 | 121 |
| 121 | *343* | *565* | 1̇71̇ | 1̇71̇ | *565* | *343* | 121 |

## Intonation Exercise 38 - Second Compass Exercise

*Drill on Tonic Chord of Major Mode:* 1 3 5 1̇

*Line 1 - Sing "help" notes;*
*Line 2 -* <u>*think*</u> *"help" notes;*
*Line 3 - omit "help" notes.*

| | | | | | | | |
|---|---|---|---|---|---|---|---|
| 121 | 343 | 565 | 1̇71̇ | 1̇71̇ | 565 | 343 | 121 |
| 1*21* | 3*43* | 5*65* | 1̇*71̇* | 1̇*71̇* | 5*65* | 3*43* | 1*21* |
| 1 | 3 | 5 | 1̇ | 1̇ | 5 | 3 | 1 |

*Repeat Intonation Exercises on* <u>Staff Notation 9.</u>

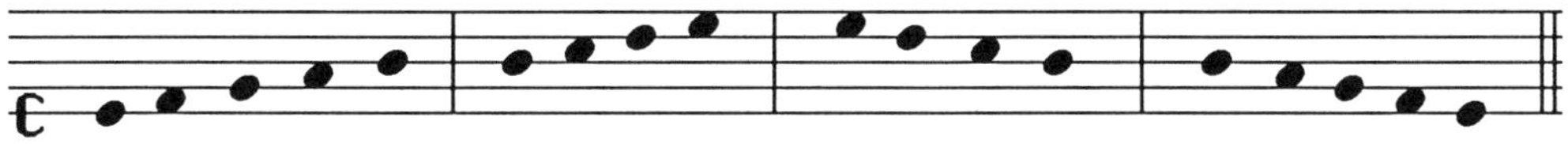

The term "children" does not necessarily mean <u>all</u> the children of the class. The Sparrows do not participate in intonation exercises with the other groups. They must listen and may take part in rhythm exercises. Periodically the teacher will test them as a group by themselves to check on their progress.

# *Rhythm*

*Review* Rhythm Patterns - Series 8

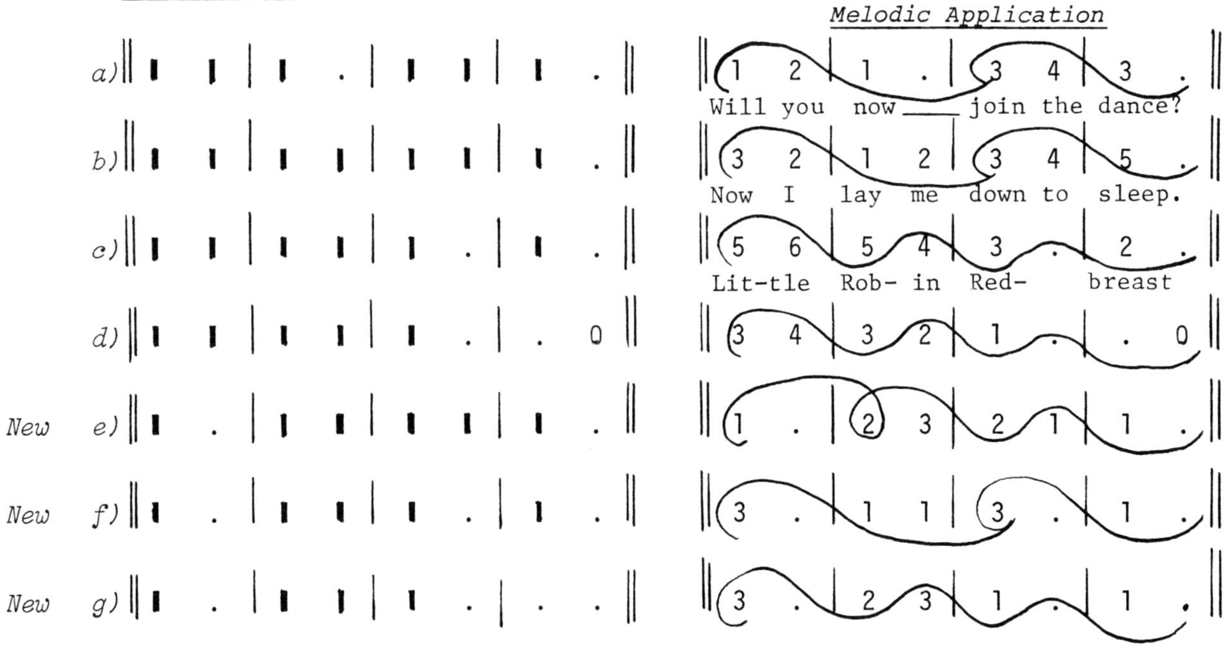


1. *Drill with* Metrical Gesture, Metrical Language, *and* Rhythm Gesture IV - Binary.

2. *Because* Rhythm Gesture IV *is still new, check children's posture, height of elbows and arms, and graceful curve of the gesture. Accompany practise of* Arsis-Thesis *with recording especially made for this purpose. Also, invite one group to sing a known song while others make the rhythm gesture.*

3. *Teacher places the following combinations of* Arsis-Thesis *on board. Children continue without stopping through all gestures, repeating each one several times as teacher points to it.*

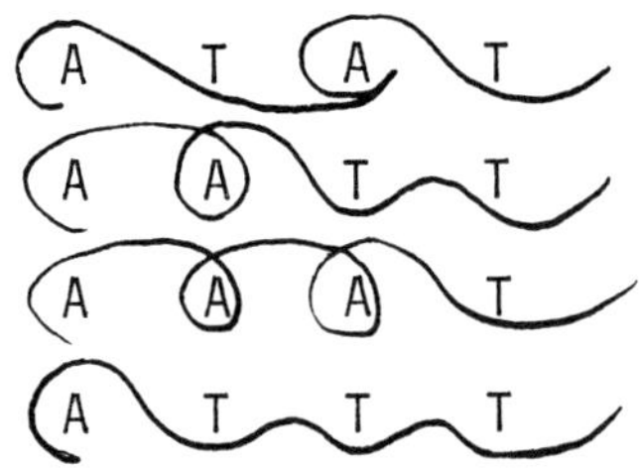

# *Notation*

*Review elements of* Staff Notation *studied thus far.*

a)

1 2 | 3 1 | 3 . | 3 4 | 5 3 | 5 . | 5 3 | 5 3 | 1 . ||

b)

1 2 | 3 5 | 3 . | 1 2 | 1 . ||

c)

1 2 | 3 2 | 3 5 | 3 . | 1 2 | 1 . ||

1. *Teacher asks children to find all* DO's; MI's; SOL's; *one-pulse notes, two-pulse notes. (Present only one line in a lesson.)*

   *Teacher extends measure bars downward to form measures for the numbers. Children indicate orally where numbers correspond to staff notes. Teacher adds rhythm wave. Children sing making appropriate rhythm gesture.*

2. *Teacher changes all two-pulse notes to one-pulse notes plus one-pulse* Rest *so that each* 𝅗𝅥 *becomes* ♩ 𝄽 *. Children indicate orally what change must now be made in the* Number Notation.

c)

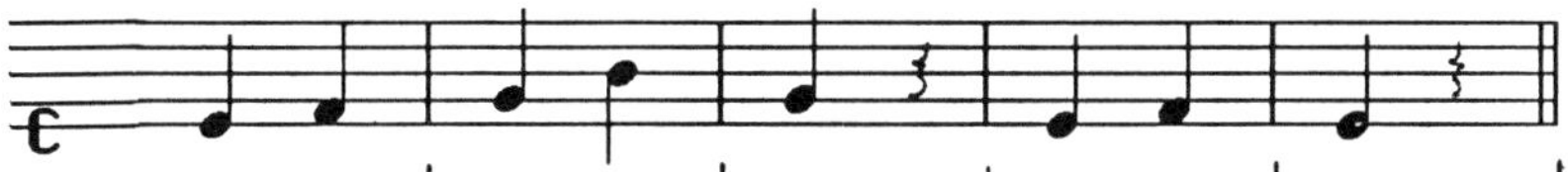

1 2 | 3 5 | 3 0 | 1 2 | 1 0 |

3. *Following each transcription, children sing melody and make correct rhythm gesture.*

# Creative Activity

*As a result of work completed thus far, children have accumulated a considerable musical vocabulary:*

- *The entire major scale;*
- *First and Second Compass Exercises;*
- *Long tones and rests;*
- *Up-pulse and down-pulse measure structures in binary rhythm;*
- *Up-pulse measures in ternary rhythm;*
- *Sense of statement and response;*
- *Four different rhythm gestures.*

1. *Using rhythm patterns of this and previous chapters, teacher suggests a form for a four-line song by writing rhythm on board (leaving space between lines so as to add melody) and inviting children to fill in melody, making use of the known vocabulary of tones.*

*SUGGESTIONS CONCERNING WRITING OF MELODIES*

*Try to avoid using* RE *and* FA *at the beginning of measures and at the end of phrases where the tones are ascending. It is perhaps better for now to use the strong tones* DO, MI *and* SOL *at these points.*

*For example, the phrase* || 2 | 1 2 | 3 4 | 5 . | . ||

*is better than* || 1 | 2 3 | 4 5 | 6 . | . ||

*When the tones of a melody are descending, however,* RE *and* FA *can effectively occupy a strong position:*

*Statement:* || 2 | 1 2 | 3 4 | 5 . | . ||

*Incomplete Response:* || 5 | 6 5 | 4 3 | 2 . | . ||

2. *Place b) of* Rhythm Patterns- Series 8 *on board:*

*Invite children to compose melody for each* Arsis-Thesis *studied up to now. Examples are given as suggestions.*

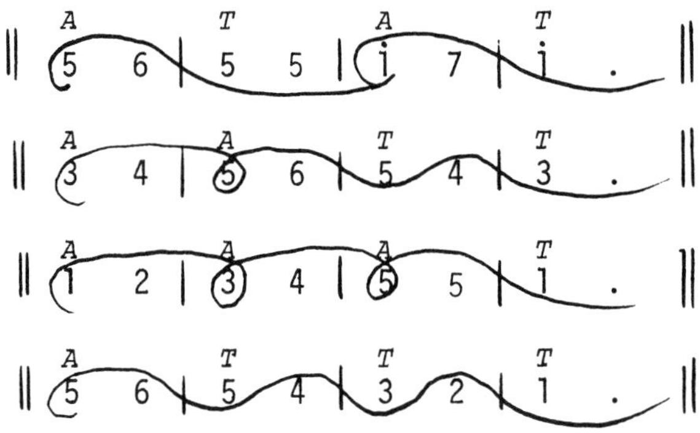

# Dictations

## Ear Tests

121 565 1̇71̇
1̇71̇ 343 12345

121 1̇71̇ 565
1̇71̇ 121 1̇71̇

121 343 565
1 3 5

11 33 44 3
3 5 1̇ 1̇71̇

1 3 5 1̇
1̇ 55 33 1

## Eye Tests

*Using* Intonation Diagram 9 *and* Staff Notation 9, *repeat patterns given under* Ear Tests.

## Rhythmic Dictation

|| A3 . | T1 2 | A3 2 | T1 . ||

|| A5 . | A6 7 | T1̇ . | T5 . ||

|| A3 4 | T3 2 | T1 . | T. 0 ||

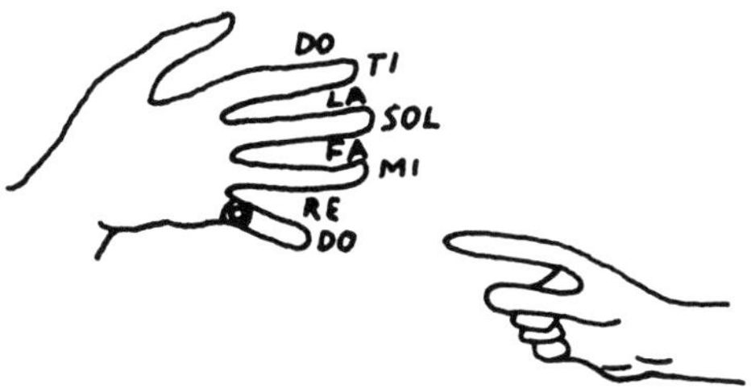


*Teacher may use hand with fingers spread out like lines of a music staff. Ring on finger suggests place of* DO.

*Dictate note-groups as eye tests using this figure.*

# Songs

## Song 42 (1 = F)

|| 3 | 1 3 | 5 4 | 3 2 | 1

3 | 1 3 | 5 6 | 5 . | .

$\dot{1}$ | 5 6 | 5

$\dot{1}$ | 5 4 | 3

4 | 3 2 | 1 2 | 1 . | . ||

## Song 43 (1 = G) *Basque melody*

*Combinations of rhythm patterns. Practise in several lessons without rhythm gestures. Then Bluebirds sing melody, others make gestures.*

*(f + c)* || 3 . | 1 1 | 3 . | 3 . | 4 3 | 2 1 | 2 . | 2 . |

*(f + d)* | 3 . | 1 1 | 3 . | 3 . | 4 3 | 2 3 | 1 . | . 0 |

*(f + c)* | 2 . | 3 4 | 5 . | 5 . | 6 5 | 4 3 | 2 . | 2 . |

*(f + d)* | 3 . | 1 1 | 3 . | 3 . | 4 3 | 2 3 | 1 . | . 0 ||

*Terminate each class with prayer learned in Lesson Sixteen:*

Let us bless the Lord. Thanks be to God. Benedicamus Domino. Deo gratias.

**Goosey, Goosey, Gander** *(1 = F)* *Mother Goose*

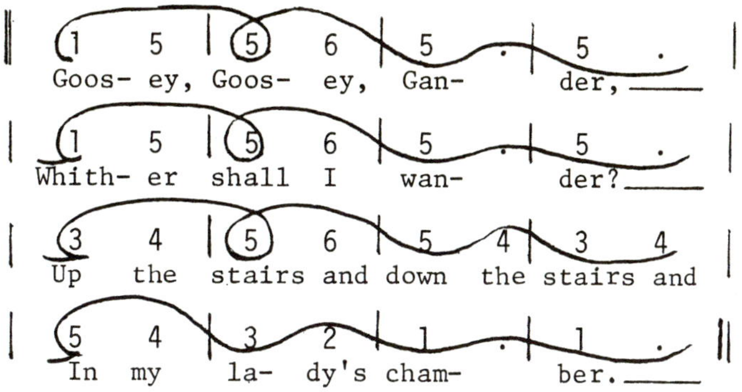


**Hark, Hark, the Dogs Do Bark** *(i = D)* *Mother Goose*

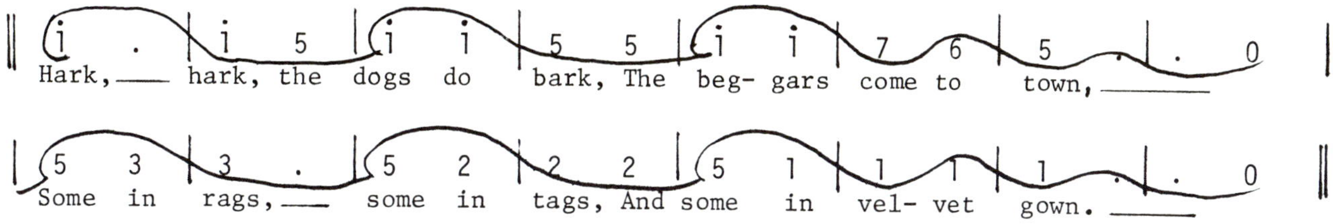

The songs offered at the end of chapters serve to develop the music technique of the children, teaching them to think rhythmically, phraseologically, to observe likenesses and contrasts, to control breath in relation to demand, and thus learn to sing with taste and beauty of tone.

# Chapter Eighteen

| | 1 | 2 | 3 | 4 | 5 |
|---|---|---|---|---|---|
| **Vocal Training** | Greeting and opening song: *Church Bells Ringing*<br>Voc. Ex. 1 Group I 1 = Eb<br>II 1 = D<br>III 1 = G | Work with individuals<br>Voc. Ex. 12 Groups I and II 1 = G | Opening song: *The Father's Love*<br>Check for accuracy of pitch at skip | → <br>→ | |
| **Intonation** | i 7 6 5 4 3 2 1<br>Int. Diag. 9a<br>Int. Ex. 39 a) and b)<br>Second Compass Ex.<br>Groups I and II<br>1 = G → | Int. Ex. 40 a) and b) → | Int. Ex. 41 1 = Eb → | Review: Int. Ex. 39, 40 and 41 in horizontal Number Notation | |
| | KEEP INTONATION DIAGRAM 9a IN FULL VIEW OF CLASS DURING DICTATIONS | | | | |
| **Dictations** Eye Tests | ‖ 1 3 5 . 6 5 5 . ‖ | Staff Notation 5 (pointer)<br>1 3 1 3 5 | ‖ 5 5 5 i . 5 5 . . ‖ | Meas. Gest. i 5 5 3 5 | Hand and fingers as staff<br>i 5 3 5 3 1 |
| **Dictations** Ear Tests | *Nu* 1 3 5 5 3 1<br>1 3 5 3 1 | 1 3 5 3 5<br>5 3 1 3 1 | 1 3 3 5 3<br>1 3 1 3 5 | 1 3 5 i 5<br>1 5 5 3 5 | 1 3 4 3 5<br>5 5 5 i 5 5 |
| **Rhythm** | **Present:** Rhythm Gesture IV – Ternary Rhythm beginning on down-pulse<br>A T A T<br>Teacher sings Song 47 or uses recording on cassette to accompany gesture practise<br>Maintain steady pace – do not rush | | | | **Review:** R. Gesture IV<br>Binary rhythm and ternary rhythm A T A T<br>A A T T |
| **Notation** | **Review:** Staff Notation 6<br>**Transcribe:** Rhythm Patterns Series 9 to Staff Notation | **Transcribe:** Song 46 Lines 3 and 4 to Staff Notation | **Transcribe:** Song 47 Line 1 to Number Notation<br>Notice repeat sign | **Transcribe:** Song 47 Lines 2 and 3<br>Sing entire song with Rhythm Gesture III | **Transcribe:** Song 48 to Staff Notation on board<br>Repeat Sign |
| **Vocal Training** | **Review:** Voc. Ex. 12 on First Compass Ex. | Voc. Ex. 13 ‖ 1 . 3 . 5 . . . 5 4 3 2 1 . . . ‖<br>Practise slowly Bluebirds (I) 1 = A<br>Robins and Sparrows make gesture | | Groups I and II 1 = G<br>Avoid slur at skips | Group III makes gestures |
| **Rhythm** | **Study:** Rhythm Patterns **Series 9** with simple Metrical Gesture and Language<br>**Dictations** | Add Melodication Applications<br>‖ 1 3 5 . i . 5 . ‖ | ‖ 1 2 1 . 3 4 3 . ‖ | ‖ 5 5 5 6 . 5 5 . ‖ | ‖ 1 . 3 5 . . 6 7 i 5 . . ‖ |
| **Creative Activity** | While making Rhythm Gesture IV in binary rhythm, improvise tunes for:<br>‖ I I \| I I \| I . \| I . ‖<br>A A T T<br>A T A A<br>All make gesture | Melodic Applications for Rhythm Series | Improvise a melody for:<br>‖ I I I \| I I I \| I I I \| I . . ‖<br>A T A T | Improvise a melody for:<br>I I I \| I I I \| I I I \| I . . ‖<br>A A T T | Improvise melodies for:<br>‖ I I I \| I I I \| I I I \| I . . ‖<br>A A A T<br>A T T T |
| | | | ALL MAKE GESTURE IV – TERNARY DURING IMPROVISATIONS | | |
| **Songs** | Song 44 or Song 45<br>*Benedicamus Domino*<br>*Deo Gratias* → | *Near to My Woodland Cottage* Last two lines → | *Near to My Woodland Cottage* Lines 1 and 2<br>**Review:** Lines 3 and 4 | Add text<br>If time permits:<br>*Hark, Hark, the Dogs Do Bark* | Song 48<br>If time permits:<br>*Goosey, Goosey, Gander* |

# Chapter Eighteen

## Vocal Training

*Review* Vocal Exercise 1

$\dot{1}$ = D ↘ G ↗ E♭

‖ $\dot{1}$ ______ ‖
Nu ______

*Review* Vocal Exercise 12

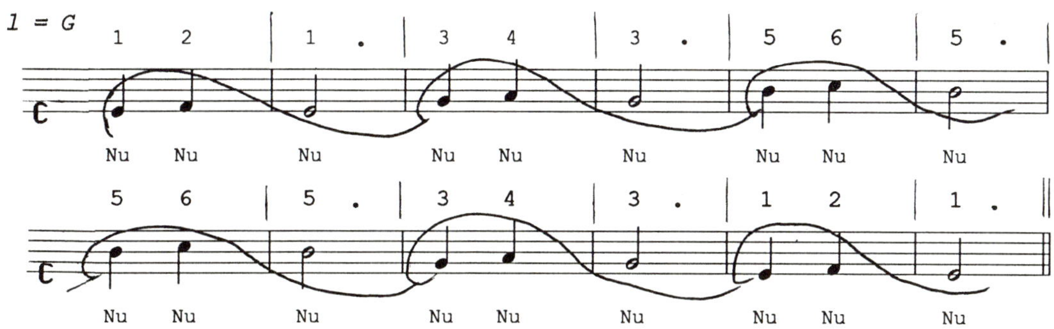


Vocal Exercise 13 *On tonic chord line* DO - MI - SOL. *Should be practised slowly, placing each note accurately as to pitch and carefully as to tonal quality. Practise at first without gesture; then with gesture.*

1 = A ↘ E

‖ 1 . | 3 . | 5 . | . . | 5 4 | 3 2 | 1 . | . . ‖
Nu __ Nu __ Nu ______ Nu Nu Nu Nu Nu ______

When drilling exercises involving skips, teacher must listen for tendency on the part of children to slur tones. This tendency must be checked as soon as it is observed.

# *Intonation*

*Drill on* Second Compass Exercise *with* Diagram 9a

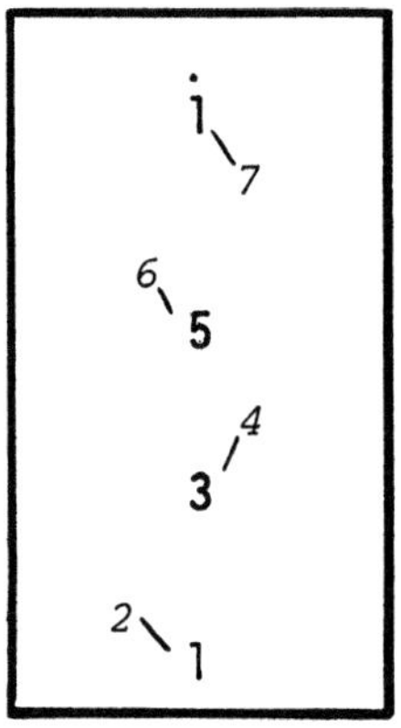


Diagram 9a

As was indicated earlier, it is not necessary to practise an intonation exercise until it can be sung perfectly by the whole class. Each subsequent exercise tends to perfect the one that precedes it. Too much repetition can be tiresome for the children.

## Intonation Exercise 39 *(1 = G )*

*Teacher must be attentive to possible slurring during these intonation exercises as with* Voc. Ex. 13.

| a) | | | | | | b) | | | | | | |
|---|---|---|---|---|---|---|---|---|---|---|---|---|
| 1 | 3 | 5 | 5 | 3 | 1 | 5 | 3 | 1 | 1 | 3 | 5 | |
| 1 | 3 | 5 | *5* | 3 | 1 | 5 | 3 | 1 | *1* | 3 | 5 | |
| 1 | 3 | 5 | | 3 | 1 | 5 | 3 | 1 | | 3 | 5 | 54321 |

## Intonation Exercise 40 *(1 = G )*

| a) | | | | | b) | | | | |
|---|---|---|---|---|---|---|---|---|---|
| 1 | 3 | 5 | 3 | 1 | 5 | 3 | 1 | 3 | 5 |
| 1 | 3 | 5 | 3 | 5 | 5 | 3 | 1 | 3 | 1 |
| 1 | 3 | 3 | 5 | 3 | 5 | 3 | 3 | 1 | 3 |
| 1 | 3 | 5 | 5 | 3 | 5 | 3 | 1 | 1 | 3 |
| 1 | 3 | 1 | 3 | 5 | 5 | 3 | 5 | 3 | 1 |

## Intonation Exercise 41 *(1 = $E^b$)*

*If $E^b$ is not on pitch pipe, teacher blows $B^b$ as* 5 - SOL *and children sing down to* DO *($E^b$) with* Measuring Gesture *or with* Finger Notation.

| | | | | | | | | | | | |
|---|---|---|---|---|---|---|---|---|---|---|---|
| 1 | 3 | 5 | | 5 | $\dot{1}$ | $\dot{1}$ | 5 | 5 | 3 | 1 | |
| 1 | 3 | 5 | $\dot{1}$ | 5 | | $\dot{1}$ | 5 | 5 | 3 | 5 | |
| 1 | 3 | 5 | $\dot{1}$ | 5 | $\dot{1}$ | $\dot{1}$ | 5 | 3 | 5 | 3 | 1 |

*Review these exercises from screen projections or chart, showing exercises in numbers on an horizontal line.*

# Rhythm

## Rhythm Gesture IV - Ternary

*In* Rhythm Gesture IV - Ternary, *each* Arsis *and each* Thesis *has* <u>*three*</u> *pulses instead of two. Teacher gives model while counting softly "one-two-three" for each* A *and each* T. *Gesture ends in a ternary thesis.*

*Practise first in combination as follows, starting on a down-pulse:*

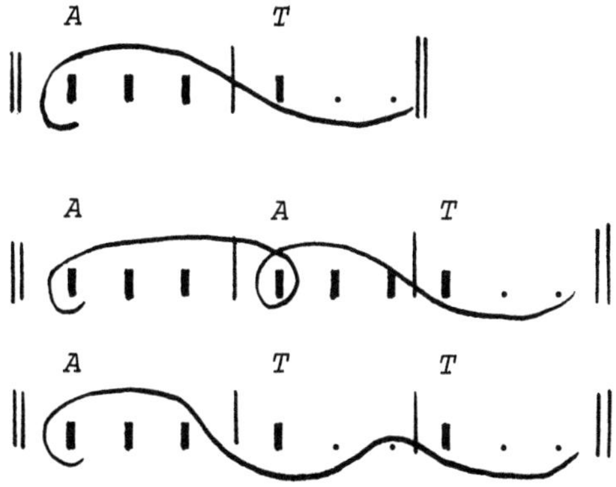


*Succession of two* T*'s in ternary rhythm will present a problem: the lift at the end of the* Thesis *gesture must not be made until the third pulse of the measure * :*

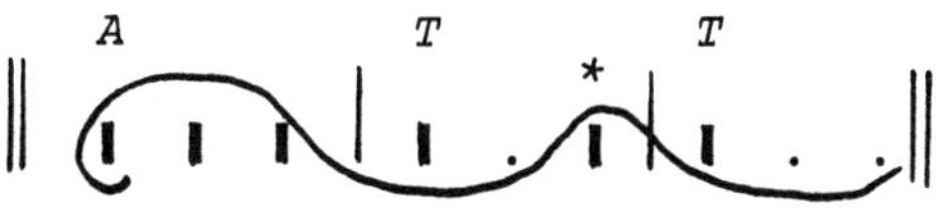


<u>Rhythm Patterns - Series 9</u> *Practise single lines and in combination with other lines as was done in previous chapters.*

<u>*Melodic Application*</u>

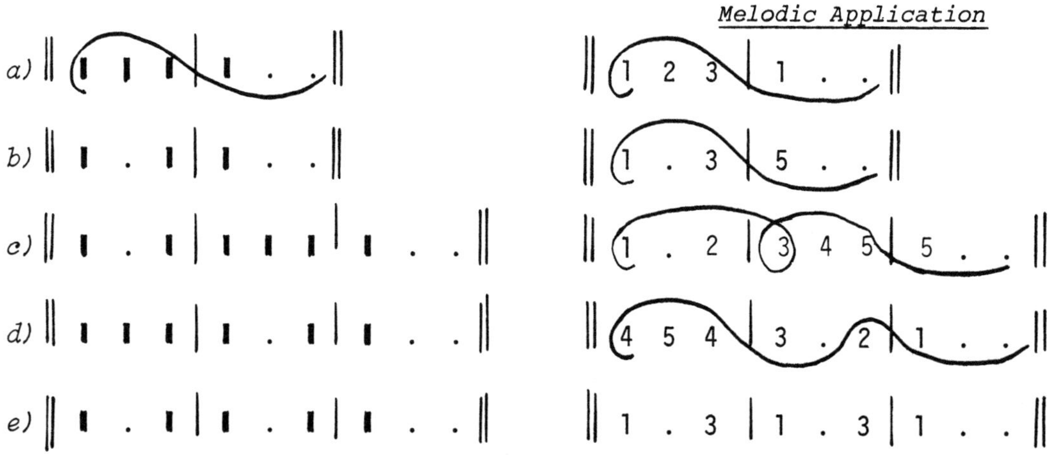

# Notation

Staff Notation 6 *Notation symbols given for transcribing* Rhythm Patterns - Series 9.

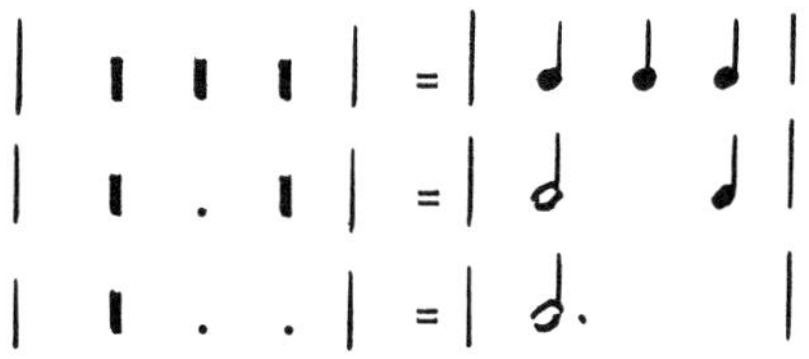

*Transcribe* Song 46 *to* Staff Notation

Staff Notation 11 - Repeat Sign *Double line and two dots at beginning and end of a phrase:* ||: ———— :||

||: 1 2 | 3 5 | 5 . | 4 4 | 3 . | 3 . :||

*Transcribe first line of* Song 47 *to* Number Notation

# Creative Activity

*Continue improvisation of melodies with* Arsis-Thesis *gestures in four-measure patterns as in previous chapter.*

*SUGGESTION concerning rhythm of improvisation.*

*All long notes should be located at beginning of measures. In notation, long notes should always be preceded by a measure bar:*

3 | 1 . | 3 2 | 1 . | .

*Other placements of long notes than at beginning of measures result in syncopations,* that is, temporary displacements of normal rhythm:*

3 | 1 . | 3 *1 | .

*If children sing their melodies softly before writing them down, this problem will often solve itself.*

# Dictations

## Ear Tests

135 531
135 31

13353
13135

135 1̇5
1̇5 535

1 343 5
55 51̇ 55

135 671̇5
4543 121

## Eye Tests

|| 1 3 | 5 . | 6 5 | 5 . ||

*Use* Staff Notation 5

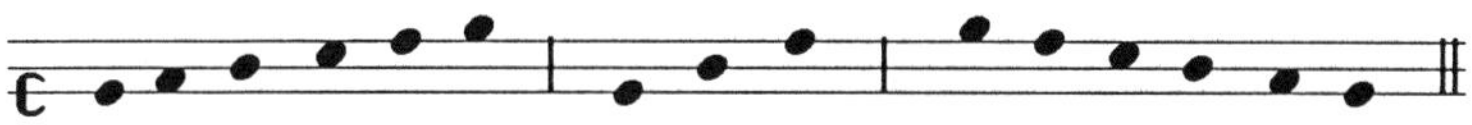

1 3 1 3 5

5 3 1 3 1

1̇ 5 5 3 5

1̇ 5 3 5 3 1

|| 1 2 | 1 . | 3 4 | 3 . |
| 5 6 | 5 4 | 3 . | 2 . ||

|| 5 5 5 | 1̇ . 5 | 5 . . ||

## Rhythmic Dictations

|| 1 3 | 5 . | 1̇ . | 5 . ||

|| 1 2 3 | 1 2 3 | 1 . . ||

|| 1 2 3 | 1 . 3 | 1 . . ||

|| 5 5 5 | 6 . 5 | 5 . . ||

|| 1 . 3 | 5 . . | 6 7 1̇ | 5 . . ||

# Songs

## Song 44 (1 = G)

*Application of Rhythm Patterns to melody for* Rhythm Gesture IV-Binary.

|| 1 2 | 3 4 | 3 . | . . |

| 3 4 | 5 6 | 5 . | . . |

| 5 6 | 5 6 | 5 . | . . |

| 3 2 | 1 2 | 1 . | . . ||

## Song 46 (1 = G)

*Application of Rhythm Patterns to melody for* Rhythm Gesture IV-Ternary.

|| 1 . 2 | 3 . . |

| 3 . 4 | 3 . 2 | 3 . . |

| 1 . 2 | 3 . . |

| 3 . 4 | 3 . 2 | 1 . . ||

## Song 45 ($\dot{1}$ = $E^b$)

*If* $E^b$ *is not on pitch pipe, teacher blows* $B^b$ *as* SOL. *Children sing* 54321 *down to* $E^b$ *with* Measuring Gesture.

|| 1 2 | 1 . | 3 4 | 3 . |

| 5 6 | 5 4 | 3 . | 2 . |

| 3 4 | 3 . | 5 6 | 5 . |

| 6 5 | 6 7 | $\dot{1}$ . | $\dot{1}$ . |

| $\dot{1}$ 7 | $\dot{1}$ . | 5 6 | 5 . |

| $\dot{1}$ $\dot{1}$ | 7 6 | 5 . | 5 . |

| 3 4 | 3 . | 5 6 | 5 . |

| 3 4 | 3 2 | 1 . | 1 . ||

## Song 47 (1 = G) *Review* Rhythm Gesture III

*French Folk Melody*

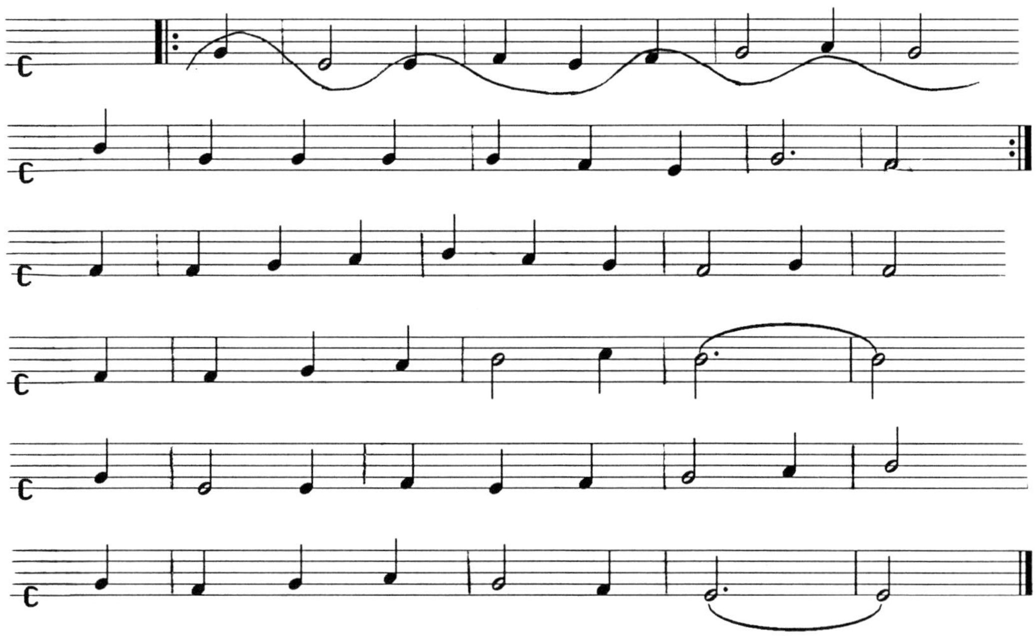

**Song 48** *(1 = G)* *Spanish Folk Song*

‖: 1 2 | 3 5 | 5 . | 4 4 | 3 . | 3 . :‖

| 5 4 | 3 . | 2 . | 3 5 | 5 4 | 3 . | . . ‖

**Near to My Woodland Cottage** *(i̇ = E$^b$)* *French Folk Song*

‖ 5 5 5 | 6 . 5 | 5 . 3 |
Near to my wood- land cot- tage,

| 5 5 5 | 6 . 5 | 5 . . |
Lis-ten, for hear you may______

| 5 5 5 | i̇ . 5 | 5 . 3 | 3 2 3 | 5 . 3 | 2 . . |
Night-in gales soft- ly sing- ing, Sing-ing both night and day______

| 1 . 3 | 5 . . | 6 7 i̇ | 5 . . |
Hear their song, their pret-ty song,

| 4 5 4 | 3 . 2 | 1 . . | . 0 0 ‖
In the sweet month of May.______

# Chapter Nineteen

## Vocal Training

*Review* Vocal Exercise 1

$\dot{1}$ = D \ / E, G

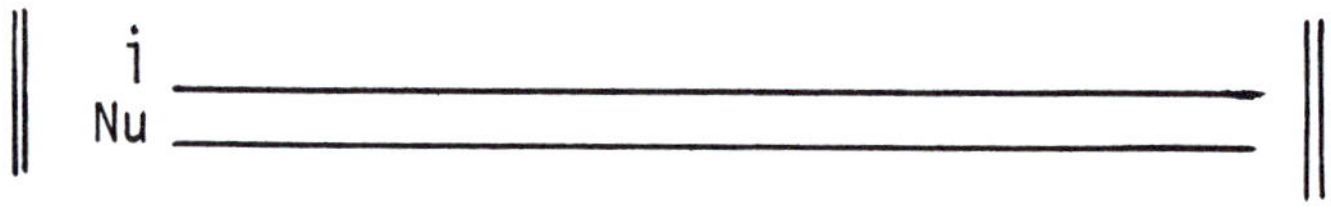


*Review* Vocal Exercise 13

$1 = A^b$

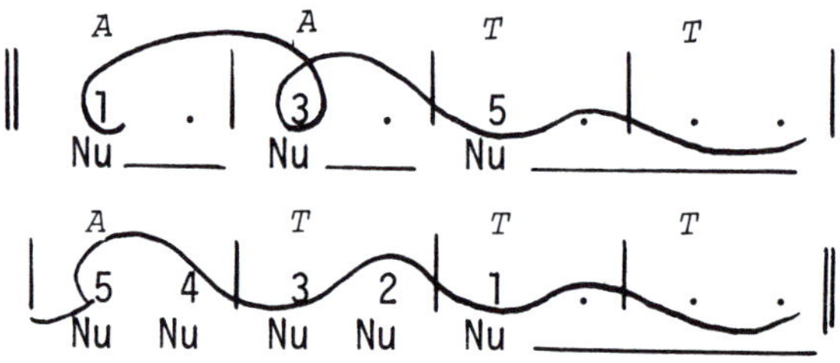


Vocal Exercise 14

$1 = A^b$

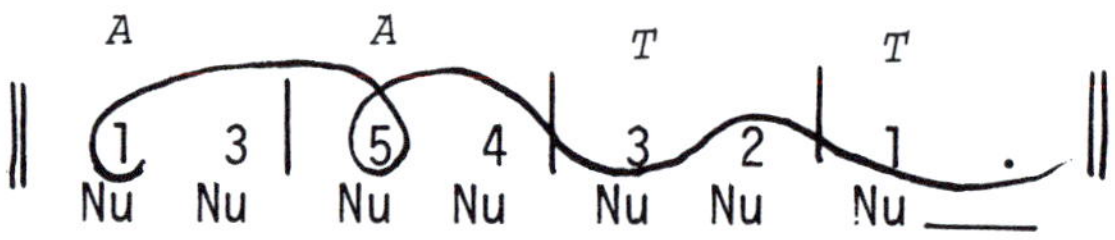


*More practise on the tonic chord. Continue to observe clear attacks on notes separated by wide skips.*

# Intonation

Diagrams 9b and 9c.

*Continuation of drills on tonic chord emphasizing the skips:* 1 - 5, 5 - 1, 1 - 1̇, 1̇ - 1.

*Practise exercises on both diagrams given.*

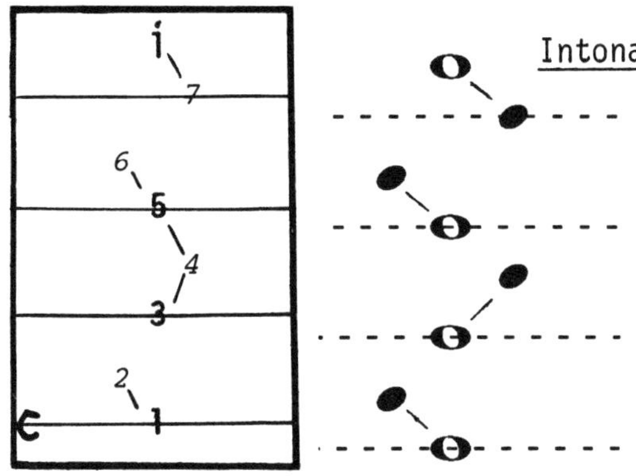


Diagram 9b

Intonation Exercise 42 *(1 = G)*

| a) | | | | | | b) | | | | | |
|---|---|---|---|---|---|---|---|---|---|---|---|
| 1 | 3 | 5 | 5 | 3 | 1 | 5 | 3 | 1 | 1 | 3 | 5 |
| 1 | 3 | 5 | 5 | *3* | 1 | 5 | *3* | 1 | 1 | 3 | 5 |
| 1 | 3 | 5 | 5 | | 1 | 5 | | 1 | 1 | 3 | 5 |
| 1 | *3* | 5 | 5 | | 1 | 5 | | 1 | 1 | *3* | 5 |
| 1 | | 5 | . | | 1 | 5 | | 1 | . | | 5 |

Intonation Exercise 43 *(1 = $E^b$)*

a)

| | | | | | | | |
|---|---|---|---|---|---|---|---|
| 1 | 3 | 5 | 1̇ | 1̇ | 5 | 3 | 1 |
| 1 | *3* | 5 | 1̇ | 1̇ | 5 | *3* | 1 |
| 1 | *3* | *5* | 1̇ | 1̇ | *5* | *3* | 1 |

Diagram 9c

b)

| | | | | | | | |
|---|---|---|---|---|---|---|---|
| 1 | | 5 | 1 | 1 | 5 | | 1̇ |
| 1 | | 5 | 3 | 3 | 5 | | 1̇ |
| 1̇ | | 5 | 3 | 3 | 5 | | 1 |

*Drills in* Eye Tests *and* Ear Tests *will help to assimilate concepts of large skips on tonic chord line.*

Ear Tests

1 3 5 5 1 | 1 5 1 1̇
5 1 1 3 5 | 1 3 5 3 1 1̇

1 2 1 1 5 5 | 1 1̇ 5 1̇
5 1 1 2 3 4 5 | 1 1̇ 1̇ 1

1 5 5 6 7 1̇
1 5 5 1̇

Eye Tests

1 5 5 3 1
1 5 5 1

*On* Diagram 9c

1 3 5 3 5
5 3 1 3 1
1 5 3 5 3 1
5 5 5 1̇ 5 5

# Rhythm

Rhythm Patterns - Series 9 *Continued*

MELODIC APPLICATION

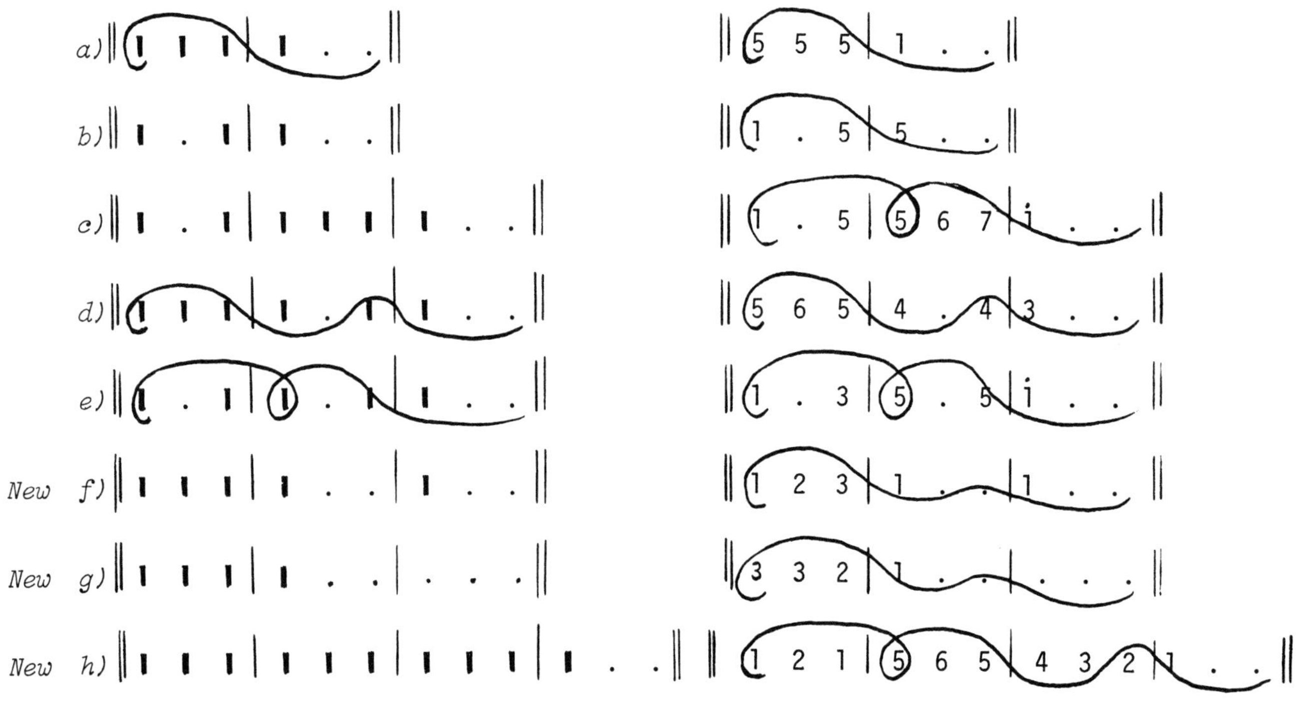


*Note especially the new pattern at g) for practise in singing long tones.*

*Teacher will plan to combine patterns for drills. For example:*

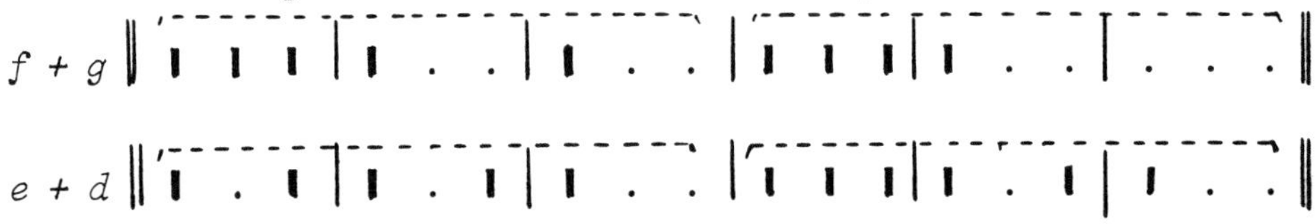


Rhythmic Dictation

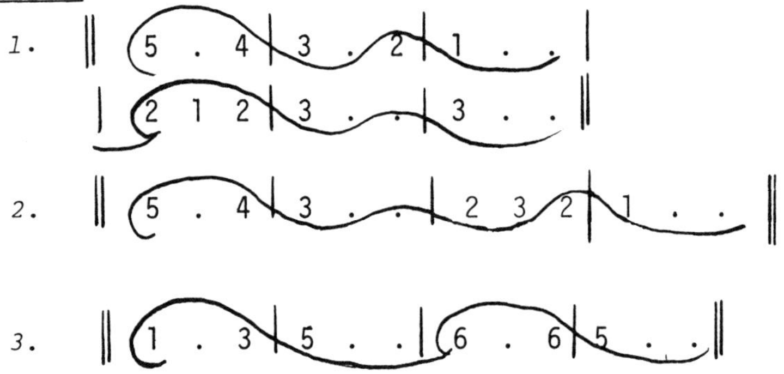

Melodic Application of Rhythm Patterns as a Four-line Song.

| | | | | | | | | | | | | | | | | | |
|---|---|---|---|---|---|---|---|---|---|---|---|---|---|---|---|---|---|
| *e + f* | 5 | . | 4 | 3 | . | 2 | 1 | . | . | 2 | 1 | 2 | 3 | . | . | 3 | . | . |
| *e + g* | 5 | . | 4 | 3 | . | 4 | 5 | . | . | 6 | . | 6 | 5 | . | . | . | . | . |
| *e + f* | 5 | . | 6 | 5 | . | 4 | 3 | . | . | 2 | 3 | 2 | 1 | . | . | 2 | . | . |
| *e + g* | 3 | . | 4 | 5 | . | 4 | 3 | . | . | 2 | 1 | 2 | 1 | . | . | . | . | . |

# *Notation*

Staff Notation 12 *The* Tie *for notes of equal pulse values.*

1. *Transcribe rhythm patterns of this chapter, especially f) and g); others in combinations.*

*Place correct staff note beneath rhythm strokes.*

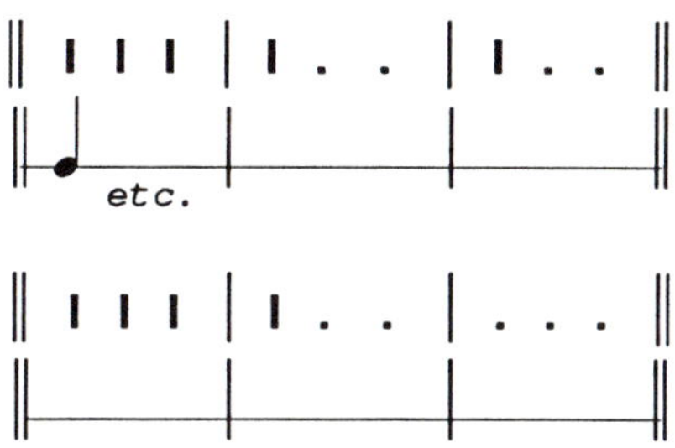


2. *Transcribe first line of* Song 51 *to* Number Notation.

## Creative Activity

Technique of Rhythmic Enlargement
Improvisation of Melodies to Rhythm Patterns

*1.*

*To show how variety can be achieved in a musical composition, the teacher demonstrates the effect of "rhythmic enlargement." At some point in the melody, selected tones are repeated and lengthened.*

*Examples*

*1.* ‖ 1 2 | ③ ④ | 3 . ‖
‖ 1 2 | 3 . | 4 . | 3 . ‖

*2.* ‖ 3 4 | ③ ② | 1 . ‖
‖ 3 4 | 3 . | 2 . | 1 . ‖

*3.* ‖ 1 . 2 | ③ 4 ③ | 2 . . | 1 . . ‖
‖ 1 . 2 | 3 . 4 | 3 . . | 2 . 0 ‖

*Sing each pair of melodies several times, so that children come to understand what takes place and feel the musical effect of the rhythmic transformation.*

*2.* Improvisation

*Place h) of* Rhythm Patterns - Series 9 *on board. Invite children to improvise melodies to each* Arsis - Thesis *keeping in mind that when the melody rises,* Arsis *is called for; when the melody descends,* Thesis *is indicated.*

*Examples given are for the teacher's use.*

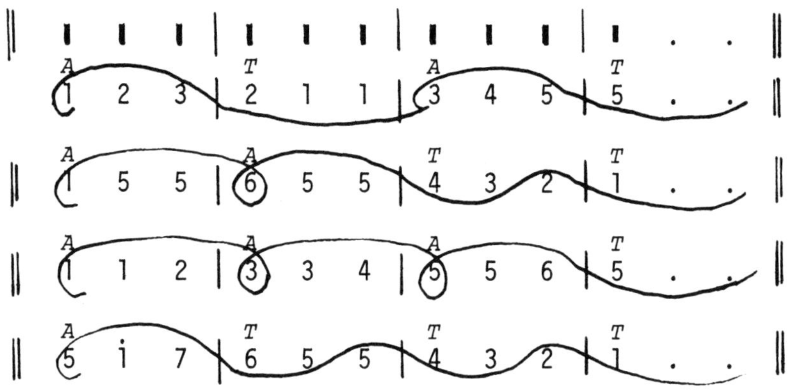

# Songs

**Song 49** ($\dot{1} = E^b$) *Notice the repeat sign*

‖: 1 3 | 5 . | $\dot{1}$ . | 5 . | 5 $\dot{1}$ | 5 4 | 3 2 | 1 . :‖

**Song 50** ($\dot{1} = E^b$) *French Folk Song*

| | | | | | | | | | | | |
|---|---|---|---|---|---|---|---|---|---|---|---|
| $\dot{1}$ | $\dot{1}$ | $\dot{1}$ | 7 | 7 | 7 | 6 | 7 | $\dot{1}$ | 5 | . | . |
| 4 | 4 | 4 | 3 | 3 | 3 | 2 | 2 | 2 | 1 | . | . |
| 1 | 2 | 3 | 1 | 2 | 3 | 1 | 2 | 3 | 4 | . | . |
| 2 | 3 | 4 | 2 | 3 | 4 | 2 | 3 | 4 | 5 | . | . |
| $\dot{1}$ | 7 | 6 | 5 | 4 | 3 | 2 | 1 | 2 | 1 | . | . |

**Song 51** (1 = G) *German Folk Song*

*This song in staff notation will require some preparation. Draw attention to first and second endings. Explain that after repeating first part, the "box" at 1 is skipped over and "we land in box at 2."*

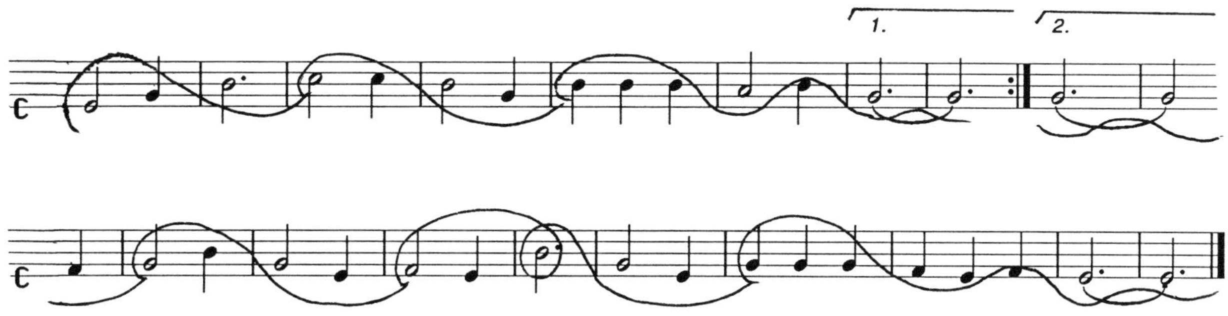

**For the Gift of Daily Bread** *($\dot{1}$ = E)* *German Folk Song*

‖ 1 1 | 3 3 | 5 5 | 3 . | 4 4 | 3 2 | 3 . | 2 . |
For the gift of dai- ly bread,__ Dear-est Lord, we thank__ you.__

| 1 1 | 3 3 | 5 5 | 3 . | 1 2 | 3 1 | 2 . | 1 . |
For your bless- ings on us shed,__ Dear-est Lord, we thank__ you.__

| 2 3 | 4 3 | 2 3 | 4 . | 3 4 | 5 4 | 3 4 | 5 . |
For the joy of songs to sing,__ For your love and ev'- ry- thing,__

| $\dot{1}$ 5 | 4 3 | 2 . | 1 . ‖
Dear- est Lord, we thank__ you.__

# Chapter Twenty

## Vocal Training

*Attack high pitch neatly from above to avoid "scooping." A crisp "N" will help to make clear attack.*

*Review* <u>Vocal Exercise 1</u> *1 = D, A, E*

|| 1 ——— ||
|| Nu ——— ||

<u>Vocal Exercise 15</u> *1 = G, A*

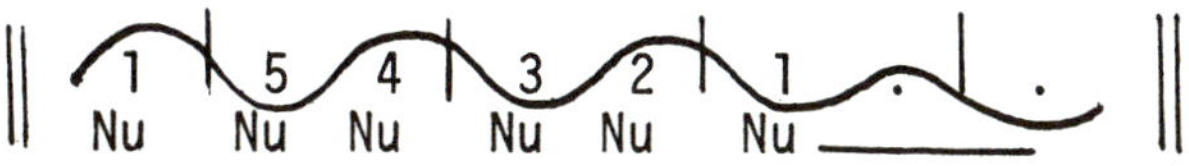


## Intonation

Third Compass Exercise

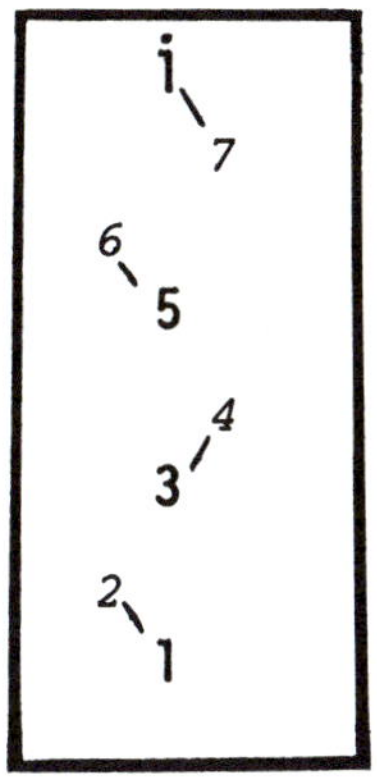


Diagram 9a

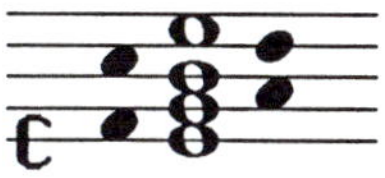

Diagram 9c

<u>Intonation Exercise 44</u> *($1 = E^{b}$) With* Diagrams 9a *and* 9c

| 121 | 343 | 565 | 1̇71̇ | 1̇71̇ | 565 | 343 | 121 |
|---|---|---|---|---|---|---|---|
| *121* | *343* | *565* | *1̇71̇* | *1̇71̇* | *565* | *343* | *121* |
| 21 | 43 | 65 | 71̇ | 71̇ | 65 | 43 | 21 |

*This exercise too, depends on <u>thinking the help tones</u>. Full attention is required to hear a tone that is not sung.*

*Practise procedure:*

*<u>Line 1.</u> Bluebirds and Robins sing straight across.*

*<u>Line 2.</u> Bluebirds sing small notes; Robins sing large notes.*

*<u>Repeat Line 2.</u> One child sings small notes softly. Bluebirds and Robins sing large notes.*

*<u>Repeat Line 2.</u> Bluebirds sing large notes and <u>think</u> small notes. Robins repeat. Sparrows listen. Teacher must allow time for <u>thinking</u> tones.*

*<u>Line 3.</u> Bluebirds and Robins sing large notes.*

<u>Ear Tests</u> *"Listen!"*

1 5 1 1̇ | 121 21 343
1 1̇ 5 5 1̇ | 343 43 565

1 21 43 65 | 1̇71̇ 65 71̇
65 71̇ 71̇ | 1 5 65 71̇

1 3 5 1̇
21 43 65 71̇

<u>Eye Tests</u> *"Look and Remember!"*

121 1̇71̇ 1 | 2211 443
1 1̇ 343 | 44 3 665

1̇71̇ 65 43 | 51 1̇1̇5
43 665 71̇ | 53 665 71̇

Use red end of pointer for <u>think</u> tones and Eye Tests.

# Rhythm

Rhythm Gesture IV - Binary *and review of* Rhythm Patterns - Series 7 *with Melodic Application*

## Rhythm Patterns - Series 7 *(Review)*

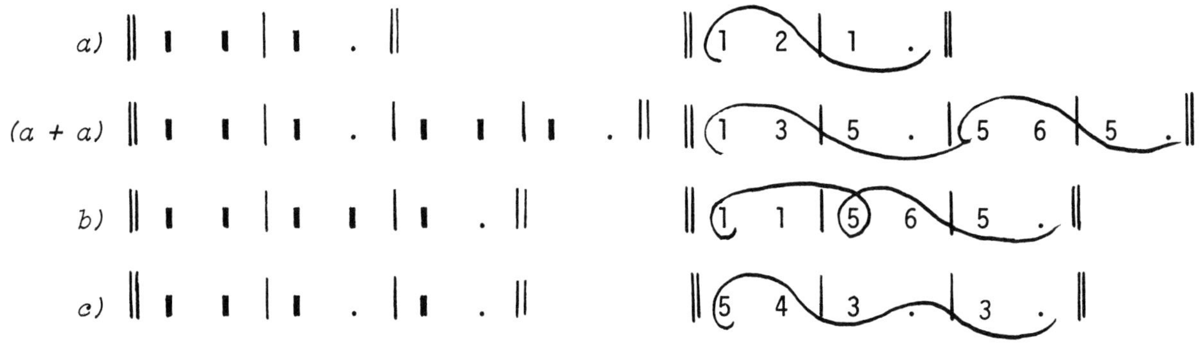


## Rhythm Gesture IV - Binary *(Review)*

**Dictation** *Teacher sings one of the melodic applications given below. Children determine how many* A*'s and* T*'s in the phrase. They also try to select rhythm patterns used. One child adds rhythm on board; another the melody. Teacher adds rhythm curve. Bluebirds and Robins sing while Sparrows make gesture.*

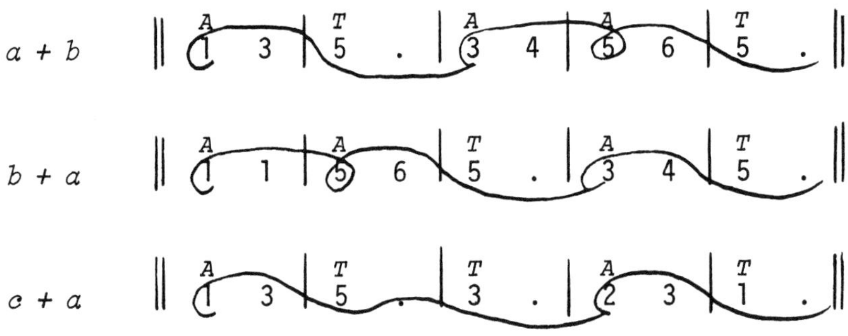

# Notation

<u>Staff Notation 17</u> *Practise in transcribing from* Staff Notation *to* Number Notation.

*Teacher shows melody on board, then extends bar lines by adding dotted lines below staff as measures for the numbers. Children - especially Sparrows - suggest correct numbers orally for notes on staff.*

*All children say notes using* Metrical Gesture.
*Bluebirds and Robins sing notes while Sparrows make gesture.*
*Bluebirds and Robins sing notes and all make* Rhythm Gesture IV.

*In the same way, transcribe single lines from staff song given at end of this chapter.*

# Creative Activity

*Review* Rhythm Patterns - Series 7 Binary

*Work consists in finding new melodic applications for rhythm patterns in combination: Melodies given are only suggestions.*

*a + b* || 1̇ 7 | 1̇ . | 5 5 | 6 7 | 1̇ . ||

*b + c* || 1 3 | 5 5 | 1̇ . | 5 6 | 5 . | 5 . ||

*c + a* || 3 2 | 1 . | 1 . | 5 5 | 3 . ||

*a + a* || 5 6 | 5 . | 5 5 | 1̇ . ||

*c + c* || 5 4 | 3 . | 5 . | 3 2 | 1 . | 1 . ||

*Use upper tetrachord* 1̇765 *as well as pentachord* 12345 *for melodies.*

# *Songs*

## Twinkle, Twinkle, Little Star (1 = G) *Folk Song*

*Practise melody alone. Then recite words rhythmically for several lessons before putting words and melody together.*

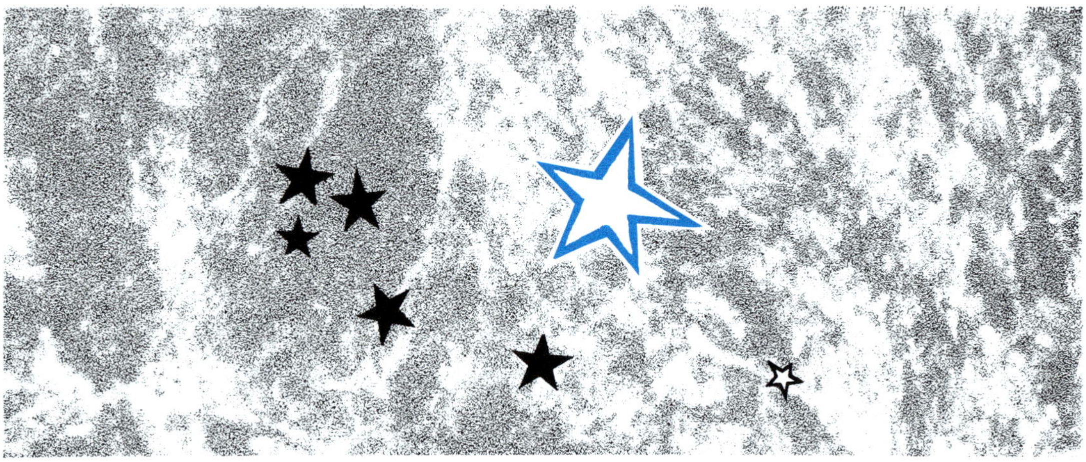

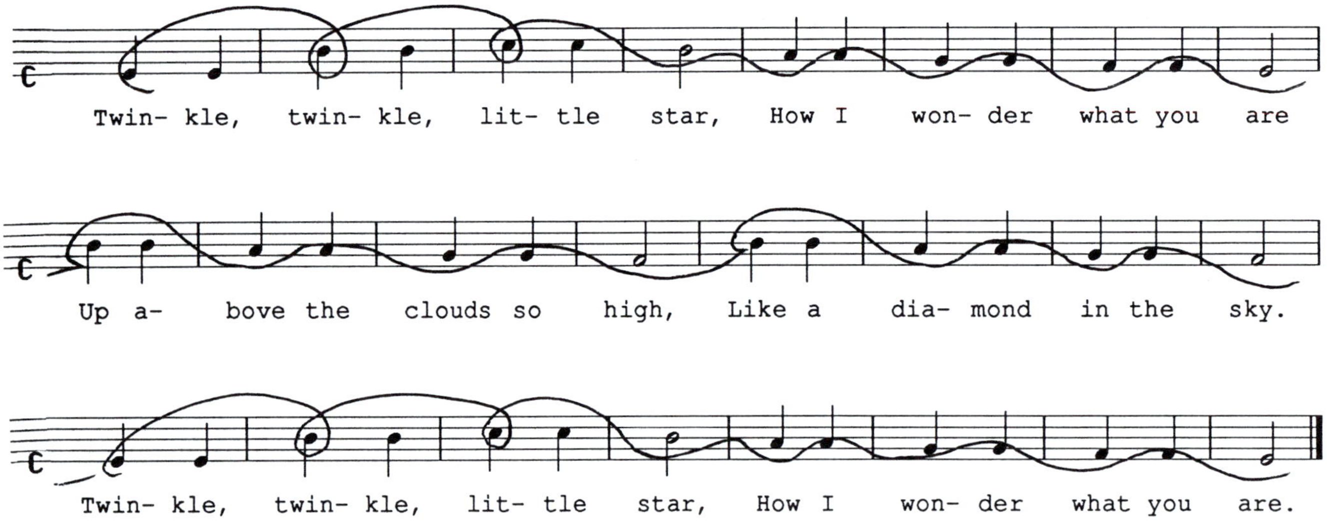

**Song 52** *(1 = G)*

A T A T A T

‖ 1 5 | 5 . | 5 4 | 3 4 | 5 6 | 5 . ‖

**Where Abideth Charity and Love** *(1 = A)* *Gregorian Chant*

‖: 1 1 | 2 3 | 3 2 | 3 4 | 3 2 | 3 2 |
Where a- bid- eth___ char- i- ty and love,___

| 1 1 | 1 2 | 2 . | 0 0 :‖ 1 . | 1 . ‖
God is ev- er there.___ A- men.___

**How Do You Like to Go Up in a Swing?** *(i̇ = E♭)* *Robert Louis Stevenson*

*Robert L. Stevenson*

‖ 1 1 2 | 3 3 4 | 5 5 6 | 5 . . |
How do you like to go up in a swing,___

| 3 3 4 | 5 6 7 | i̇ . . | . . . |
Up in the air___ so blue? ___

| i̇ 7 6 | 5 5 5 | i̇ 7 6 | 5 . . |
O, I do think it's the pleas-ant - est thing___

| 3 4 5 | 3 . 2 | 1 . . | . . . ‖
Ev- er a child___ can do. ___

# Chapter Twenty One

## Vocal Training

*Review* Vocal Exercise 1

$\dot{1}$ = D \ A / E

‖ $\dot{1}$ ——— ‖
Nu ———

*Review* Vocal Exercise 15

1 = G / A

‖ 1 | 5 4 | 3 2 | 1 | . | . ‖
Nu Nu Nu Nu Nu Nu ———

## Intonation

*Combines horizontal and vertical reading in* Number *and* Staff Notation *with* Diagrams 10a *and* 10b.

| | |
|---|---|
| 5 | 6 |
| | 4 |
| 3 | |
| | 2 |
| 1 | |

Diagram 10a

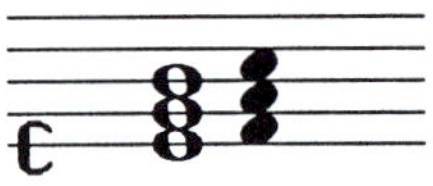

Diagram 10b

Intonation Exercise 45 *(1 = G)*

*Contains fragments of* Second *and* Third Compass Exercises. *"Help" notes are necessary in early training of children. Teacher takes only two or three lines at a time.*

| | | | | | | | | | | |
|---|---|---|---|---|---|---|---|---|---|---|
| 1 | 2 | 3 | 1 | 2 | | 1 | | 34 | | 3 |
| 1 | 3 | 5 | 1 | | 34 | | 3 | | 56 | 5 |
| 1 | 3 | 5 | 1 | | | | 3 | | 6 | 5 |
| | | | | | | | | | | |
| 5 | 3 | 5 | 5 | 4 | 3 | | | | 56 | 5 |
| 5 | 3 | 5 | 5 | | 3 | | | | 56 | 5 |
| | | | | | | | | | | |
| 3 | 1 | 5 | 3 | 2 | 1 | | | | 56 | 5 |
| 3 | 1 | 5 | 3 | | 1 | | | | 56 | 5 |
| 3 | 5 | 1 | 3 | *5* | 6 | | | 5 | *32* | 1 |

*Sing "help" notes - Think "help" notes - Omit "help" notes*

Intonation Exercise 46 *(1 = G)* *Discovering* RE- FA - LA *as stopping places.*

Fourth Compass Exercise

| | | | | | | | | | | | | | | | | | |
|---|---|---|---|---|---|---|---|---|---|---|---|---|---|---|---|---|---|
| 1 | 2 | 1 | 2 | 1 | 4 | 3 | 6 | 5 | 6 | 5 | 4 | 3 | 2 | 1 | 1 | 2 | 1 |
| 1 | 2 | 1 | 2 | *1* | 4 | *3* | 6 | *5* | 6 | *5* | 4 | *3* | 2 | *1* | 1 | 2 | 1 |
| 1 | 2 | 1 | 2 | | 4 | | 6 | | 6 | | 4 | | 2 | | 1 | 2 | 1 |

*Memorize last line.*

*For practise in vertical reading use* Diagram 9c. *For practise in oblique reading use* Diagram 11.

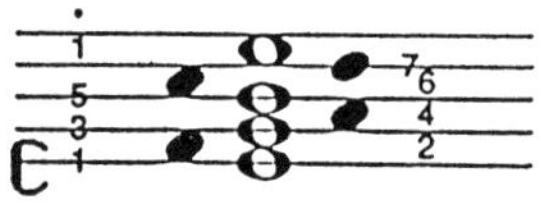


Diagram 9c

*Review* Intonation Exercise 34 *(1 = F)*

First Compass Exercise *(With* Diagram 11*)*

| 121 | 123 | 343 | 345 | 565 | 565 | 543 | 343 | 321 | 121 |
|---|---|---|---|---|---|---|---|---|---|
| 121 | *123* | 343 | *345* | 565 | 565 | *543* | 343 | *321* | 121 |
| 121 | | 343 | | 565 | 565 | | 343 | | 121 |

*Review* Intonation Exercise 35 *(1̇ = E♭)*

First Compass Exercise (Upper Tetrachord)

| 1̇71̇ | 1̇765 | 565 | 565 | 5671̇ | 1̇71̇ |
|---|---|---|---|---|---|
| 1̇71̇ | *1̇765* | 565 | 565 | *5671̇* | 1̇71̇ |
| 1̇71̇ | | 565 | 565 | | 1̇71̇ |

*Review* Intonation Exercise 38 *(1 = E♭)*

Second Compass Exercise *(*Diagrams 9c *and* 11*)*

| 121 | 343 | 565 | 1̇71̇ | 1̇71̇ | 565 | 343 | 121 |
|---|---|---|---|---|---|---|---|
| 1*21* | *343* | *565* | 1̇*71̇* | 1̇*71̇* | *565* | *343* | 1*21* |
| 1 | 3 | 5 | 1̇ | 1̇ | 5 | 3 | 1 |

# Dictations

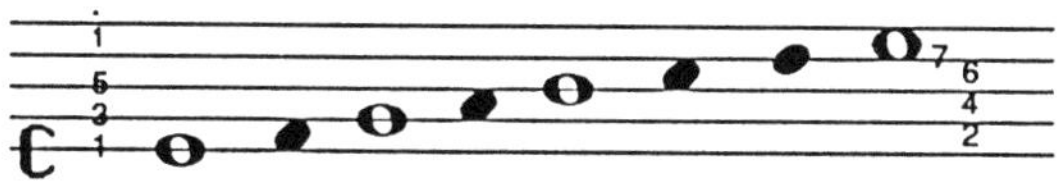


Diagram 11

Ear Tests *(With* Diagram 11*)*

151 1 121 | 21 343 | 1 21 43 65
115 51 343 | 43 565 | 65 71̇ 71̇

1̇71̇ 65 71̇ | 1 3 5 1̇
1 5 65 71̇ | 21 43 65 71̇

Eye Tests *(With* Diagrams 9c *and* 11*)*

121 1̇71̇ 1 | 2211 443 | 1̇71̇ 65 43 |
1 1 343 | 44 3 665 | 43 665 71̇ |

51 115 |
53 665 71̇ |

|| 2 2 | 1 1 | 2 . | 1 . ||
|| 4 3 | 3 3 | 4 . | 3 . ||

# *Creative Activity*

1. *Review* Rhythm Patterns - Series 9 *(See Chapter Nineteen)*

*Work consists in finding new melodic applications for ternary rhythm patterns in combination.*

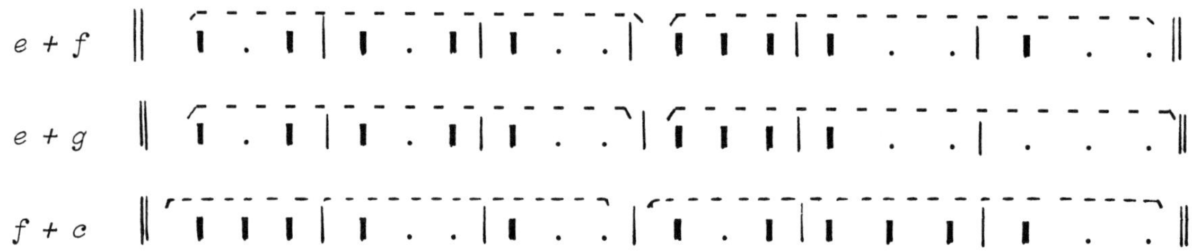


2. *Technique of* Rhythmic Enlargement *continued*

*Teacher writes a rhythm pattern on board taken from a line of a song studied, for example: "Twinkle, Twinkle, Little Star."*

*Children suggest a new melodic application:*

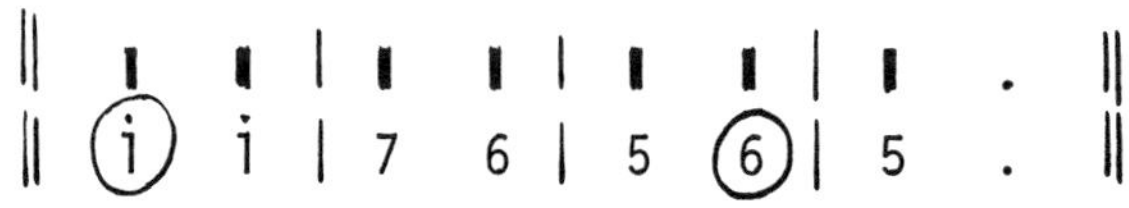

*Double time values of several single-pulse notes as shown in circles:*

‖ i̇ . | i̇ 7 | 6 5 | 6 . | 5 . ‖

*To make a longer melody, select two rhythm patterns; make new melodic application; repeat process of rhythmic enlargement, that is, notes in circles are lengthened. Sing with simple gesture.*

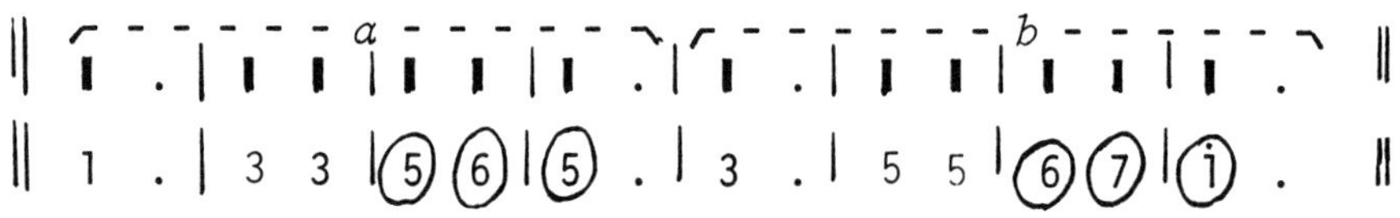

*a)* 1 . | 3 3 | 5 . | 6 . | 5 . | . . |

*b)* 3 . | 5 5 | 6 . | 7 . | i̇ . | . . ‖

*Select other patterns and repeat.*

# Songs

**Song 53** *Melodic Application of Third Compass Exercise.* Rhythm Gesture III.

(1 = G)

‖ 2 | 1 . 2 | 1 . 4 | 3 . . | . 0
2 | 1 . 4 | 3 . 6 | 5 . . | . 0
6 | 5 . 4 | 3 . 6 | 5 . . | . 0
6 | 5 . 4 | 3 . 2 | 1 . . | . 0 ‖

## O How We Love the Month of May

*French Singing Game*

*French Singing Game*
*Divide class into two groups of singers:*
*Group I - Sing with* Rhythm Gesture II;
*Group II- Sing with* Rhythm Gesture IV - Binary

(1̇ = E)

*(Notice the repeat signs.)*

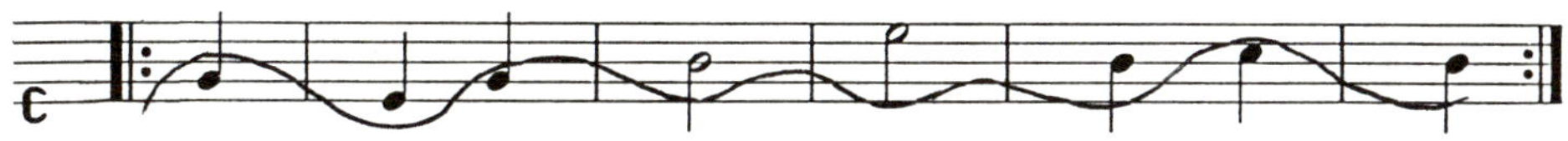

O how we love the month of May
When we go out to sing and play;

To sing and dance out in the sun Is

just the time for hav- ing fun.

Month of May, ev'- ry day, Sing and dance out in the sun;
Month of May, ev'- ry day, Just the time for hav- ing

fun. ——

**Song 54** *(1 = G)* *Santa Catalina – Spanish Folk Song*

**Now That Daylight Fills the Sky** *(1 = F)* *Gregorian Chant*

|| 3 | 1 3 | 5 5 | 6 4 | 5
Now that the day- light fills the sky,

5 | 6 4 | 5 4 | 3 2 | 3 . | .
We lift our hearts to God on high, ______

5 | 4 2 | 3 4 | 3 2 | 1
That He, in all we do or say,

1 | 3 4 | 5 4 | 3 2 | 3 . | . ||
Would keep us free from harm to- day. ______

# Chapter Twenty-Two

## Vocal Training

*Review* Vocal Exercise 1

*1 = D \ G / E*

‖ 1 ——————— ‖
Nu ———————

*Review* Vocal Exercise 15

*1 = A \ F / B♭*

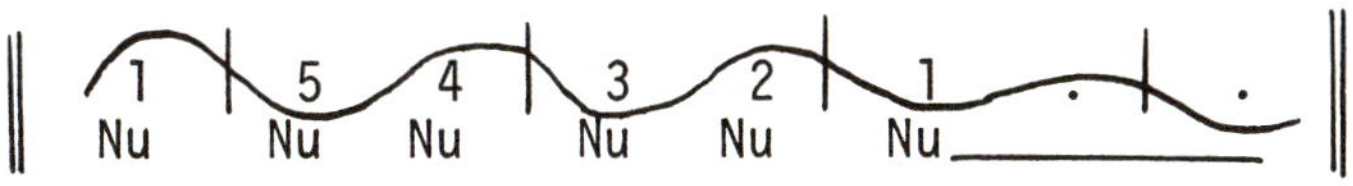


## Intonation

*Having memorized last line of* Fourth Compass Exercise *in Lesson Twenty-One, children are ready for drills on* Diagrams 10a *and* 10b. *Practise as follows:*

| | | |
|---|---|---|
| *Up one column and down the other:* | 1 3 5<br>2 4 6 | 6 4 2<br>5 3 1 |
| *Repeat last note of each column:* | 1 3 5 5<br>2 4 6 6 | 6 4 2 2<br>5 3 1 1 |
| *Repeat middle note of each column:* | 1 3 3 5<br>2 4 4 6 | 6 4 4 2<br>5 3 3 1 |

| | |
|---|---|
| 5 | 6 |
| | 4 |
| 3 | |
| | 2 |
| 1 | |

Diagram 10a

Diagram 10b

Intonation Exercise 47 *(1 = A) Continue to deal with fragments of* Third *and* Fourth Compass Exercises, *establishing relationship between strong* (1 3 5) *and weak* (2 4 6) *tones.*

| a) | | b) | |
|---|---|---|---|
| 1 2 3 | 4 2 1 | 3 4 5 | 4 2 3 |
| 1 3 | 4 2 1 | 3 5 | 4 2 3 |
| 1 3 | 2 4 3 | 5 3 | 4 2 3 |
| 3 1 | 2 4 3 | 5 3 | 2 4 3 |

Intonation Exercise 48 *(1 = G)*

| | |
|---|---|
| 1 3 5 | 6 5 4 3 |
| 1 3 5 | 6 4 3 |
| 1 3 5 | 4 5 6 5 |
| 1 3 5 | 4 6 5 4 3 |
| 1 3 5 | 6 4 5 6 5 |

> Where there are skips from one weak note to another, do not hesitate to supply strong note as a "help" note. Thus, for 2 4 6 or 6 4 2, supply 5 before 6 so that intervals can be sung on pitch.

# Rhythm

## Aural Training in Rhythm

*In this chapter, a beginning is made in an important aspect of ear training. By successive steps, the teacher will lead the children to discover the rhythmic character of a melody solely by hearing it.*

*Step One. Rhythm determined by cadence.*

*RULE: The last note of a melody is always on the down-pulse. A bar-line will therefore always be placed before it. Other notes will be grouped into measures of two or three pulses while counting backwards from the last note. We begin with a search for a cadence sense.*

*Problem in measures of duple (binary) time:*

*Does the rhythm correspond to* Rhythm Gesture II*?*
*Does the rhythm correspond to* Arsis-Thesis Gesture (Binary)*?*

*At the outset, the procedure is purely mechanical:*

| | |
|---|---|
| *Teacher writes 4, 5, 6, or 7 notes on board -* | I I I I I |
| *Measure bar is added before last note and other bars are added by two's counting from the end -* | I I I I \| I |
| *To which gesture is the rhythm best adapted?* II *or* IV*? Sing on* Nu. | I I \| I I \| I |
| *Add length to the last note to finish the measure. Sing on note-names.* | \| I I \| I I \| I . \|<br>\| 1 3 \| 5 4 \| 3 . \| |
| *If rhythm proposed corresponds to* Rhythm Gesture II *beginning on the up-pulse, then two dots are added at the end -* | I \| I I \| I I \| I . \| .<br>2 \| 1 4 \| 3 2 \| 1 . \| . |

*Under no circumstances will the teacher give special stress to the first pulse of a measure!*

| *Dictations without melody* | *Dictations with melody* |
|---|---|
| I I I I | 3 1 3 5 |
| I I I I I | 1 3 5 4 3 |
| I I I I I I | 2 1 4 3 2 1 |
| I I I I I I I | 5 6 5 4 3 2 1 |

# *Notation*

*Review* Function of Five-Line Staff

*"Why do we need five lines instead of three?"*

*"Could we write whole scale on three lines?"*

1. *Teacher writes* DO - MI - SOL *on three-line staff.*

*"Where do we put* LA - TI - DO*?"*

*"Where does* DO *live?"*

*"What are names of lines and spaces?"*

*"What are names of notes shown on staff?"*

2. *Name long notes; name short notes; sing all notes.*

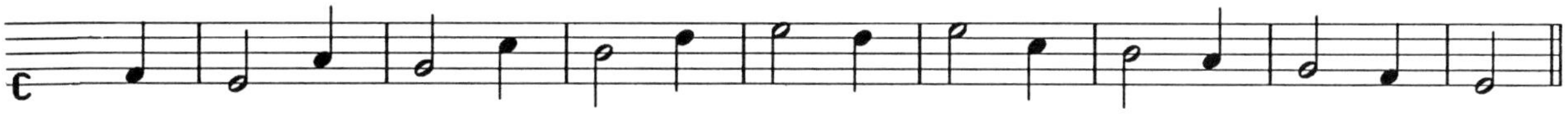

*Extend measure bars below staff to make measures for* Number Notation. *Transcribe.*

*Sing exercise on note names while making* Rhythm Gesture III.

> Do not work on these drills for more than a few minutes. It is better to return to them frequently.

# Creative Activity

1. *Musical conversations using tones of* Diagrams 10a *or* 10b

*Question* - *on strong tones*

‖ 1 3 | 5 6 | 5 . |

*Answer* -*(incomplete) on weak tones*

| 6 5 | 4 3 | 2 . |

*Question* - *on weak tones*

| 2 3 | 4 3 | 2 . |

*Answer* - *(complete) on strong tones*

| 3 5 | 3 2 | 1 . ‖

*Be sure that diagram is in view of class during conversations.*

*Endings usually occur on strong tone phrase.*

2. *To encourage children to learn to use* 2 4 6 *from right hand column of* Diagrams 10a *or* 10b, *invite them to fill in "help" notes in the following melody:*

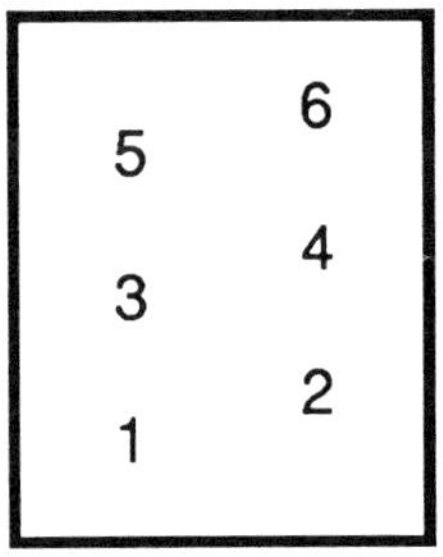


Diagram 10a

‖ 3 | 1 2 | 3 4 | 3 . | .
x | 4 x | 2 x | 2 . | .
x | 2 x | 4 x | 6 . | .
x | 5 x | 3 x | 1 . | . ‖

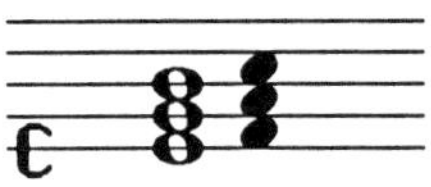

Diagram 10b

# Dictations

## Ear Tests

1 3 5 6 4 2 1

5 3 1 2 4 6 5

1 2 3 4 2 1

1 2 3 2 4 2 3

1 3 5 4 6 4 5

5 3 5 4 4 6 6 5

1 3 5 4 6 5

3 3 5 4 2 1

## Eye Tests

1 2 3 4 5 4 6 5

1 2 3 4 5 6 4 5

1 5 4 3 2 4 2 3

1 5 4 3 4 2 4 3

1 3 5 6 4 6 5

5 6 5 4 5 4 6 5

5 6 5 3 5 4 2 3

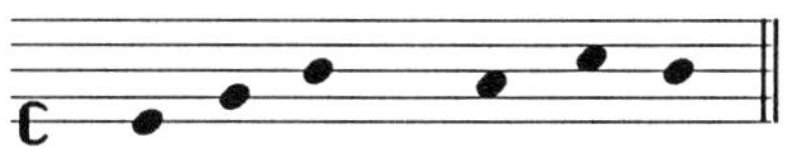

## Rhythmic Dictations

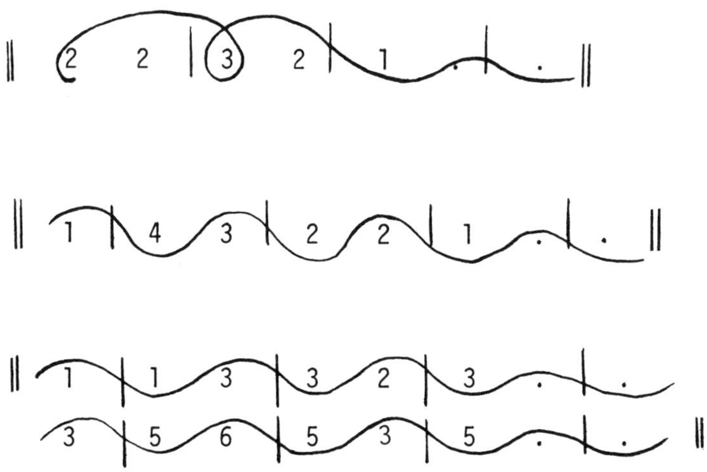

# Songs

**Go and Tell Aunt Nancy** *(1 = G)* *American Folk Song from the Appalachian Mountains*

‖ 3 3 | 3 2 | 1 . | 1 . |
Go and tell Aunt Nan- cy,

| 2 2 | 2 4 | 3 2 | 1 . |
Go and tell Aunt Nan- cy,

| 5 5 | 5 4 | 3 . | 3 1 |
Go and tell Aunt Nan- cy The

| 2 2 | 3 2 | 1 . | . 0 ‖
old grey goose is dead.

**O Cock-A-Doodle Doo!** *($\dot{1}$ = $E^b$)* *English Folk Song*

‖ 3 | 1 3 | 3 2 | 3 . | .
O cock- a- doo- dle doo!

3 | 1 3 | 3 2 | 3 . | .
My dame has lost her shoe!

5 | $\dot{1}$ $\dot{1}$ | 7 6 | 5 3 | 1
My mas-ter's lost his fid-dling stick,

2 | 3 5 | 3 2 | 1 . | .
They don't know what to do,

3 | 1 3 | 3 2 | 3 . | .
They don't know what to do,

3 | 5 6 | 5 3 | 5 . .
They don't know what to do;

5 | $\dot{1}$ $\dot{1}$ | 7 6 | 5 3 | 1
My mas-ter's lost his fid- dling stick,

2 | 3 5 | 3 2 | 1 . | . ‖
They don't know what to do.

## O Holy Spirit, Lord of Grace *($\dot{1}$ = E)*

‖ 1 | 3 4 | 5 5 | 6 6 | 5

O Ho- ly Spi- rit, Lord of Grace,

5 | $\dot{1}$ 7 | 6 6 | 5 . | .

E- ter- nal source of love,______

1 | 3 4 | 5 5 | 6 6 | 5

In- flame, we pray, our in- most heart

5 | 4 3 | 2 2 | 1 . | . ‖

With fire from heav'n a- bove.______

# Chapter Twenty-Three

## Vocal Training

*Review* Vocal Exercise 1

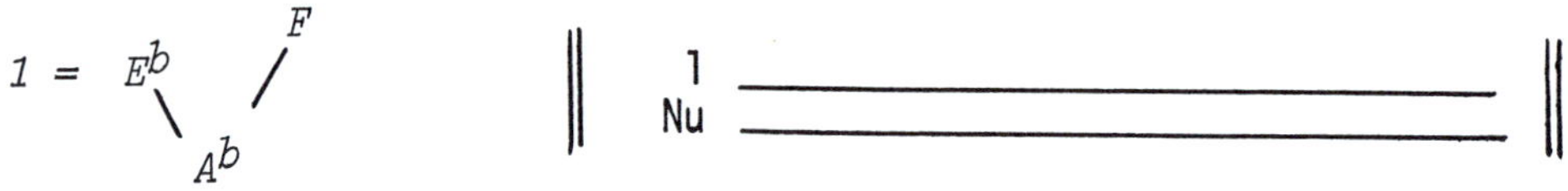


Vocal Exercise 16 *Sing at first with breath in the middle. Then sing straight across on a single breath, legato, with a soft ending.*

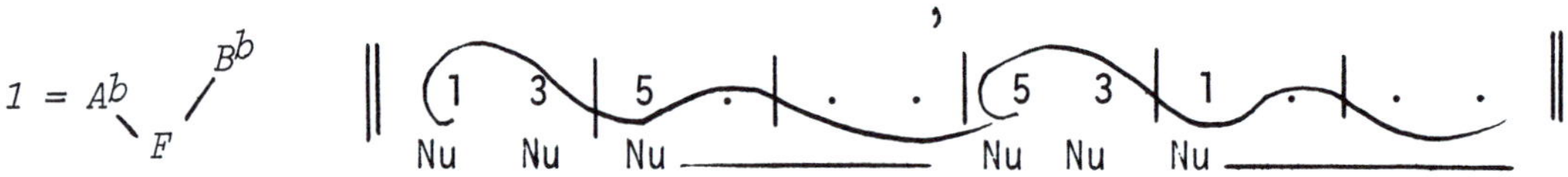


## Intonation

*No new material in this chapter. Work here is directed toward assimilation of* Third *and* Fourth Compass Exercises.

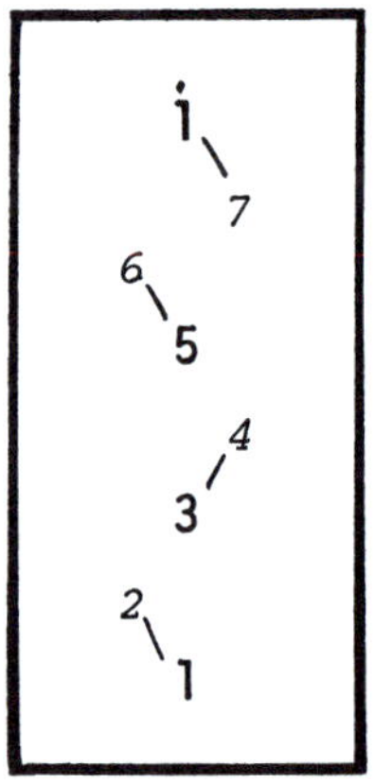


Diagram 9a

Intonation Exercise 49 *on* Diagrams 9a *and* 10a.
*(1 = G)*

| | | | | | | | | |
|---|---|---|---|---|---|---|---|---|
| 1 | 3 | 5 | 6 | 4 | 3 | | | |
| 1 | 3 | 5 | 6 | 4 | 5 | | | |
| 1 | 3 | 5 | 6 | 4 | 2 | | | 1 |
| 1 | 3 | 5 | 6 | 4 | 5 | 3 | 2 | 1 |

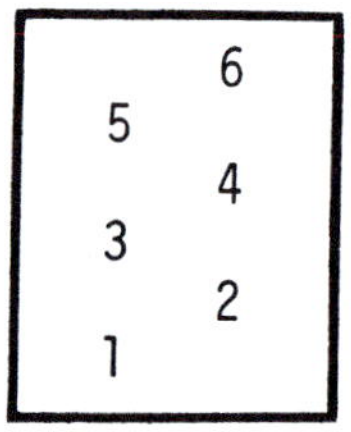


Diagram 10a

Diagram 9c

Intonation Exercise 50 *on* Diagrams 9a *and* 9c.
*(1 = E♭)*

| | | | | | | | | | |
|---|---|---|---|---|---|---|---|---|---|
| 5 | 1̇ | 5 | 5 | 6 | 7 | 1̇ | 6 | 5 | |
| 5 | 1̇ | 5 | 5 | 6 | | 1̇ | 6 | 5 | |
| 5 | 1̇ | 5 | 6 5 | 4 | 3 | 6 | 5 | | |
| 5 | 1̇ | 5 | 4 3 | 5 | 6 | 5 | 4 | 3 | 5 |

*These Intonation Exercises should be taken only a few lines at a time. Teacher should plan to return to them often.*

*For the convenience of teachers, herewith is a summary of last lines of the Compass Exercises:*

| | | | | | |
|---|---|---|---|---|---|
| *First* | 1 2 1 | 3 4 3 | 5 6 5 | 1̇ 7 1̇ | *and return* |
| *Second* | 1 | 3 | 5 | 1̇ | *and return* |
| *Third* | 2 1 | 4 3 | 6 5 | 7 1̇ | *and return* |
| *Fourth* | 2 | 4 | 6 | | *and return* |

*It is well to begin a lesson with something familiar such as a Compass Exercise that helps to establish a tonality.*

# Dictations

*Same as in Chapter Twenty-Two but using* Diagrams 9a, 9c *or* 10a.

| Ear Tests | | Eye Tests | |
|---|---|---|---|
| 1 3 5 | 6 4 21 | 1 2 3 4 5 | 4 6 5 |
| 5 3 1 | 2 4 65 | 1 2 3 4 5 | 6 4 5 |
| 1 2 3 | 4 2 1 | 1 5 4 3 2 | 4 2 3 |
| 1 2 3 | 2 4 2 3 | 1 5 4 3 4 | 2 4 3 |
| 1 3 5 | 4 6 4 5 | 1 3 5 | 6 4 6 5 |
| 5 3 5 | 4 4 6 6 5 | 5 6 5 4 5 | 4 6 5 |
| 5 6 7 1̇ 5 | 6 4 5 | 5 6 5 3 5 | 4 2 3 |
| 5 1̇ 5 | 5 4 6 5 | | |
| 1 3 5 | 4 6 5 | 1̇ 5 4 6 | 5 5 1̇ |
| 3 3 5 | 4 2 1 | | |

Rhythmic Dictations

*Transcribe to staff.*

# *Rhythm*

*1.* Rhythm Patterns - Series 10 *Study with* Arsis-Thesis *gesture and melodic application.*

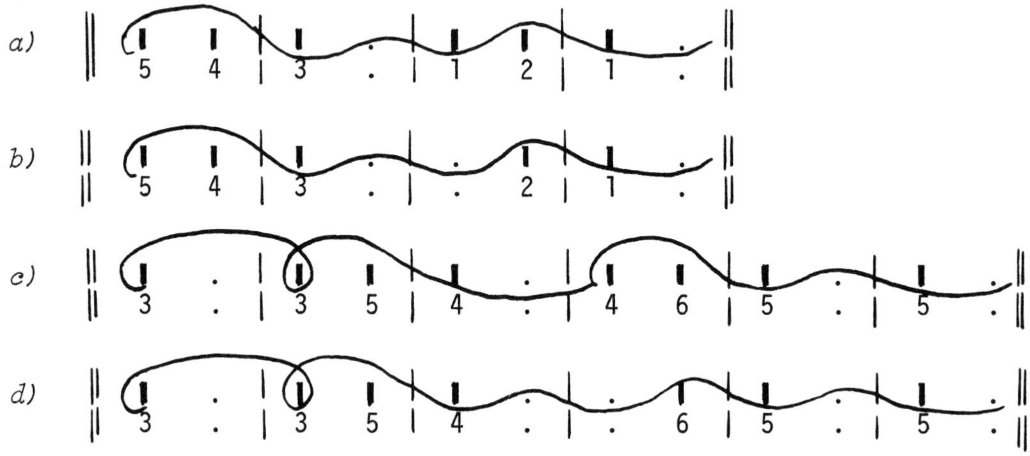


*2.* Aural Training in Rhythm (*Cont'd.*)

*Consider problems of measures in triple time:*

*"Does rhythm correspond to* Rhythm Gesture III?"
*"Does rhythm correspond to* Rhythm Gesture IV - Ternary?"

*Proceed as in previous chapter.*

*Teacher writes a series of single-pulse notes on board. Children add bar-lines according to rule: last note is a down pulse, therefore, bar-line precedes it. Then count back by threes, adding bar-lines after each group of three notes.*

*Length of last note:* *If rhythm corresponds to* Rhythm Gesture III, *one dot is added.*

*If rhythm corresponds to* Rhythm Gesture IV, *two dots are added.*

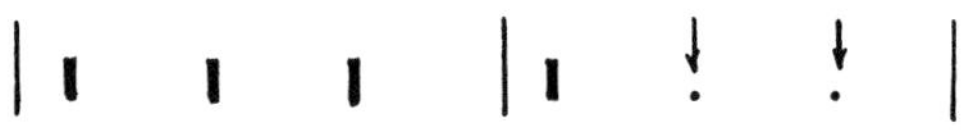

*N.B. If a rhythmic phrase begins with a part of a measure, then it will also end with a part of the measure, that is, the remainder of the very first measure. If the first measure is complete, then the last measure will also be complete.*

*As soon as this principle is understood, teacher dictates groups with melody.*

*Without Melody*

*With Melody*

3 3 4 3 5

5 1 1 1 2 2 2 3

3 2 3 1

# Creative Activity

1.
*Continue with musical conversations in ternary rhythm using* 1 3 5 *and* 6 4 2.

2.
*For drills in melodic invention, use longer rhythm patterns (ternary) from* Rhythm Patterns Series 9 *as given in Chapter Nineteen.*

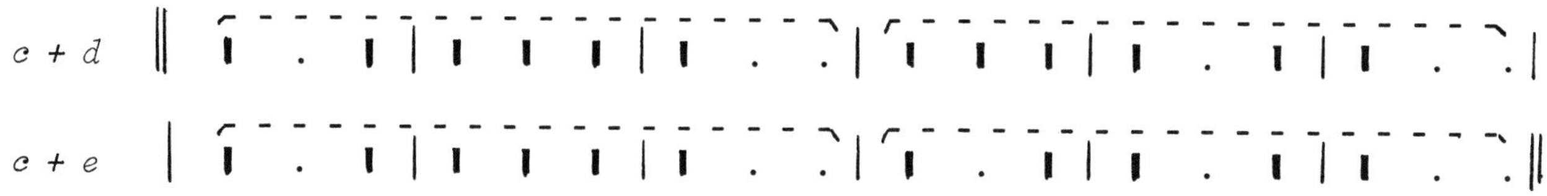


# Notation

1. *Transcribe Lines 1 and 2 of* Intonation Ex. 49 *to* Staff Notation.

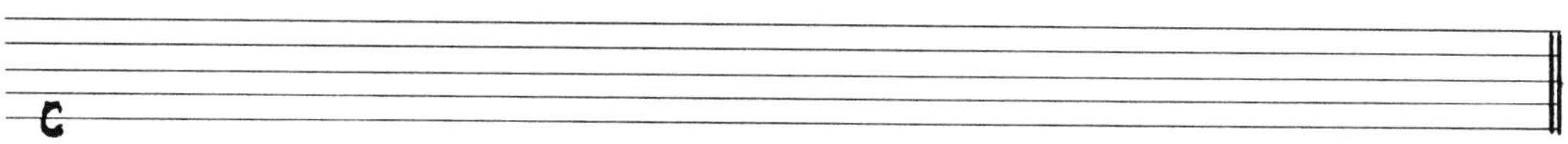

1 3 5 6 4 3 1 3 5 6 4 5

2. *Review transcription of time values:*

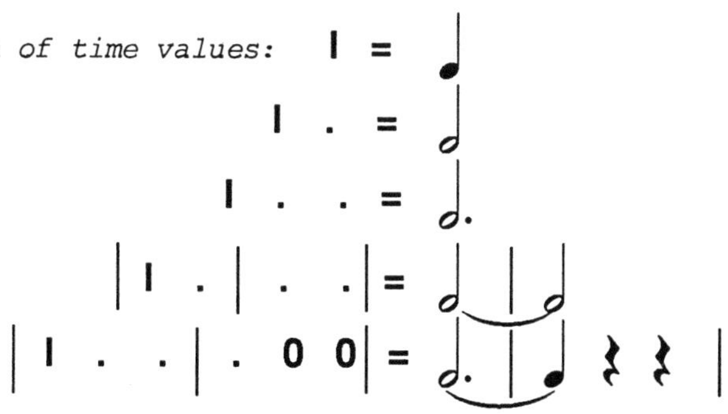

*Transcribe* Song 55 *to* Number Notation.

*Transcribe* Song 56 *to* Staff Notation.

# *Songs*

**Song 55** *(1 = A)* *Spanish Lullabye*

**Song 56** *($\dot{1}$ = E)* *Basque Melody*

‖ 5 5 | $\dot{1}$ $\dot{1}$ | 5 5 | 6 . | 5 5 | $\dot{1}$ $\dot{1}$ | 6 6 | 5 . |<br>
| 5 5 | $\dot{1}$ $\dot{1}$ | 5 5 | 6 . | 5 4 | 3 2 | 1 . | 1 . |<br>
| 3 . | 3 . | 4 . | 6 . | 5 4 | 3 2 | 3 . | 1 . |<br>
| 3 . | 3 . | 4 . | 6 . | 5 4 | 3 2 | 1 . | . . ‖

**Song 57** *(1 = G)* *Catalan Melody*

‖ 3 . | 3 5 | 4 . | . 6 | 5 . | 5 . |<br>
| 3 . | 3 5 | 4 . | . 6 | 5 . | . . |<br>
| 3 . | 3 5 | 4 . | . 2 | 1 . | 2 . |<br>
| 3 . | 3 5 | 4 . | . 2 | 1 . | . . ‖

**Regina Caeli** *(1 = G)* *(Queen of Heaven)* *Gregorian Chant*

*Group One:* ‖ 1 2 | 1 2 | 3 . | 4 3 | 2 .
Re-gí- na cáe- li, lae-tá- re

*Group Two:* 4 | 3 2 | 1 . ‖
al- le-lú- ia.

**Children of Your Heav'nly King** *($\dot{1}$ = $E^b$)*

‖ 1 . 1 | 5 . 3 | 4 5 6 | 5 . . |
Chil- dren of your heav'n - ly King,

| 1 . 1 | 5 . 3 | 4 5 6 | 5 . . |
As you jour- ney, sweet- ly sing;

| 5 . 5 | $\dot{1}$ 7 6 | 5 . 4 | 3 . . |
Sing your Sa- vior's worth- y praise,

| 4 5 6 | 5 . 3 | 2 1 2 | 1 . . ‖
Glo- rious in his works and ways.

*John Cennick, 1742*

# APPENDIX I - "HOW TO..."

## Plan a Lesson

The WARD METHOD recommends a short daily music period. For this reason the chapters of this book contain material for five twenty-minute lessons, enough for one full week's program of study. Many capable class teachers find time to fit in a short period of music every day with the result that all the children's work benefits from this splendid training in intelligent listening, co-ordination, concentration, and self-expression.

A well-planned lesson is the teacher's personal contribution to the method. He will arrange his material so that activities requiring great concentration will alternate with relaxing or semi-relaxing ones. Every activity will lead quite naturally towards the discovery of a song to be sung by the children at the end of their twenty-minute lesson.

General Plan of a Typical Twenty-minute Lesson by the Ward Method.

Vocal Training (2 minutes, semi-relaxing). To place the voice and to develop the child's vocal quality, aiming at purity, resonance and perfect intonation.

Pitch Training (2 minutes, maximum concentration). To train the child to pitch notes correctly and to study the relationship of the different degrees of the scale in the Major Mode.

Rhythmic Training (3 minutes, relaxing). To arouse and develop the child's latent sense of rhythm through gestures and the study of rhythmic patterns.

Listening Games (1 minute, maximum concentration). A preparation for musical dictation, and an essential part of the child's aural training.

Looking and Remembering Games (1 minute, maximum concentration). Training in rapid observation and memorization, to prepare good sightreaders.

Vocal Training (2 minutes, semi-relaxing). As above, and half way through the lesson this activity will freshen up the children's voices.

Rhythmic Dictation (3 minutes, semi-relaxing). To teach the child to write down rhythmic patterns as he recognizes them, and to do so at the same tempo.

Staff Notation (2 minutes, semi-relaxing). To teach the child to read and write music from staff notation.

Creative work (2 minutes, relaxing). To enable the child to express himself in music: improvisation and composition.

Performance of a Song (2 minutes, relaxing). This is the synthesis of the whole lesson.

## Teach Vocal Exercises

The teacher - or a child - sings the vocal exercise, using the appropriate gesture (expressive or rhythmic).

A group of children (Group I or Group II) repeats the exercise several times with the gesture. The teacher gives the pitch of the first note but does not sing with the children.

The same group of children sings the vocal exercise once more, but without the gesture, and the teacher tells the children to "let us hear the gesture." These gestures are not an end in themselves, but a means to an end - namely, the musical result they bring about.

The teacher then does the same work with the other group. Each time a group has sung the listening groups will give an opinion on the vocal quality produced by the singers.

The teacher now plays a few pitch-matching games with individual members of Group III ("non-singers").

## Help the "Non-singers" to Find Their Singing Voices

The teacher demonstrates to the children the difference between simply reciting the words of a well-known song and singing it with the tune. Once the children have grasped the difference the teacher shows them how to produce a musical sound themselves. He teaches the children to open their mouths with round lips and guides their first attempts at singing Vocal Exercise 1 (Ab). As they do so, he will notice which children cannot produce a musical note at the right pitch and will proceed to group these children in the front of the class with the singers behind them. In this way he will be able to give them plenty of individual help.

Game of Pitch-calls.

The teacher calls to one of these children and sings him a short bird-call, such as "cuckoo," in the highest part of a young child's natural register, e.g.,

The child tries to imitate the call. If he cannot do so the call is repeated and he tries again.

When the child has came as near as he can to matching the teacher's notes, the teacher brings his own pitch down to match the child's and sings an easy question to him at the lower pitch, e.g.,

The child tries to answer in a singing voice, and a short dialogue, or

"nonsense-conversation," follows between the teacher and himself, to help him to get the feel of controlling a note within his range.

Finally, the teacher sings him a clear model for Vocal Exercise 1, still at the child's own pitch. The child tries to imitate; and his efforts praised, whether successful or not.

As the weeks go by, the gap between the child's pitch and the teacher's model will diminish, and soon the great day will come when he suddenly finds he can match the teacher's notes perfectly. All the class is absolutely delighted when this happens. The ability to pitch notes correctly comes as a natural part of a child's co-ordinational development. Some children take longer than others to learn how to do this - just as some take longer than others to learn how to ride a bicycle. But every child is capable of it unless he has some serious physical handicap, such as defective hearing. There is no such thing as "tone deafness" among normally healthy children.

## Teach an Intonation Exercise

N.B. All Pitch Exercises are sung with the names of the notes, using the solfa syllables.

The teacher sings the pitch of the first note, taking the key indicated in the book. The children show the note with the measuring gesture and observe the group of notes to be sung.

The children sing the lines of the exercise as the teacher points with the green end of the pointer. A note shown with the red end is to be thought, or "sung in their heads," but not out loud. The children sing collectively, in groups, or individually, using the measuring gesture.

The teacher checks the pitch at the end of each group of notes. He never sings with the children.

The teacher should insist on perfect accuracy. However, although the exercise is to be studied with great care, the teacher need not stay too long on each one: each is a foundation for the exercise to follow, which in its turn perfects what has been learnt in the preceding lessons.

## Play "Listening" Games

The teacher chooses one or two phrases that are a good illustration of the pitch exercise studied during the lesson and which may be a preparation for the final song to be discovered at the end of the lesson. The corresponding diagram should be up on the board.

The teacher sings the first note, giving its name, e.g., "Here is DO." The children show the position of this note with the measuring gesture.

The teacher sings the phrase on "NU." The children listen attentively, keeping their eyes on the diagram, and they try to follow the rise and fall of the phrase with their measuring gesture.

The teacher gives the pitch of the first note again and the children repeat the phrase on "NU," using the measuring gesture.

The teacher gives the pitch of the first note once more and the children repeat the phrase, singing this time on the SOLFA names, with the measuring gesture.

The children repeat the phrase on the SOLFA names, using finger notation. They sing it for the last time on their fingers with their eyes shut.

After the first few weeks, a phrase from a listening game may finally be written on the board, in number or in staff notation.

## Play "Look-and-Remember" Games

One or two suitable phrases are chosen for these games, as for the listening games. As the children become more experienced, these phrases may be slightly longer than the ones for the listening games.

The teacher sings the first note, giving its name, e.g., "Here is DO." The children show the position of this note with the measuring gesture.

The teacher points rapidly to a series of notes on the diagram - the notes of the phrase he has chosen. He uses the red end of the pointer, as these notes are to be "thought." The children observe in silence, then at a sign from the teacher they sing them from memory, using the measuring gesture.

The same game may be played using finger notation. The teacher shows the notes silently on his fingers, holding his hand close to his shoulder ("think notes"). The children watch, then sing the notes out loud, showing them on their fingers with arms extended forwards ("notes to be sung").

Another way of playing this game is to write a short phrase on the board in number notation - later in staff notation. The teacher sings the name of the first note. The children observe in silence. The teacher rubs out the phrase (from left to right) and the children sing it from memory with the measuring gesture.

In all these games, when the children reach the point when they sing the phrase from memory, the teacher should listen attentively but should refrain from pointing to the notes or making any gesture to help the children. Otherwise the whole point of the game would be lost.

## Study Rhythm Patterns

The children start by practising the gesture corresponding to the rhythm to be studied. These rhythmic gestures may be practised silently, or with the help of a song, or to the accompaniment of a record or tape.

The teacher chooses a well-known pattern closely related to the one he wishes the children to learn. He writes the familiar pattern on the board, and the children identify it. They sing it to a simple melody suggested by the teacher. The children sing together, in groups, or individually, using the rhythmic gesture first, then the metrical gesture, and finally the metrical gesture and metrical language.

The teacher sings the new pattern from the series to be studied. He uses the appropriate gesture.

The children repeat the new pattern several times, as above.

The teacher writes the new pattern on the board exactly below the old pattern and then invites the children to point out the difference between the two.

The children now practise both patterns several times until they are absolutely sure of both. They may then begin to use the new pattern in their creative work, so that it becomes completely assimilated into their musical vocabulary.

### Metrical Language

For a note lasting one beat: "LA"

For a note lasting two or more beats: "LONG"

Examples:

*a)*
1 | 1 2 | 3
I | I I | I
la la la la

*b)*
| 3 . | 4 . | 5 .
| I . | I . | I .
long__ long__ long__

*c)*
1 | 3 . . | 2 . 3 | 1 . . | . .
I | I . . | I . I | I . . | . .
la long___ long__ la long______

## Give Rhythm Dictation

The teacher chooses a pattern the children already know, one that has been practised earlier in the lesson. The rhythm series containing the chosen pattern is on the board - or projected on a screen - visible to the whole class. Toward the end of the first year, the rhythm series could be erased before the dictation is given, but in the early stages it is important to leave it on the board in order to avoid confusion.

One child comes to the board and stands facing it.

The teacher sings the pattern to a simple melody once or several times with the rhythmic gesture. The child identifies the pattern among those of the rhythmic series.

The children repeat the pattern once with the rhythmic gesture.

The children repeat the pattern once with the metrical gesture.

The children sing the pattern once again with the metrical gesture and the metrical language.

The children sing the pattern again with the metrical language while the child at the board writes it down. Be sure he does so without slackening the tempo. To avoid this make him sing, too, as he writes.

The child at the board puts in the bar-lines in the following order: The first bar-line is placed before the last note. The child then counts back, two by two pulses, or three by three, according to the time chosen, in order to place the other bar-lines. He looks to see whether the last note of the pattern needs an extra bar-line because of its length. If it does, he adds it. The numbers in brackets refer to the order in which the bar-lines are added.

All the children sing the pattern again with the rhythmic gesture, while the child at the board draws the rhythmic curve, singing as he does so, and keeping to the same tempo.

The whole class sings it once again, to make sure that the written pattern is correct.

It takes time to explain rhythmic dictation, but daily practise of all the above points will give the children much ease and rapidity in their subsequent work.

## Teach a Song Without Words

The teacher selects a song that relates to the rhythm and scale tones being studied in a given lesson. Teacher must not sing the song first. The children should be allowed to "discover" the song themselves step by step.

Examine the rhythm by reading the time values of the notes while making Metrical Gesture I. In this way the short and long notes will be found.

Sing the pitches of the song while making the measuring gesture or from the intonation diagram.

Combine rhythm and pitches while making the appropriate rhythm gesture.

Invite children who succeed in combining tones and rhythm whle making correct rhythm gesture to set the model for the others. All repeat.

## Teach a Song With Words

Children are invited to read the text of the song together. Teacher explains any strange words that the children may not understand.

Words of the song are then recited in correct rhythm and tempo. Note well the syllables that are short and those that are long.

Pitches are "discovered' by means of the measuring gesture.

Melody is then sung while making simple metrical gesture. Melody is repeated while making appropriate rhythm gesture.

Add words to the melody.

# CHAPTER SUMMARIES

| | Vocal Training | Intonation | Rhythm | Dictations | Notation | Creative Activity | Songs |
|---|---|---|---|---|---|---|---|
| **1** Pages 1–25 | Voc. Ex. 1<br>1 ____<br>Nu ____<br>Long tones on *Nu* for timbre<br>Various pitches from F to C.<br>Classify voices into Groups I - II - III<br>Voc. Ex. 2 for timbre and rhythm<br>1 1<br>Nu Nu | Int. Diagram 1<br>2<br>1<br>Int. Ex. 1 and 2<br>Drills on DO and RE | Rhythm Gestures I and II<br>Rhythm Patterns Series I<br>Up-pulse binary rhythm<br>Metrical Language<br>Metrical Gesture I | *Look and Remember Games* (Eye Tests) on DO and RE<br>*Think* Games (Ear Tests) on DO and RE<br>Rhythm Dictations | Pulse lines<br>Measure bars<br>Rhythm wave<br>Dot for prolongation<br>Number Notation<br>1 = DO<br>2 = RE<br>Finger Notation and Measuring Gesture for DO and RE | Improvisation<br>Step 1<br>Musical Conversations<br>Pitch Calls<br>Tone-Matching Games | Songs 1 and 2<br>Two-line songs DO and RE<br>Melodic Application of Rhythm Patterns Series I |
| **2** Pages 26–35 | **Rev.** Voc. Ex. 1 and 2<br>Voc. Ex. 3<br>Nu Nu Nu Nu ____<br>Continue classifying voices into groups<br>Pitches range from A♭ - C | Int. Diagram 2<br>3<br>2<br>1<br>Int. Ex. 3<br>Drills on DO, RE, MI | **Rev.** Rhythm Gestures I and II<br>Melodic Application of Rhythm Patterns Series I<br>Up-pulse binary groupings<br>Teacher-Pupil dialogue | Eye and Ear tests on DO, RE, MI<br>Rhythm Dictations on DO, RE, MI as melodies | Number and Finger Notation for MI<br>Measuring Gesture for MI 3 = MI | **Rev.** Improvisation Step 1<br>Answers on same tones as question<br>Add new verbal phrases | Songs 3, 4, 5, 6<br>Melodic Application of Rhythm Patterns on DO, RE, MI<br>Teacher's dialogue Songs: *Hail, Mary Hail, Holy Queen*<br>Melodies for *Amen* and *Alleluia* |
| **3** Pages 36–43 | **Rev.** Vocal Ex. 1<br>Voc. Ex. 4 Pitch and Rhythm<br>2 1 2 1<br>Nu Nu Nu Nu ____<br>Vocalise by groups — not entire class at once.<br>Refine tone quality | **Rev.** Int. Diagram 2 using<br>Int. Ex. 4 with *think* tones<br>Present Int. Diagram 3<br>5<br>4<br>3<br>2<br>1<br>Int. Ex. 5 | Rhythm Patterns Series 2<br>Longer patterns for Up-pulse binary groupings<br>**Rev.** Rhythm Gestures I and II for precision<br>Metrical Language<br>Metrical Gesture I | Ear and Eye Tests DO to SOL (1 - 5)<br>Rhythm Dictations with Melodic Applications of Rhythm Patterns Series 2 | Add FA(4) and SOL(5)<br>to: Number Notation<br>Finger Notation<br>Measuring Gestures<br>Rhythm Notation<br>Pulse Lines<br>Measure Bars<br>Long Tones | **Rev.** Step 1<br>Begin Step 2<br>Musical answer is different from question | Songs 7, 8, 9, 10<br>Melodic Application of Patterns of Series 2 DO to SOL (1 - 5)<br>*The Flowers Awake* |
| **4** Pages 44–49 | **Rev.** Voc. Ex. 1 and 2<br>Voc. Ex. 5<br>2 1 2 3 2 1<br>Stress good tone quality together with accurate pitch and rhythm | Int. Diagram 3 Cont'd.<br>Intonation Exercises 6, 7, 8<br>Stopping and repeating various tones of the pentachord | R. P. Series 2 with new longer pattern (combining patterns)<br>Melodic Applications<br>Continue on up-pulse binary rhythms | Ear and eye tests DO to SOL cont'd<br>Rhythm Dictations on melodies 1 - 5 | **Review as in Chapter Three** | Step 3 Musical Conversation with words | Songs 11, 12, 13<br>Four-line melodies on longer patterns<br>**Review songs of previous chapters** |

# CHAPTER SUMMARIES

| | Vocal Training | Intonation | Rhythm | Dictations | Notation | Creative Activity | Songs |
|---|---|---|---|---|---|---|---|
| **5** Pages 50–55 | **Rev.** Voc. Ex. 1 and 5<br><br>Concentrate work with groups and individuals<br><br>Good legato in Voc. Ex. 5<br><br>Pitches:<br>Gr. I – B or C<br>Gr. II – G or A<br>Gr. III – E or F | Intonation Diagram 3 cont'd.<br><br>Int. Ex. 9, 10, 11<br><br>*Think notes*<br>Stop, repeat, change direction | Rhythm Patterns Series 3<br><br>Long note in middle of pattern.<br>**Review:** Rhythm Gesture II | Ear and eye tests for Int. Ex. 9, 10, 11<br><br>Rhythmic dictations from melody – children write pulse lines | Introduce DO and RE on staff of one line<br><br>St. Notation 1<br>1 2<br><br>**Rev.** Int. Ex. 1 and 2 Chapter One | Musical Conversation Step 3<br><br>Variety of answers to question<br><br>Children:<br>1 1 2 3<br><br>Teacher: offers several answers (1 to 5) | Songs 14 and 15<br><br>Melodic Applications of Rhythm Patterns |
| **6** Pages 56–62 | **Rev.** Voc. Ex. 1<br>High pitches to Gr. I<br>B♭ C<br><br>Voc. Ex. 6 (Nu)<br>2 1 2 3 4 5<br>5 5 4 3 2 1<br><br>Exaggerate Nnnn for each new note | Int. Diagram 3 cont'd.<br><br>Int. Ex. 12, 13, 14<br><br>Pentachord ascending and descending<br><br>Special attention to DO and RE | R. Patterns Series 4<br><br>Adds new pattern to series<br><br>Combine patterns Melodic Applications<br><br>Continue up-pulse binary rhythms Gestures I and II | Ear and eye tests on pentachord<br><br>Rhythmic Dictations from Series 4 with Melodic Applications | **Rev.** DO and RE on Staff Notation 1<br><br>Present MI on staff Staff Notation 2<br>1 2 3<br>**Rev.** Int. Ex. 3 and 4 on Staff Notation 2 | Step 3<br><br>Teacher asks question and student replies<br><br>Gesture II<br>Invite many to participate | Songs 16 and 17<br><br>Melodic Application of materials of chapter<br><br>*Before I Go to Sleep* (Song 14 with words) |
| **7** Pages 63–69 | **Rev.** Voc. Ex. 1 and 6<br><br>Work for smoothness and beauty of tone<br><br>Voc. Ex. 7<br>1 3 2 1<br>Nu Nu Nu Nu<br>Introduces skip DO – MI | Int. Diagram 3 cont'd.<br><br>**Rev.** Int. Ex. 13 and 14<br><br>Int. Ex. 15 and 16<br><br>Special drills on RE–MI and DO–MI | **Rev.** R. Gestures I and II<br><br>**Rev.** R. P. Series 4<br><br>New combinations and Melodic Applications using DO–MI and MI–DO | Eye and ear tests as drills on DO–MI<br><br>Rhythm Dictations identifying and singing patterns in combination | **Staff Notation 3**<br><br>One and two-pulse notes<br>Transcribe pulse lines.<br><br>Adding FA to staff<br>1 2 3 4 | Longer questions and answers<br><br>Combining longer Rhythm Patterns for Melodic Applications | Songs 18 and 19<br><br>New settings of *Alleluia*<br>5 5 4 3 3<br>Al - le - lu - ia<br>1 2 3 1<br>Al - le - lu ia |
| **8** Pages 70–77 | **Rev.** Voc. Ex. 1, 6, 7<br><br>Work for exactness of interval DO – MI and correctness of Rhythm Gesture II | Int. Diagram 4<br>1 2 3 4 5 6<br><br>Int. Ex. 17, 18, 19<br><br>New Finger Notation and Measuring Gesture for LA | **Rev.** Rhythm Gestures I and II<br><br>R. P. Series 4<br><br>Add verbal phrases to Rhythm Patterns<br><br>New combinations | Eye and ear tests concentrate on new note LA using Int. D. 4 and St. Notation 4 | Staff Notation 4<br><br>SOL and LA on staff<br>1 2 3 4 5 6<br><br>Rev. Int. Ex. 5, 6, 7, 8<br><br>**Rev.** Staff Not. 3<br>Transcribe Rhythm Patterns | Step 3 cont'd<br><br>Family of birds conversing<br><br>Continuing a conversation by not stopping on DO | Songs 20 and 21<br><br>New Melody for *Amen*<br>6 5 6<br>A – men.<br><br>*We Thank You God, for Everything*<br><br>**Review:** *The Flowers Awake*<br>*Before I Go to Sleep*<br>*Hail, Holy Queen* |

# CHAPTER SUMMARIES

| | Vocal Training | Intonation | Rhythm | Dictations | Notation | Creative Activity | Songs |
|---|---|---|---|---|---|---|---|
| **9**<br>*Pages 78–86* | **Rev.** Voc. Ex. 1, 6, 7<br><br>Special attention to individuals | Int. Diagram 4 cont'd.<br><br>Int. Ex. 20 *think* and *held* tones<br><br>**Rev.** Int. Ex. 6, 7, 8 on Staff Notation 4<br><br>Int. Diagram 5 [ i̇ 7 6 5 ]<br><br>Int. Ex. 21 | Rhythm Gesture III<br>Begin on up-pulse<br><br>Rhythm Patterns Series 5 with Melodic Application | Eye and ear tests Staff Notation 4 and Int. Diagram 5<br><br>Rhythm Dictation Series 4<br><br>Mel. Application of Int. Ex. 21 | Staff Notation 5<br><br>**Rev.** Staff Not. 3<br>Transcribe new rhythm patterns to staff notation | Step 3 cont'd.<br><br>Reverse direction of question and answer. | Song 22 Up-pulse binary rhythm with tones of upper tetrachord<br><br>Song 23 Up-pulse ternary rhythm using tones of penta – chord<br><br>*I Saw a Ship A-sailing* |
| **10**<br>*Pages 87–93* | **Rev.** Voc. Ex. 1<br>Stress placement of voice in resonating cavity<br><br>Voc. Ex. 8<br>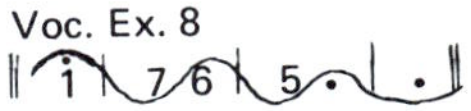<br>Work for accurate pitch of 1 - 7<br>Clean attack on highest pitch | Int. Diagram 5 cont'd.<br><br>Int. Ex. 22, 23, 24<br><br>Int. Ex. 25 with Finger Notation | Rhythm Gesture III cont'd.<br><br>R. Patterns Series 6 with Melodic Application<br><br>Combine patterns in triple meter | Ear and eye tests on notes of upper tetrachord<br><br>R. Dictations in ternary rhythm beginning on up-pulse<br><br>Eye tests from Staff Not. 4 | Staff Notation 6<br>Ternary measures<br>Three-pulse note<br>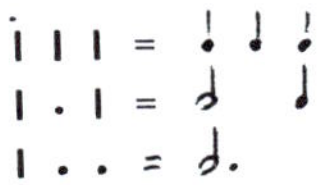<br>**Rev.** Staff Notation 4 | Musical conversations using tones of upper tetrachord | Song 24 Up-pulse ternary using tones of upper tetrachord<br><br>Song 25 Up-pulse binary rhythm using tones of upper tetrachord (Work on visual memory)<br><br>Advent Prayer Part I<br>*O Come, O Come, Emmanuel* |
| **11**<br>*Pages 94–100* | **Rev.** Voc. Ex. 1<br>Test Group III<br><br>Voc. Ex. 9<br><br>Practise slowly but with steady pulse | Int. Diagram 5 cont'd.<br><br>Int. Ex. 26 and 27<br><br>Repeat on Staff Not. 7 | Rhythm Gesture III cont'd.<br>R. Patterns Series 6 with new line added<br><br>Continue combining patterns for Melodic Applications | Ear and eye tests derived from exercises of the chapter | St. Notation 7<br><br>Upper tetrachord on staff<br><br>**Rev.** Int. Ex. 26, 27 on St. Not. 7 | Improvise melody on Rhythm Patterns of Chapter<br><br>Find verbal phrases that fit patterns | Song 26 Up-pulse ternary<br><br>Song 27 Up-pulse ternary<br><br>Advent Prayer Part II<br>*Rejoice, rejoice, O Israel* |
| **12**<br>*Pages 101–106* | **Rev.** Voc. Ex. 1 and 9<br><br>Work for clear tone and smooth progression | Int. Diagram 5 cont'd.<br><br>Int. Ex. 28, 29, 30<br><br>**Rev.** Int. Ex. 23 and 24 on Staff Notation 7 | R. Gesture III cont'd.<br><br>R. Patterns Series 6 cont'd.<br><br>Melodic Applications and *rhythm words* | Ear and eye tests derived from exercises of the chapter | Staff Notation 8<br>The Tie<br>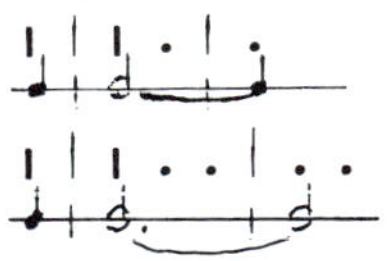<br>Exercises in transcription<br><br>R. Patterns Series 2 | Musical conversations with Rhythm Gestures II and III | Song 28 Up-pulse binary<br><br>Song 29 Up-pulse ternary<br><br>Songs 30 and 31 in Staff Notation<br><br>*A Christmas Carol* |

# CHAPTER SUMMARIES

| | Vocal Training | Intonation | Rhythm | Dictations | Notation | Creative Activity | Songs |
|---|---|---|---|---|---|---|---|
| **13**<br>Pages 107–113 | **Rev.** Voc. Ex. 1, 4, 5, 6<br><br>Stress proper placement of Nnnn before *oo*<br>Quiet breath control<br><br>Sing Voc. Ex. 4, 5, 6 from same DO<br><br>Voc. Ex. 10<br>1 1̇ 7 6 5 1̇ | Int. Diagram 6<br>entire scale<br><br>1 7 6 5 (5) 4 3 2 1<br><br>Int. Ex. 31 and 32 on Int. Diagram 6 and Staff Notation 9 | Longer combinations of Series 6<br><br>Melodic Application of combined rhythm patterns to make two-line song | Tonal and rhythmic dictations in upper and lower segments of scale<br><br>from Int. Diagram and Staff Notation | St. Notation 9<br><br>Transcribe melodic application of rhythm patterns to Staff Notation | Composing two and four-line songs on combinations of rhythm patterns in binary rhythm | Song 32 Up-pulse binary using entire scale<br><br>Song 33 Staff notation<br><br>*If All the World Were Paper* |
| **14**<br>Pages 114–121 | **Rev.** Voc. Ex. 1, 6, 10<br><br>Check for good posture<br>Note shape of lips for *oo* sound | Int. Diagram 6 cont'd.<br><br>Int. Ex. 33 and 33a<br><br>Repeat on Staff Notation 9 | **Rev.** Rhythmic Patterns Series 2 and 3<br><br>Rhythm Gesture II<br><br>**Rev.** R. Patterns Series 6<br>Melodic Applications and guessing game | Eye and ear tests on entire scale from ex. of chapter | **Rev.** Position of notes on five-line staff.<br><br>Transcribe Number Notation to Staff Notation using fragments of songs of chapter | Composing two and four-line songs in ternary up-pulse rhythms | Song 34 Entire scale in up-pulse ternary meter<br><br>Song 35 Up-pulse binary rhythm<br><br>Song 36 Up-pulse ternary in Staff Notation<br><br>*The World Is So Full of a Number of Things* |
| **15**<br>Pages 122–130 | **Rev.** Voc. Ex. 1 and 10<br><br>Work for clear resonance in high ranges<br><br>Voc. Ex. 11 (Nu)<br>1 1̇ 7 1̇<br><br>Note quality of tone | Int. Diagram 7<br><br>6 5 4 3 2 1<br><br>Int. Ex. 34 — First Compass Ex. | Binary Rhythm beginning on down pulse.<br><br>R. Patterns Series 7<br><br>Rhythm Gesture IV — Binary<br>Arsis-Thesis<br>Melodic Application | Ear and eye tests on fragments of First Compass Ex.<br><br>Rhythmic dictation on Arsis-Thesis binary rhythms | **Rev.** Staff Notation 8<br><br>Transcribe R. Patterns Series 7<br>Also Compass Ex. and Song 35 to Staff Notation | Musical Conversations on tones of First Compass Ex. with R. Gesture IV-Binary | Song 37 Down-pulse binary<br><br>Song 38 Down-pulse binary<br><br>Song 39 Down-pulse binary<br><br>*Ave Maria*<br>*Ubi Caritas* |
| **16**<br>Pages 131–137 | **Rev.** Voc. Ex. 1 and 10<br><br>Voc. Ex. 12 (Nu)<br>1 2 1. 3 4 3. 5 6 5.<br>5 6 5. 3 4 3. 1 2 1.<br><br>Tones of First Compass Ex. with R. G. IV — binary | Int. Diagram 8<br>1̇ 7 6 5<br><br>Int. Ex. 35<br><br>Int. Diagram 9a<br>1̇ 7 6 5 4 3 2 1<br><br>Int. Ex. 36 — First Compass Ex. Entire scale | R. G. IV — Binary<br>Study of 4 rhythms:<br>A T A T<br>A A T T<br>A A A T<br>A T T T<br><br>Mel. Application of Series 8 | Ear and eye tests from chapter materials<br><br>R. dictations with A-T binary rhythms | Staff Notation 10<br>The Rest<br><br><br>Transcription Ex. | Musical Conversation using the entire scale<br><br>Writing on board from rhythm patterns<br>Four lines | Song 40 Down pulse Binary<br><br>Song 41 Down pulse Binary<br><br>*Church Bells Ringing*<br><br>*The Father's Love*<br><br>*Benedicamus Domino* |

# CHAPTER SUMMARIES

| | Vocal Training | Intonation | Rhythm | Dictations | Notation | Creative Activity | Songs |
|---|---|---|---|---|---|---|---|
| **17**<br>Pages 138–145 | **Rev.** Voc. Ex. 1, 11, 12<br><br>Check accuracy of pitch on tones of DO MI SOL<br><br>Work for clean attack and skip | Int. Diagram 9a cont'd.<br><br>Int. Ex. 37 First Compass Ex.<br><br>Int. Ex. 38 Second Compass Ex.<br><br>Repeat Int. Ex. on Staff Notation 9<br><br>Drills on tonic chord of Major Mode | Rhythm Gesture IV Binary Rhythm<br><br>**Rev.** R. P. Series 8 with Melodic Application<br><br>**Rev.** Arsis-Thesis Gesture | Ear and eye tests on First and Second Compass Exercises<br><br>Rhythmic Dictations from R. Patterns Series 8<br><br>Using fingers of hand as a staff | **Rev.** Elements of Staff Notation studied thus far<br><br>Transcriptions to Staff Notation | Composing four-line melodies using 1 - 3 - 5 as first beats of measures<br><br>Compose melodies to Rhythm Patterns Series 8 to Arsis and Thesis | Song 42 Up-pulse binary<br><br>Song 43 (Basque Melody) Down pulse binary<br><br>*Goosey, Goosey Gander*<br><br>*Hark, Hark, the Dogs Do Bark* |
| **18**<br>Pages 146–153 | **Rev.** Voc. Ex. 1 and 12<br><br>Voc. Ex. 13<br>‖ 1 · \| 3 · 5 · \| 1 · · ‖<br>\| 5 4 3 2 \| 1 · \| · · ‖<br><br>Practise slowly at first | Int. Diagram 9a cont'd<br><br>Int. Ex. 39, 40, 41<br><br>Be careful to avoid slurring when making skips | Rhythm Gesture IV Ternary Rhythm<br><br>Rhythm Patterns Series 9 | Ear and eye tests from materials of chapter | **Rev.** Staff Notation 6 Transcribe Rhythm Patterns Series 9<br><br>Staff Notation 11 Repeat Sign<br>‖: :‖<br>Transcribe Song 46 to Staff Notation<br>Transcribe Song 48 to Number Notation | Suggestions for composing melodies long notes at beginning of lines<br><br>Compose melodies to Rhythm Pattern Series 9<br><br>Add verbal phrases to patterns | Song 44 Down-pulse binary<br><br>Song 45 Down-pulse binary<br><br>Song 46 Down-pulse ternary<br><br>Song 47 (French) Up-pulse ternary<br><br>Song 48 (Spanish)<br><br>*Near to My Woodland Cottage* (French) |
| **19**<br>Pages 154–160 | **Rev.** Voc. Ex. 1 and 13<br><br>Voc. Ex. 14<br>‖ 1 3 \| 5 4 3 2 \| 1 · ‖<br><br>Rhythm Gesture IV binary<br><br>Continue to work for accuracy in skips | Int. Diagrams 9b and 9c<br>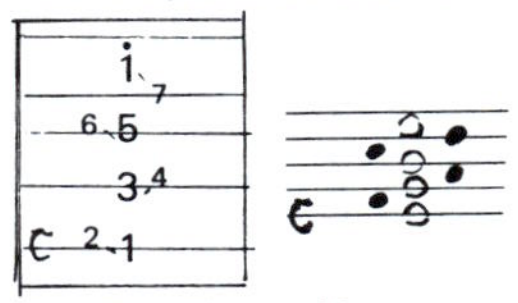<br>Int. Ex. 42 and 43 | Rhythm Patterns Series 9 new patterns added<br><br>Rhythm Gesture IV – Ternary with Melodic Applications<br><br>Long tones | Ear and eye tests from materials of chapter | Ties for notes of equal length<br><br>Transcription exercises | Technique of rhythmic enlargement | Song 49 Down-pulse binary<br>Song 50 (French) Down-pulse ternary<br><br>Song 51 (German) Down-pulse ternary<br><br>*For the Gift of Daily Bread* |
| **20**<br>Pages 161–165 | **Rev.** Voc. Ex. 1<br><br>Voc. Ex. 15<br>‖ 1 5 4 3 2 \| 1 · \| · ‖<br><br>Avoid scoop when singing the interval 1-5 | Int. Diagram 9a cont'd.<br><br>Int. Ex. 44<br><br>Dialogue form for practising *think* tones of Compass Ex.<br><br>Third Compass Ex. | **Rev.** Rhythm Patterns Series 7<br><br>**Rev.** Rhythm Gesture IV binary | Arsis-Thesis dictation<br><br>Ear and eye tests from Third Compass Ex. | **Rev.** Staff Notation Transcriptions to Number Notation | New Melodic Applications to Rhythm Patterns in combinations. | Song 52 Down-pulse binary<br><br>*Twinkle, Twinkle Little Star*<br>*Where Abideth Charity and Love*<br>*How Do You Like to Go Up in a Swing?* |

# CHAPTER SUMMARIES

| | Vocal Training | Intonation | Rhythm | Dictations | Notation | Creative Activity | Songs |
|---|---|---|---|---|---|---|---|
| **21** Pages 166–170 | **Rev.** Voc. Ex. 1 and 15 | Intonation Diagram 10a 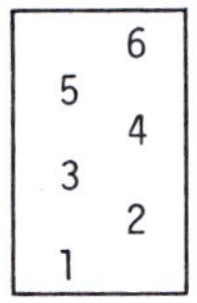 Int. Ex. 45<br>Int. Ex. 46 Fourth Compass Ex.<br>Int. Diagram 10b 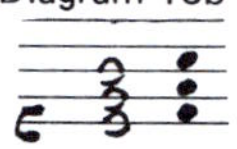<br>RE FA LA as stopping places | Rhythm Patterns Series 9 in combinations<br><br>(See under Creative Activity) | Tests on all four Compass Ex. | **Rev.** Staff notation Rests, Ties, repeat sign. | New combinations of rhythms and Melodic Applications.<br><br>Rhythmic enlargement cont'd. | **Song 53** Up-pulse ternary<br><br>**Song 54** (Spanish) Down-pulse ternary<br><br>*O How We Love the Month of May*<br>*Now That the Daylight Fills the Sky* |
| **22** Pages 171–177 | **Rev.** Voc. Ex. 1 and 15 | Int. Diagrams 10a and 10b cont'd.<br><br>Int. Ex. 47 and 48 | Aural training in rhythm<br><br>Recognizing rhythm of a melody — binary | Dictations on materials of the chapter | **Rev.** All Staff Notation signs | Musical Conversation on strong and weak tones of Int. Diagram 10a or 10b<br><br>Discovering the *help* notes of a melody | *O Cock-a-doodle-Doo*<br><br>*Go and Tell Aunt Nancy*<br><br>*O Holy Spirit, Lord of Grace* |
| **23** Pages 178–183 | **Rev.** Voc. Ex. 1<br><br>Voc. Ex. 16 <br><br>Sing on one breath | Int. Diagrams 9a and 9c<br><br>Int. Ex. 49 and 50<br><br>**Rev.** Four Compass Ex.<br>Int. Diagram 11 for oblique reading 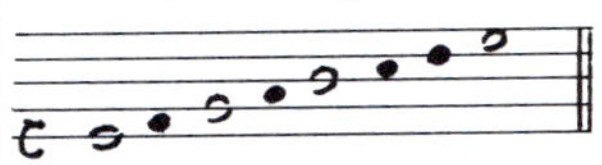<br>**Rev.** Int. Ex. 49 and 50 | Rhythm Patterns Series 10<br><br>Study with Arsis-Thesis gesture and Melodic Application<br><br>Aural training in rhythms — ternary | Ear and eye tests using both Int. Diagrams 9a and 10a | Transcription and review — Staff Notation | Musical Conversation on 135 and 246<br><br>Longer patterns for melodic invention | **Song 55** (Spanish) Down-pulse ternary<br>**Song 56** (Basque) Down-pulse binary<br>**Song 57** (Catalan) Down-pulse binary<br>*Regina Caeli*<br>*Children of Your Heavenly King* |